COLUMBIA CRITICAL GUIDES

W9-ABN-317

Virginia Woolf

To the Lighthouse
The Waves

EDITED BY JANE GOLDMAN

Series editor: Richard Beynon

COLUMBIA UNIVERSITY PRESS ◣◢ NEW YORK

Columbia University Press
Publishers Since 1893
New York
Editor's text copyright © 1998 Jane Goldman

First published in the Icon Critical Guides series in 1998
by Icon Books Ltd.

Library of Congress Cataloging-in-Publication Data
Virginia Woolf — To the lighthouse, The waves / edited by Jane
   Goldman.
      p.   cm. — (Columbia critical guides)
   Includes bibliographical references and index.
   ISBN 0–231–11532–6 (cloth : alk. paper). —
   ISBN 0–231–11533–4 (pbk. : alk. paper)
   1. Woolf, Virginia, 1882–1941.   To the lighthouse.   2. Woolf,
Virginia, 1882–1941.   Waves.   I. Goldman, Jane, 1960–   .
II. Series.
PR6045.072T628   1998
823'.912—dc21   98–39509

Casebound editions of Columbia University Press books are printed
on permanent and durable acid-free paper.

Printed in the United States of America

c 10 9 8 7 6 5 4 3 2 1
p 10 9 8 7 6 5 4 3 2 1

Contents

desire to come up with a unifying way of understanding Woolf's work – whether by looking for a totalising Woolfian philosophy evident throughout the *œuvre*, or by scrutinising individual works in terms of a unifying philosophical, mythic, psychoanalytic or psychological approach. In 1953 selections from Woolf's diary were published in *A Writer's Diary* which had considerable impact on such attempts to account for her achievement. The four main extracts are from: Joseph Blotner's (1956) essay, offering a mythic and Freudian analysis of *To the Lighthouse*; Shiv Kumar's (1962) study of Bergsonism and modern fiction; extracts on *To the Lighthouse* and *The Waves* from Guiguet's classic study of Woolf's *œuvre* (1962); and Frank McConnell's (1968) essay on romanticism and phenomenology in *The Waves.*

CHAPTER FOUR   86

The 1970s and 80s: Diverging Approaches – Androgyny, Art, Feminism

This discusses the groundwork done in the 1970s for the major developments in feminist criticism that followed in the 1980s and 90s. The three main extracts are from readings which make use of important spheres of influence on Woolf's work: Allen McLaurin, in *Virginia Woolf: The Echoes Enslaved* (1973), draws on the visual arts and the aesthetic theories of Roger Fry; Perry Meisel's book, *The Absent Father: Virginia Woolf and Walter Pater* (1980), is a fascinating meditation on literary influence; and Gillian Beer's essay, 'Hume, Stephen, and Elegy in *To the Lighthouse*' (1984), looks at the combining influences of the philosophical, biographical and elegiac.

CHAPTER FIVE   109

The 1980s: Sexual/Textual Readings

This chapter is devoted to textually based, deconstructive, and psychoanalytic approaches. The four main extracts from the work of Toril Moi, Gayatri Chakravorti Spivak, Garrett Stewart and Rachel Bowlby, are all from the 1980s, but their arguments and concerns continue in much criticism of the 1990s.

CHAPTER SIX   148

The 1990s: Historical, Materialist, Post-colonialist Readings

This chapter looks at contextually based, historical and post-colonialist readings. The extracts are from Jane Marcus's ground-breaking essay on *The Waves* as anti-imperialist text (1992); and Janet Winston's recent analysis of imperial discourses in *To the Lighthouse* (1996).

Introduction

YOU'RE REAL to some – I to others. Who's to decide what reality is? Not dear Harold, anyhow, whom I've not heard, but if as you say, he sweeps us all into separate schools one hostile to the other, then he's utterly and damnably wrong, and to teach the public that's the way to read us is a crime and a scandal, and accounts for the imbecility which makes all criticism worthless. Lord – how tired I am of being caged with Aldous, Joyce and Lawrence! Can't we exchange cages for a lark? How horrified all the professors would be! Yes, greatly to my surprise The Waves is selling better than any of my novels, which pleases me, and E.M. Forster says it moves him more than any of them, which pleases me still more. Otherwise, opinions good and bad, seem to me increasingly futile and beside the mark.

(Virginia Woolf to Hugh Walpole, 8 November 1931)[1]

Cage the Woolf – who would dare? Her disdain for critical confinement has not deterred any number of us from such 'imbecility' in the six decades since she passed these comments showing scant respect for the bars of Harold Nicolson's 'modernism', from behind which she flirtatiously calls to Hugh Walpole, himself detained on quite a different charge ('old-fashioned' realism).[2] Woolf's writing has gloriously survived and defied a variety of critical internments which it is the business of this book to sample and explore. To the Lighthouse (1927) and The Waves (1931) stand at the zenith of Woolf's achievements as a novelist, and remain dominant landmarks in twentieth century writing. Commanding critical attention since first publication, they have been the focus of a number of important critical and theoretical debates which also extend beyond Woolf studies. The sheer enormity and proliferation of Woolf studies alone, however, may daunt not only student beginners but more experienced academics too.[3] It is not proposed that we will safely cage an authentic Woolf in this guide, nor arrive at a single, authoritative account of the novels, for that would be an injustice to the range and wealth of available readings and approaches. Rather, we will map out, in the following discussion and selection of extracts, the broad, shifting, critical demarcations by which To the Lighthouse and The Waves have been understood as well as sample some of the most influential and discerning critical readings. The finest of Woolf criticism, as we will see, resembles not a cage but a key – by which her work has been opened up (rather than merely unlocked, deciphered), and by which further readings, debates and theories have been released. This is not to suggest that there has been a harmonious flow – one school of approach growing out of another without friction or dissent – for criticism of Woolf's work has always been diverse, sometimes radically divergent. The following pages will identify the important arguments, debates and differences, turning-points and stakes of argument to have emerged in criticism of *To the Lighthouse* and *The Waves*.

To the Lighthouse – the third in a sequence of formally experimental, increasingly lyric, novels beginning with *Jacob's Room* (1922) and *Mrs Dalloway* (1925)[4] – constitutes a significant breakthrough for Woolf, as her diary famously records: '(But while I try to write, I am making up "To the Lighthouse" – the sea is to be heard all through it. I have an idea that I will invent a new name for my books to supplant "novel". A new – – by Virginia Woolf. But what? Elegy?).'[5] Critics, as we shall see, have spilled a deal of ink meditating on just what this departure from the novel entails and on the precise elegiac qualities of Woolf's work. Perversely Woolf subtitled not as elegy but as biography her next novel, *Orlando* (1928).[6] But this 'escapade after these serious poetic experimental books' culminating in *To the Lighthouse* may also be regarded as a preparatory clearing towards *The Waves*, which is for some Woolf's greatest achievement in the elegiac: 'I want to kick up my heels & be off . . . I think this will be great fun to write; & it will rest my head before starting the very serious, mystical poetical work which I want to come next'.[7] But *To the Lighthouse* and *The Waves* are more directly connected in Woolf's creative processes by a vision she records, while completing the earlier work, of 'a fin passing far out' which she guesses 'may be the impulse behind another book'[8] and to which she returns on completing *The Waves*: 'I have finally netted that fin in the waste of waters which appeared to me . . . when I was coming to an end of *To the Lighthouse*.'[9] *The Waves*, which she wrote 'to a rhythm and not to a plot',[10] was understood by Woolf as a new departure: 'Oh yes, between 50 & 60 I think I shall write out some very singular books,' she noted on its completion, 'if I live; I mean I think I am about to embody, at last, the exact shapes my brain holds. What a long toil to reach this beginning – if The Waves is my first work in my own style!'[11] It is, for many, her definitive work.

Criticism of Woolf's fiction has broadly fallen between the poles of modernism, feminism and postmodernism, and these will be kept in view in the organisation of this book. *To the Lighthouse* and *The Waves* have been understood as exemplary high modernist texts, applauded (and occasionally castigated) for their rich poetic language and formal experimentation, and explored and debated, for example, not only in terms of aesthetics (neoplatonism, phenomenology, the visual aesthetics of post-impressionism and so on), but also in terms of the biographical, psychoanalytical and the political. Formalist and structuralist readings have given way to poststructuralist and deconstructive, modernist readings have met with postmodernist, aesthetic countered by Marxist, and many of these have been challenged and negotiated by feminist readings. More recently these works have been reconsidered in relation to materialist, historical, and post-colonialist criticism and contexts. Although *To the Lighthouse* and *The Waves* hold the main focus of attention, then, this guide will also be helpful in offering orientation more generally within Woolf studies.

Already, one or two cages may be rattling. Woolf's comments, above, to Walpole may have unsettled, perhaps, received understanding of Woolf as a high modernist and scourge of the very kind of writer she seems here so ready to join ranks with: isn't Walpole one of those 'materialist' authors to be reviled, as are Wells, Galsworthy and Bennett in Woolf's most cited of essays, 'Mr Bennett and Mrs Brown'?[12] It may also surprise some readers to learn of the immediate commercial success and general popularity of *The Waves*, so often considered her most difficult, aestheticised, and abstract work. Over the decades, preconceptions about Woolf have, of course, come and gone, as well as occasionally stuck – from contemporary assessments, where the author was politely referred to as 'Mrs Woolf' (a chill subsuming of her achievements to those of her husband, perhaps), to the present wealth of scholarship, where 'Virginia Woolf' (as in 'who's afraid of . . .') has yielded either to just plain, magnificent, 'Woolf' (eclipsing Leonard as the more distinguished in the partnership), or even sometimes to the more intimate 'Virginia'. Readers in the 1940s were helped to a particularly enduring stereotyped view of her achievements, however, by shorthand portraits such as Robert Graves' and Alan Hodge's rather cheeky summation:

■ [Joyce's] 'stream of consciousness' was a method of writing in which the thoughts and feelings of characters were more important than action or dialogue. The method was also adopted by Virginia Woolf, daughter of a Victorian man-of-letters, in her novel To the Lighthouse, and others. Like E.M. Forster, she wrote with her nervous sensibilities, so that her readers shrank sympathetically at each painfully composed paragraph. She was married to Leonard Woolf, author of The Jungle, a competent novel about Ceylon, founder of the Hogarth Press (with money won in a Calcutta Sweep), and the man responsible for the working system of the International Labour Office at Geneva – which was the most practically successful of the League's undertakings.[13] □

Woolf is here defined, at every turn, with reference to the achievements of men – whether in the form of her modernist rival's (Joyce's) literary innovation, her father, Leslie Stephen's literary reputation, her friend Forster's sensibilities, or her husband Leonard's career as author, publisher and politician. Her apparently excruciating method of composition positions her as an other-worldly upper-class aesthete, too sensitive, too remote, to stray from the 'aesthetic clique' (another early critic's term for Bloomsbury)[14] she inhabits into the more robust realm of hard reality. If we have more considered, feminist, scholarship to thank for correcting many of these presumptions – for example, Woolf's literary innovations may also be compared with those of women writers such as Dorothy Richardson (to whose work, incidentally, was first applied the term 'stream-of-consciousness' – by another woman, May Sinclair),[15] Woolf acknowledged the influence of several literary 'mothers' as well as showing ambivalence towards that of her father, she was in fact co-founder and active partner in the Hogarth Press,[16] and she enjoyed a full, social and sometimes political, life in the 'real world'[17] and so on – yet we have also been in receipt of further stereotypical views from some feminist quarters: for example, Woolf as 'guerrilla fighter in a Victorian skirt',[18] or as suicide case and victim of childhood sexual abuse.[19]

In the following introduction to the material covered in this guide, I will discuss my selection of extracts with reference to three main areas of criticism of Woolf's novels: modernism, feminism and postmodernism. There are many other categories and subcategories, distinct and inter-relating, which may also be invoked, as we have seen, but (since other categories such as psychoanalytical or Marxist may be understood to traverse them) these three remain more useful points of departure. The chapters proceed through criticism of the novels more or less chrono-logically, and the selection of extracts is organised to highlight key areas of debate as they come to the fore, become consolidated or reach an interesting pass. There are a number of issues recurrent throughout Woolf criticism: attention will be paid to where they meet with signifi-cantly differing critical emphasis, and to alternative links and later developments.

Before turning to our three main areas, I would first like to say a little about Woolf's own critical work and about her biography and auto-biography. Biography, although an area of criticism not directly about the fiction, has had enormous impact on approaches to the novels – not least *To the Lighthouse* and *The Waves*, as we shall see. Quentin Bell's excellent biography of his aunt remains the standard authority,[20] and Hermione Lee's recent, and already classic, *Virginia Woolf* offers a wealth of new insights and material.[21] *Moments of Being*, a collection of Woolf's autobiographical reflections, published posthumously, has also been an important influence on criticism of her work.[22] Just as her biography (more appropriately, perhaps, biograph*ies*) and autobiographical writings have been put to work in readings of her fiction, Woolf's impressive body of criticism has also been intensively exploited. Students of Woolf's novels may now readily consult essays, diaries, letters, memoirs, notebooks, and drafts of various works, including *To the Lighthouse* and *The Waves*. A deal of archive material is now available on microfilm and CD-ROM.[23]

Woolf has become for many critics her own greatest authority – not merely because so much of her private and public writing on writing is available, but because it is so stimulating and illuminating of her work and so eminently quotable. By the time *To the Lighthouse* was published, Woolf, who worked from an early age as a reviewer, had gained recognition as an essayist and critic following the success of her first collection, *The Common Reader* (1925). She published a second collection in 1932,[24] and several collections have appeared since her death.[25] Critics have put them to great use, along with the two longer, critical and polemical works, *A Room of One's Own* (1929) and *Three Guineas* (1938).[26]

'Most of the important things for a critic to say about Mrs Woolf,' according to William Empson, 'have been said by herself in *A Room of One's Own*, and centre round a peculiar attitude to feminism'.[27] *A Room of One's Own* (1929), published two years after *To the Lighthouse* and two years before *The Waves*, is certainly an important resource for interpretations of these works, and is more widely regarded as a founding text for twentieth-century feminist aesthetics, not least because it is also a source of many, often conflicting, theoretical positions. This stimulating and contradictory work is cited as *locus classicus* for a number of important modern feminist debates concerning: materialism, education, patriarchy, androgyny, subjectivity, the feminine sentence, the notion of 'Shakespeare's sister', the canon, the body, race, class, and so on. Like readers of Woolf's fiction, students of her critics will find it enormously helpful. Other pieces by Woolf which students of *To the Lighthouse* and *The Waves* will find useful, and find frequently cited in secondary criticism, include: 'Modern Fiction' (1919), 'Mr Bennett and Mrs Brown' (1924),[28] 'The Moment: Summer's Night' (c. 1929), 'Memories of a Working Women's Guild' (1930),[29] 'The Leaning Tower' (1940), and *Three Guineas* (1938). I have resisted the temptation to reproduce sizeable extracts from Woolf's writings since, *pace* Empson, the focus of this guide is not her own but that massive body of other people's criticism her work has inspired. The most significant of her statements are quoted, however, where they assist in following particular standpoints on the novels.

Woolf's criticism has also been used to adumbrate the work of other contemporary writers and, most significantly, in connection with defining modernist aesthetics. Unlike other women modernists who have recently been rediscovered by various feminist scholars,[30] Woolf has not suffered the same degree of exclusion, at mid-century and after, from the modernist canon erected by male critics.[31] But her status has occasionally been reduced to that of handmaiden to the men of modernism – Joyce, Lawrence, Conrad, Ford, Lewis, Eliot, Yeats, Pound and so on – whose work has been read through the filter of her most famous statements on modern writing. Her declaration, in 'Mr Bennett and Mrs Brown', that 'on or about December 1910 human character changed',[32] has been widely invoked in surveys not only of modernist literature but of other arts, and more generally of culture and politics too. One passage from 'Modern Fiction', however, is possibly *the* most quoted of her statements on avant-garde practice:

■ Look within and life, it seems, is very far from being 'like this'. Examine for a moment an ordinary mind on an ordinary day. The mind receives a myriad impressions – trivial, fantastic, evanescent, or engraved with the sharpness of steel. From all sides they come, an incessant shower of innumerable atoms . . . . Life is not a series of gig lamps symmetrically arranged; life is a luminous halo, a semi-transparent envelope surrounding us from the beginning of consciousness to the end. Is it not the task of the novelist to convey this varying, this unknown and uncircumscribed spirit, whatever aberration or complexity it may display, with as little mixture of the alien and external as possible?[33] □

William Troy's early essay on *The Waves* and *To the Lighthouse*, 'Virginia Woolf: The Novel of Sensibility', may be seen as a critical template in the use of this statement as epigraph and in attributing it to 'the voice of Henri Bergson'.[34] Readers of this guide will find frequent allusions to this passage, particularly in the early chapters. But if Woolf's essay provides for many 'one of the most comprehensive and celebrated statements of the priorities of modernism',[35] it has also been held up for derision as everything that the work of a certain kind of male modernist is not. M.H. Levenson, for example, makes scant reference to Woolf in his *Genealogy of Modernism*, ruling that her metaphors 'imply an art that rejects precise statement and moral certainty in favour of the suggestiveness and imprecision usually associated with symbolism or Impressionism. Pound on the other hand, opposed all "mushy technique" and "emotional slither", preferring a poetry "as much like granite as it could possibly be".'[36] In quoting from Pound's essay, 'The Hard and the Soft in French Poetry',[37] and reflecting T.E. Hulme's taste for 'hard' poetry,[38] Levenson is aligning his argument with one side of a critical divide dating back to the ruptures of the period such as the 1914 Ideal Home Exhibition 'rumpus' between Wyndham Lewis' Vorticists and the Bloomsbury Group.[39] The many different, and hostile factions in the early avant-garde cannot readily be homogenised under the rubric of a coherent modernist movement: 'the Pound era', as Hugh Kenner termed it, indeed may not be the same as the Woolf era after all.

Chapter 1 of this guide looks briefly at both Woolf's private reflections and the informal reviews supplied to her by friends and family, before turning to the first published reviews of *To the Lighthouse* and *The Waves*, and reveals that Woolf's modernism was first understood in relation to her contemporaries' innovations in plot and character and 'stream-of-consciousness' and to the theories of Henri Bergson (which remain dominant in both Woolf and modernist criticism), as well as in relation to Bloomsbury Group aesthetics. The latter are defined with special reference, in later studies, to the philosophy of G.E. Moore,[40] and to the theories and achievements of male Bloomsbury: Roger Fry, Clive Bell, Lytton Strachey, Duncan Grant, Desmond MacCarthy, Maynard Keynes, and Leonard Woolf.[41] Bloomsbury aesthetics are given special focus in Chapter 4 where the innovative work of Allen McLaurin is represented. Recently more detailed attention has been paid to the influence of women such as Vanessa Bell, Ray Strachey, Jane Harrison, and Dora Carrington.[42] But early reviewers and many critics through to the 1950s and 60s, as we will see in Chapters 2 and 3, had a much more nebulous understanding of Woolf's modernism. 'It quickly became an established orthodoxy,' Su Reid observes, that Woolf 'was an "experimental" novelist whose readers should look for symbols and evocations of mood in her work rather than sequences of events, for stories.' It took until the 1970s for this orthodoxy to break up, although some critics still persist with the tendency 'to impose complex symbolic meanings on to the novels, and, at the same time, to regard them as an often-baffling experience without direct relevance to recognisable events'.[43] Chapter 4 of this guide marks the turning point in the 1970s. But the first few chapters also record the exceptional works in the earlier period which, for their rigour and clarity, as well as for their innovations in critical methodology, stand out from the nebulous mass. Erich Auerbach's classic chapter, from *Mimesis* (1946), on *To the Lighthouse* (in Chapter 2 below) is *the* shining example. Chapter 3 also examines the critical impulse to find a unifying Woolfian philosophy, and a totalising account of her *œuvre*. The classic here is Jean Guiguet's monumental and thoroughgoing existentialist study of Woolf's works.

The apparent 'indeterminacy' of Woolf's style, so repellent to Levenson's understanding of modernism, becomes a virtue when reinterpreted in terms of postmodernism. But the arena in which the debate over Woolf's apparent postmodernist practice has been most important, and most interestingly played out, and in which post-structuralist and post-Freudian psychoanalytical theories have been tested in readings of her work, is that of feminism. Chapter 5, which begins from the controversial intervention of Toril Moi's *Sexual/Textual Politics*, addresses the shift in the 1980s in feminist criticism from debates surrounding Woolf's theory of androgyny and her materialist feminism to debates on textuality and subjectivity. Chapter 6 explores more context-based readings, also emerging in the 1980s and coming to dominance in the 1990s, in which historical, political, and cultural factors dominate, and the influence of post-colonialist theories is discerned. A reading of *The Waves* as anti-imperialist by the prolific and provocative Woolf scholar, Jane Marcus, is the centre-piece.

Shortly after the publication of *The Waves* in 1931, Woolf confided to her diary: 'I'm the hare, a long way ahead of the hounds my critics.'[44] This guide sets out to follow the tracks of the many hounds, in the six decades since, to have taken chase after her.

CHAPTER ONE

Contemporary Reviews

To the Lighthouse and *The Waves* were not just successful in aesthetic terms, they also sold widely and well. They mark a period of consolidating commercial success for Woolf in which she took great pride as writer *and* publisher. Whether as reviewer, essayist or novelist, her status as a professional writer was always important to her, even as she distinguished between her aesthetic and commissioned writings. By this period she was commanding impressive fees for her stories and essays on both sides of the Atlantic, and recorded her pleasure at the spending power she earned by the pen.[1] *To the Lighthouse*, which was awarded the *Prix Femina* in 1928, sold 3,873 copies in its first year, and Woolf splashed out on a new car in the summer after its publication.[2] *Orlando* was an even greater success. *The Waves* too sold very well. This chapter records some of Woolf's private projections in composition and reflections on completion of *To the Lighthouse* and *The Waves*, as well as the responses, on publication, of some of those close to her. These private reviews, which years later found their way into print when the Bloomsbury industry took off, are discussed alongside a selection from the published critical reception, for which *Virginia Woolf: The Critical Heritage*, edited by Robin Majumdar and Allen McLaurin, remains the standard source.[3]

Reviews of *To the Lighthouse*

The formal innovation of *To the Lighthouse*, augured in Woolf's early conception of its triadic structure as 'two blocks joined by a corridor',[4] has dominated critical responses from the moment it was published. More conventional, novelistic, interpretations, and an interest in stable meaning, are certainly subsumed to formal concerns in the kind of critical response Woolf herself outlines to her friend Roger Fry, the influential theorist of formalism in the visual arts:[5]

■ I meant *nothing* by The Lighthouse. One has to have a central line down the middle of the book to hold the design together. I saw that all sorts of feelings would accrue to this, but I refused to think them out, and trusted that people would make it the deposit for their own emotions – which they have done, one thinking it means one thing another another. I can't manage Symbolism except in this vague, generalised way. Whether its right or wrong I don't know, but directly I'm told what a thing means, it becomes hateful to me.[6] □

This statement, once available in published form to a wider audience, has encouraged numerous readings of the novel and its imagery as enigmatic, mystical, and nebulously symbolic. But it should be recalled that Woolf directed these remarks to Fry whose approval she seems to court by echoing his formalist, aesthetic terms, as well as those of his associate Clive Bell (Woolf's brother-in-law), who made famous the theory of 'Significant Form'. The influence on Woolf's work of Fry's and Bell's (sometimes closely allied, sometimes differing) contributions to formalist theories has been of lasting interest to critics, and will be discussed in more detail in a later chapter.[7] Yet equally stimulating to later criticism are her early formulations in which she envisages the work as an elegy on her parents:

■ I'm now all on a strain with desire to stop journalism & get on to To the Lighthouse. This is going to be fairly short: to have father's character done complete in it; and mother's & St. Ives; & childhood; & all the usual things I try to put in – life, death &c.. But the centre is father's character, sitting in a boat, reciting We perished each alone while he crushes a dying mackerel.[8] □

Woolf indeed was to look back on the writing of *To the Lighthouse* as a kind of exorcism of her parents' ghosts,[9] while, somewhat conversely, her sister Vanessa thanks her, on its publication, for having raised them from the dead in its pages.[10] These private exchanges, once available in archives and published form, led many later critics to understand the novel as 'frankly biographical',[11] and most introductions to the novel lend them considerable emphasis. But this was not the assessment of the first reviewers of *To the Lighthouse*, one of whom even went so far as to assert that Woolf's writing, here and in the earlier *Mrs Dalloway*, 'is as objective as *Ulysses* is autobiographical and observational . . . Neither Clarissa [Dalloway] nor Mrs Ramsay has anything autobiographical about her'.[12] Whereas privately Woolf may have thought in terms of portraying, if not herself, her family and friends,[13] it was for a later generation of critics, informed by psychoanalytical theories and with a thirst for psychobiography, to make something of this in interpreting the novel. Although *To the Lighthouse* was to be for F.R. Leavis Woolf's 'one good novel' because of its recognisable portrayal of her father,[14] what occupied most early reviewers was not the equating of Mr and Mrs Ramsay with Leslie and Julia Stephen, nor Lily Briscoe with Vanessa Bell, but technical comparisons with the earlier works, particularly *Mrs Dalloway*. The important (interrelated) factors here were, above all, character, plot, and form. Woolf's innovations in these areas tend to elicit from the first reviewers mainly positive responses – sometimes mixed with mild anxiety, sometimes ranging to utter intolerance.

The first extract, taken from an anonymous review in the *Times Literary Supplement*, is typical of many contemporary reviews in admiring the book's form, worrying a little over its portrayal of character, and emphasising its central preoccupation with philosophical inquiry:

■ In form *To the Lighthouse* is as elastic as a novel can be. It has no plot, though it has a scheme and a motive; it shows characters in outline rather than in the round; and while it depends almost entirely on the passing of time, it expands or contracts the time-sense very freely. . . . It is a reflective book, with an ironical or wistful questioning of life and reality. Somehow this steals into the pages, whether there is a sunny peace in the garden, or Mr Ramsay is interrupted in a fairy-tale, or a couple is late for dinner, so that one is inclined to say that this question of the meaning of things, however masked, is not only the essence but the real protagonist in the story. . . . Perhaps this is one reason why you are less conscious of Mrs Woolf's characters than they are of each other. They have an acute consciousness which reminds you of the people in Henry James, but with a difference. The characters of Henry James are so absorbed in each other that they have no problem beyond the truth, or otherwise, of their relations; and they are so intensely seen as persons that they are real. But the people in Mrs Woolf's book seem to be looking through each other at some farther question; and, although they interact vividly, they are not completely real. . . . [In 'Time Passes'] Mrs Woolf's detachment seems a little strained, and, in fact, this transitional part of the book is not its strongest part. One comes back, however, to the charm and pleasure of her design.[15] □

Woolf's attempts at the depiction of multiple, possibly collective, subjective consciousnesses, implicitly mark her out as pushing 'stream-of-consciousness' in new directions, to the point where the term may not be adequate in accounting for her method. Louis Kronenberger, in the *New York Times*, suggests that 'Mrs Woolf' has utilised for different ends, 'the method of *Mrs Dalloway*', that is, 'her strikingly individual mingling of inward thought with outward action – in which the "stream of consciousness" style is liberated from its usual chaos and, by means of selection and sense of order, made formally compact'. He is typical of his generation of reviewers here in using as a benchmark for Woolf's work the 'Ulysses school'. But whereas the consciousness of one particular character dominates Mrs Dalloway, 'To the Lighthouse, on the other hand, is a book of interrelationships among people.' Troubled by the 'minor note' struck in Part Three, 'The Lighthouse', Kronenberger finds

■ the rest of the book has its excellencies. Like Mrs Dalloway it is underlaid with Mrs Woolf's ironic feeling toward life, though here character is not pitted against manners, but against other character. Once again Mrs Woolf makes use of her remarkable method of charac-terisation, a method not based on observation or personal experience, but purely synthetic, purely creational. . . . In To the Lighthouse there is nobody who even approaches Clarissa Dalloway in completeness and memorability, but on a smaller and perhaps more persuasive scale Mrs Ramsay achieves powerful reality. The other characters are not fully alive because they are not whole enough. Most of them are one-dimensional fragments that have been created with great insight but insufficient vitality. They have minds, moods, emotions – but they get all three through creative intellect. For passion Mrs Woolf has no gift – her people never invade the field of elementary emotions: they are hardly animal at all.

It is, I think, in the superb interlude called 'Time Passes' that Mrs Woolf reaches the most impressive height of the book, and there one can find a new note in her work, something beyond the ironic sophis-tication and civilised human values of Mrs Dalloway. In this description of the unused house in the Hebrides, entered for ten years only by old and forlorn women caretakers and the wind and the sea air and the light of the lighthouse lamp, she has told the story of all life passing on, of change and destruction and solitude and waste – the story which more than a little embodies the plot action of the rest of the book, but above all the story which has for man the profoundest human values of all, though for ten years the house itself never received a human guest. The great beauty of these eighteen pages of prose carries in it an emotional and ironical undertone that is superior to anything else that the first-class technician, the expert stylist, the deft student of human life in Mrs Woolf ever has done. Here is prose of extraordinary distinction in our time: here is poetry . . . [16] □

Arnold Bennett, Woolf's literary sparring partner, was not as impressed as Kronenberger with her method. He sums up, in his Evening Standard review, the dissenting view of her sacrifice of plot to the poetic: 'The scheme of the story is rather wilful – designed seemingly, but perhaps not really, to exhibit virtuosity. A group of people plan to sail in a small boat to a lighthouse. At the end some of them reach the lighthouse in a small boat. That is the externality of the plot.'[17] But the poetic dimension of Woolf's novel, particularly in 'Time Passes', is everything to other readers. For the poet Edwin Muir, 'one cannot regret that Mrs Woolf wrote the second section in this book' because of the 'imagination and beauty of writing . . . probably not surpassed in contemporary prose', yet he does worry 'how this kind of imagination can be applied, as one feels sure it can, to the business of the novelist, the shadowing forth of human life'. As if Woolf were on the verge of an important scientific discovery, he concludes: 'It is still a problem to be solved.'[18] Bennett, on the other hand, is not at all convinced by 'Time Passes' which he dismisses as 'a novel device to give the reader the impression of the passing of time – a sort of cataloguing of intermediate events. In my opinion it does not succeed.' He grudgingly concludes:

■ I have heard a good deal about the wonders of Mrs Woolf's style. She sometimes discovers a truly brilliant simile. She often chooses her adjectives and adverbs with beautiful felicity. But there is more in style than this. The form of her sentences is rather tryingly monotonous, and the distance between her nominatives and her verbs is steadily increasing. Still, *To the Lighthouse* has stuff in it strong enough to withstand quite a lot of adverse criticism.[19] □

In the following extract the American reviewer, Conrad Aitken, makes some perceptive comments on Woolf's technical achievements in comparison with those of Joyce *and* – possibly a surprise to today's readers – Dorothy Richardson and Jules Romains. In doing so he raises the issue of class in Woolf's work, and, although praising her technical achievements, allows to emerge a picture of Woolf as a charming 'lady' novelist, of fine sensibilities, removed from the real world and real lives of ordinary people. Class-based censure, implicit here, gathers force in later seams of Woolf criticism.

■ Among contemporary writers of fiction, Mrs Woolf is a curious and anomalous figure. In some respects, she is as 'modern', as radical, as Mr Joyce or Miss Richardson or M. Jules Romains; she is a highly self-conscious examiner of consciousness, a bold and original experimenter with the technique of novel-writing; but she is also, and just as strikingly, in other respects 'old-fashioned'. This anomaly does not defy analysis. The aroma of 'old-fashionedness' that rises from these highly original and modern novels . . . is a quality of attitude; a quality, to use a word which is itself nowadays old-fashioned, but none the less fragrant, of spirit. For in this regard, Mrs Woolf is no more modern than Jane Austen: she breathes the same air of gentility, of sequestration, of tradition; of life and people and things all brought, by the slow polish of centuries of tradition and use, to a pervasive refinement in which discrimination, on every conceivable plane, has become as instinctive and easy as the beat of the wing. Her people are 'gentle' people; her houses are the houses of gentlefolk; and the consciousness that informs both is a consciousness of well-being and culture, of the richness and lustre and dignity of tradition; a disciplined consciousness, in which emotions and feelings find their appropriate attitudes as easily and naturally – as *habitually*, one is tempted to say – as a skilled writer finds words.

It is this tightly circumscribed choice of scene – to use 'scene' in a social sense – that gives to Mrs Woolf's novels, despite her modernity of technique and insight, their odd and delicious air of parochialism, as of some small village-world, as bright and vivid and perfect in its tininess as a miniature: a small complete world which time has somehow missed. Going into these houses, one would almost expect to find antimacassars on the chair-backs and daguerreotype albums on the tables. For these people – these Clarissa Dalloways and Mrs Ramsays and Lily Briscoes – are all vibrantly and saturatedly conscious of background. And they all have the curious innocence that accompanies that sort of awareness. They are the creatures of seclusion, the creatures of shelter; they are exquisite beings, so perfectly and elaborately adapted to their environment that they have taken on something of the roundness and perfection of works of art. Their life, in a sense, is a sea-pool life: unruffled and secret: almost, if we can share the cool illusion of the sea-pool's occupants, inviolable. They hear rumours of the sea itself, that vast and terrifying force that lies somewhere beyond them, or around them, but they cherish a sublime faith that it will not disturb them; and if it does, at last, break in upon them with a cataclysmic force, a chaos of disorder and undisciplined violence, they can find no language for the disaster: they are simply bewildered.

But if, choosing such people, and such a *mise en scène*, for her material, Mrs Woolf inevitably makes her readers think of *Pride and Prejudice* and *Mansfield Park*, she compels us just as sharply, by her method of evoking them, to think of *Pilgrimage* and *Ulysses* and *The Death of a Nobody*. Mrs Woolf is an excellent critic, an extremely conscious and brilliant craftsman in prose; she is intensely interested in the technique of fiction; and one has at times wondered, so vividly from her prose has arisen a kind of *self-consciousness* of adroitness, whether she might not lose her way and give us a mere series of virtuosities or *tours de force*. It is easy to understand why Katherine Mansfield distrusted 'Mr Bennett and Mrs Brown'. She felt a kind of sterility in this dextrous holding of the raw stuff of life at arm's length, this playing with it as if it were a toy. Why not be more immediate – why not surrender to it? And one did indeed feel a rather baffling aloofness in this attitude: it was as if Mrs Woolf were a little afraid to come to grips with anything so coarse, preferred to see it through a safe thickness of plate-glass. . . . Now, in her new novel, *To the Lighthouse*, she relieves one's doubts, on this score, almost entirely.

For, if one still feels, during the first part of this novel almost depressingly, and intermittently thereafter, Mrs Woolf's irritating air as of carrying an enormous technical burden: her air of saying 'See how easily I do this!' or 'This is incomparably complex and difficult, but I have the brains for it': nevertheless, one's irritation is soon lost in the growing sense that Mrs Woolf has at last found a complexity and force of theme which is commensurate with the elaborateness and self-consciousness of her technical 'pattern'. By degrees, one forgets the manner in the matter. One resists the manner, petulantly objects to it, in vain: the moment comes when at last one ceases to be aware of something persistently artificial in this highly feminine style, and finds oneself simply immersed in the vividness and actuality of this world of Mrs Woolf's – believing in it, in fact, with the utmost intensity, and feeling it with that completeness of surrender with which one feels the most moving of poetry. It is not easy to say whether this abdication of 'distance' on the reader's part indicates that Mrs Woolf has now achieved a depth of poetic understanding, a vitality, which was somehow just lacking in the earlier novels, or whether it merely indicates a final triumph of technique. Can one profitably try to make a distinction between work that is manufactured, bitterly and strenuously, by sheer *will* to imagination, and work that is born of imagination all complete – assuming that the former is, in the upshot, just as convincing as the latter? Certainly one feels everywhere in Mrs Woolf's work this will to imagine, this canvassing of possibilities by a restless and searching and brilliant mind: one feels this mind at work, matching and selecting, rejecting this colour and accepting that, saying, 'It is this that the heroine would say, it is this that she would think'; and nevertheless Mrs Woolf's step is so sure, her choice is so nearly invariably right, and her imagination, even if deliberately willed, is so imaginative, that in the end she makes a beautiful success of it. She makes her Mrs Ramsay – by giving us her stream of consciousness – amazingly alive; and she supplements this just sufficiently, from *outside*, as it were, by giving us also, intermittently, the streams of consciousness of her husband, of her friend Lily Briscoe, of her children: so that we are documented, as to Mrs Ramsay, from every quarter and arrive at a solid vision of her by a process of triangulation. The richness and copiousness and ease, with which this is done, are a delight. These people are astoundingly real: they belong to a special 'class', as Mrs Woolf's characters nearly always do, and exhale a Jane-Austenish aroma of smallness and lostness and incompleteness: but they are magnificently real. We live in that delicious house with them – we feel the minute textures of their lives with their own vivid senses – we imagine with their extraordinary imaginations, are self-conscious with their self-consciousness – and ultimately we know them as well, as terribly, as we know ourselves.

Thus, curiously, Mrs Woolf has rounded the circle. Apparently, at the outset of her work, avoiding any attempt to present life 'immediately', as Chekhov and Katherine Mansfield preferred to do; and choosing instead a medium more sophisticated and conscious, as if she never for a moment wished us to forget the *frame* of the picture, and the fact that the picture *was* a picture; she has finally brought this method to such perfection, or so perfectly allowed it to flower of itself, that the artificial has become natural, the mediate has become immediate. The technical brilliance glows, melts, falls away; and there remains a poetic apprehension of life of extraordinary loveliness. Nothing happens, in this houseful of odd nice people, and yet all of life happens. The tragic futility, the absurdity, the pathetic beauty, of life – we experience all of this in our sharing of seven hours of Mrs Ramsay's wasted or not wasted existence. We have seen, through her, the world.[20] □

Reviews of *To the Lighthouse*, whether entirely positive or evidencing reservations, pay serious attention to Woolf's new lyric novel for its innovations in form, experimentalism with character and apparent abandonment of plot. Even her most hostile critic, Arnold Bennett, finds the work not without virtue. It has been for later criticism to pick up on the ramifications of Woolf's private meditations on elegy and the more personal elegiac significance of this work. Her departure from the conventions of traditional realism, however, did infuriate some readers not so willing to grant the novel poetic licence. Whereas most reviewers and most later criticism, pay little attention to the Hebridean setting of *To the Lighthouse*, some private readers were sufficiently incensed by Woolf's depiction of it to point out her errors. Shortly after it was published Woolf complains to Vita Sackville-West that 'an old creature writes to say that all my fauna and flora of the Hebrides is totally inaccurate'.[21] Exasperated by the pedantic corrections of Lord Olivier, who 'writes that my horticulture and natural history is in every instance wrong: there are no rooks, elms, or dahlias in the Hebrides; my sparrows are wrong; so are my carnations', she confides to her sister: 'This is the sort of thing that painters know nothing of.'[22] An early review of Woolf's more traditional realist novel, *Night and Day*, points to 'little slips' and 'inaccuracies',[23] and these traits become associated in later criticism with a discerned stylistic vagueness and, again, Woolf's letter to Fry gathers significance. Joan Bennett, in her 1945 study of Woolf, suggests such 'vagaries', 'deliberate carelessness' and 'inaccuracy of fact' are 'due to the essential feminineness of her mind',[24] and goes on to liken the workings of Woolf's mind to those of her own creations, Mrs Dalloway and Mrs Ramsay. In such ways, the attribution of an aura of feminine mysticism to Woolf's work begins to emerge in the criticism. One work, above all others, has been the focus of this tendency: *The Waves*.[25] Whereas readers of *To the Lighthouse* may find vestigial elements of an old realism in the prose, readers of *The Waves* find themselves more firmly in the terrain of poetry.

Reviews of *The Waves*

■ What interests me in the last stage was the freedom & boldness with which my imagination picked up used & tossed aside all the images & symbols which I had prepared. I am sure that this is the right way of using them – not in set pieces, as I had tried at first, coherently, but simply as images; never making them work out; only suggest. Thus I hope to have kept the sound of the sea & the birds, dawn, & garden subconsciously present, doing their work under ground.[26] □

Woolf's own private review of *The Waves* is couched in terms of a new, poetic, sense of freedom in her handling of formal, aesthetic elements. The lyricism of the work similarly dominates the first critical responses, and concern over the notion that 'nothing happens' in Woolf's novels evaporates to awed acceptance in many early reviews of *The Waves*. According to Woolf herself, canvassing family and friends (some of whom did go into print on the subject), 'no two people think alike about it',[27] but we may discern in fact a strong consensus among reviewers, whether they love it or loathe it, that *The Waves*, embodying a more fully sustained attempt at the lyric prose promised in some of the flights of language in *To the Lighthouse*, is, in the words of Harold Nicolson, 'a literary sensation', taking to the brink her experimentalism in plot, lyric, and character:

■ Mrs Woolf has carried 'the internal monologue' a stage further than was dreamt of even by Joyce. It forms the entire apparatus of her story. It expands the lyrical note which lurks always as the undertone to her writings into something antiphonal, sacerdotal, vatic. . . . Mrs Woolf has not attempted to give a consecutive narrative or to isolate distinct characters. Her aim is to convey the half-lights of human experience and the fluid edges of personal identity. Her six characters fuse, towards the end, into a synthesis of sensation.[28] □

The minority opinion, it seems, was with Vita Sackville-West (Nicolson's wife, and Woolf's lover), who – to Woolf's great delight – considered *The Waves* 'so bad that only a small dog that had been fed on gin could have written it'.[29] Woolf's sister, Vanessa Bell, responded to the more personal aspects of its elegiac dimension, for the novel is in part an elegy on their brother Thoby, as Woolf's diary entry on the completion of the manuscript reveals: 'Anyhow it is done; & I have been sitting these 15 minutes in a state of glory, & calm, & some tears, thinking of Thoby & if I could write Julian Thoby Stephen 1881–1906 on the first page. I suppose not.' [30] Although Woolf resists this temptation, her sister confirms an implicit homage to Thoby when she surfaces from her first reading of *The Waves*:

■ Of course there's the personal side, the feelings you describe on what I must take to be Thoby's death (though I know that it is only what it means to me, and perhaps you). But that's not very important, and it's accidental that I can't help such feelings coming in and giving an added meaning. Even then I know it's only because of your art that I am so moved. I think you have made one's human feelings into something less personal – if you wouldn't think me foolish I should say you have found the 'lullaby capable of singing him to rest.' But that's only a small bit.[31] □

Her feelings about Thoby in connection with *The Waves*, although powerful, are personal and partial, Bell emphasises, and she goes on to discuss the novel in comparison with her own painting technique. This recognition of the shifting away from the biographical and autobiographical in the work is a perceptive anticipation of an important strand of thought in the novel's critical reception, concerned with the idea of 'impersonality'. Woolf's organisation of *The Waves* into subjective passages by six soliloquists, punctuated by objective, pastoral, passages without a marked narrator, suggests a concern both with subjectivity (individual and collective) and phenomenology, with subjective engagement and objective detachment, with processes of the self, as well as absence of the self. 'I did mean that in some vague way we are the same person, and not separate people', she tells G. Lowes Dickinson:

■ The six characters were supposed to be one. I'm getting old myself . . . and I come to feel more and more how difficult it is to collect oneself into one Virginia; even though the special Virginia in whose body I live for the moment is violently susceptible to all sorts of separate feelings. Therefore I wanted to give the sense of continuity, instead of which most people say, no you've given the sense of flowing and passing away and that nothing matters.[32] □

Vanessa Bell's response has come to dominate interpretations – after being 'completely submerged in *The Waves*' she finds herself 'gasping, out of breath, choking, half-drowned . . . so overcome by the beauty'.[33]

Many readers and critics find themselves concurring with Gerald Bullett's summation: 'It is impossible to describe, impossible to do more than salute, the richness, the strangeness, the poetic illumination of this book.'[34] Mystical and aesthetic analogies abound. Before lapsing back into mystical silence, one reviewer finds *The Waves* 'a pointillist picture, alive with golden notes',[35] while for another it is 'a kind of symphonic poem' inhabited by 'six imagist poets, six facets of the imagist poet that Mrs Woolf is herself.'[36] Others find Woolf's aestheticism has gone too far: for Storm Jameson, 'the convention which Mrs Woolf has adopted for this book is one that a clever writer might have thought of and a great writer would have rejected as – clever'.[37] For Robert Herrick *The Waves* is 'style and very little more', but his tongue-in-cheek references to the imagined reflections of a 'convinced communist' critic on its engagement with 'English imperialism' may be seen to anticipate very recent developments in post-colonial criticism of this novel.[38] Earl Daniels, on the other hand, anticipates the dominant and lasting strand of Bergsonism in Woolf criticism when he defines the basis of *The Waves* to be 'the eternal drama of subject and object, of inner and outer, of the eternal and the flux.'[39]

The anonymous reviewer for the *Times Literary Supplement* is one of the earliest critics to cite Woolf's own criticism (that famous passage from 'Modern Fiction') as an authority for her fiction: 'One might say that in Mrs Woolf's novel life has turned into what she once described it as being – "a luminous halo, a semi-transparent envelope surrounding us from the beginning of consciousness to the end". And the novel has turned into something very like a poem.' The reviewer goes on to draw attention to the novel's concern with character and impersonality, and seems impressed by its technical achievements and capacity to move, but, in keeping with those Woolf finds to have sensed from *The Waves* that 'nothing matters', also appears troubled by an immanent 'sense of a void':

■ This incisive and unflagging prose is as rapid as verse, and the utterances follow one another with a sort of rhythmical incantation. Sometimes they are frankly antiphons, and one always has that sense of a response; the book moves to that measure. This formal effect recurs with the further settings which have given it its title; prefixed to each movement of it there is a background of the sea, with changes from dawn to sunset. Here, it seems to us, the effect of a complete detachment does not quite succeed. It may be because Mrs Woolf does not keep our eyes on the sea, but diverts them to birds and fields and gardens; or it may simply be that these elaborate, often exquisite, passages are too deliberate altogether.

A poetic novel, as it certainly is, it is still – however peculiarly – a novel. The six people all have their idiosyncrasy of nature; Bernard, with his communicative, affable receptiveness; Louis, very conscious of humiliations; but with a kind of ruthless romanticism below his business efficiency; Neville, who lives with a concentrated inwardness and makes, we infer, a name; and the women – Jinny, who lives for her body and the sparkle of life; Susan, embedded in the country rhythm and motherhood; and Rhoda, a flying nymph of solitude. We watch them unfolding, and are aware of the silence under their speech, movement without action, and the flickering of that inmost flame of personality call it spirit or ego – whose place is often vacant even in a novel of character. Mrs Woolf's uncommon achievement is to have made this visible, and it is hardly less of a feat, perhaps, to have shown life in a texture which matches it. It seems a proof by example that the matter of fiction can be changed and distilled to a new transparency. Yet there is as certainly a cost in the process. The book, with all its imaginativeness and often poignant feeling, leaves some sense of a void behind, if not of an actual desolation. It is not merely, perhaps, that we have been deprived of the usual comfortable upholsterings but that creative experience in life is of a closer tissue than this and demands a fuller view of its attachments. Alive as the novel is with the vividness of things, one feels in more than one sense that its spirits roam through empty places. Yet it is simpler, after all, to be grateful for a book that achieves its own aim and that no one else could have written.[40] □

Frank Swinnerton, an early negative critic of Woolf's work on grounds of class,[41] does not altogether share this sense of gratitude in his review for the *Evening News*:

■ I find the present book as bloodless as its predecessors; but it would be idle to deny great distinction to the style, great beauty to many of the similes, and much subtlety and penetration to the author's intuitions. If to these qualities life had been added, I should have been lost in admiration of Mrs Woolf's gifts. . . . Though we ourselves may be lost in sensations and reveries, we are not therefore, to others, the amorphous creatures of the Woolfian novel. And the characters in *The Waves* have, for the reader, no such personalities as those known to their friends. Seen, as it were, as receptive sensationalists, from within, they never live. Once, therefore, one is past the beauty of the author's writing, and the ingenuity of her associative power, one is conscious only of a luminous transparency which bears no relation to flesh and blood. Yet these characters are offered as human beings.[42] □

In labelling 'Mrs Woolf . . . a metaphysical poet who has chosen prose-fiction for her medium', Gerald Bullett seems to be invoking the criticism of Woolf's friend, T.S. Eliot, whose own interest in poetic impersonality and the poetry of the Metaphysicals was highly influential, and who is understood to be the model for the poet Louis in *The Waves*.[43] He also anticipates David Daiches' Yeatsian interpretation[44] in observing: 'Every novelist speaks through his various masks; but her masks on this occasion – Bernard, Susan, and so on – are confessed as such, and the voice speaking through them never varies, never disguises itself, speaks always in its own subtle literary idiom, and gives utterance to thoughts which the character in question (a child, let us say) could not, in nature, have had.'[45] Gerald Sykes anticipates the chauvinism of the later canon-makers of modernism by first squarely defining *The Waves* as modernist, only to diminish Woolf's achievements in a patronising comparison with Joyce's.

■ The word 'modern' has more significance today than it probably ever had before. No century can have been so conscious of its difference from other centuries as the twentieth. To go into this consciousness, this 'modernism', would require a great deal of space; but if we confine ourselves to the arts, and to a very brief glance at them, we observe, beginning several years ago, a considerable number of clever people – not necessarily artists – who nevertheless desired to 'express themselves'. (Some began in poetry or painting and ended in advertising or lampshades.) They were much too ingenious, too renascent to be content with the art forms that they found. Change, unconventionality, experiment were in the air. In literature, in prose, the old novel form displeased them. They wanted 'new forms'. It irked them to be confined to realistic narration, which precluded a language like that of the Elizabethans, which they envied.

The present volume is one of the culminations of that movement. In *The Waves* Mrs Woolf has carried her well-known experiments to their farthest. It is unquestionably a new form, a novel told entirely in soliloquies. . . . Culturally, despite its lofty traditionalism, *The Waves* suggests a pretty lampshade – a well-educated lampshade, smart, original, advanced. Not an ordinary lampshade by any means, but one that has been a mode of self-expression. A confusion peculiar to our country makes it necessary to point out the important differences between a desire for self-expression and the true creative urge. It is not the latter, it is not an artist's passion, that we discern in *The Waves*. There is beauty – one has the sensation of being smothered in beauty – but it is synthetic. Unfortunately, criticism of new imaginative literature is in such bad shape today that most people, hearing that *The Waves* has a 'new form', will lump it indiscriminately with the rest of 'modernist' fiction, and particularly with *Ulysses* by James Joyce. No two books could better exemplify the difference between a desire for self expression and the true creative urge. In *The Waves* we see what happens to an amiable talent that lacks an inner drive; we see virtuosity that has finally become disconnected from inspiration, virtuosity therefore that has lost its original charm and turned into a formula; we see a torrent of imagery because the imagist tap has been left running. In *Ulysses* we see a genuine work of art. It has nothing to do with the tea-room modernism that we have been discussing.[46] □

The last extract in this chapter, appropriately, is from a review by a poet. Edwin Muir begins with a survey of Woolf's *œuvre*, singling out 'Time Passes' as 'perhaps the best thing Mrs. Woolf wrote before *The Waves*'.

■ It describes the gradual dilapidation of the house where the action has passed and will pass again. The house is beset by countless great and little forces, by wind, rain, mice, dust, neglect, its own age. A very powerful sense of time is conveyed in this way. But when Mrs. Woolf writes about time she is carried away; the middle section of *To the Lighthouse* is consequently far too strong for the other two: it did not need all this, one feels, to make a few characters a few years older. The time she evokes has hardly anything to do with individual human life at all, except accidentally, like evolution, for example; it is so much too powerful that it seems to have no effect at all, like an electric charge which, multiplied a thousand times, passes through one's body without one's feeling it, whereas, reduced to the right voltage, it would act devastatingly. □

Muir passes perceptive comment on Woolf's innovation in characterisation, and makes useful and sympathetic comparison of her work with that of Pirandello and Lawrence. He concludes with a close comparative analysis of her style in selected passages from *Mrs Dalloway* and *The Waves*. In so doing he anticipates the high standard of close reading that Woolf's work, as we will see, has elicited from some of her best critics.

■ Mrs. Woolf quite discards characterisation in the ordinary sense in *The Waves*, and her vision of life at last stands out clearly. She seems no longer concerned with temporal attributes in this book, but with permanent things: the problem of time which she has pursued for so long has yielded her here a resolution. The six figures whose monologues make it up are beings freed from the illusions of time. They stand beyond time and see themselves within it; they incarnate something in the spirit which in the midst of change is not deceived. They have been blamed for not being characters, and very ignorantly; for to such beings character is merely a costume they put on, and have to put on, before they go on the temporal stage to play their parts. If they are to be called characters at all, then they are characters who have awakened.

It is difficult to find any parallels in literature for these six figures, or for the dimension in which they move. One may be reminded now and then of Pirandello's much overpraised *Six Characters in Search of an Author*; but the resemblance is only a surface one. For Pirandello merely presents schematically a few aspects of illusion, whereas Mrs. Woolf has pierced to something deeper, to that part of us which refuses to be deceived. Is there a part of us which refuses to be deceived? If there is, it exists where consciousness is most intense, alert and magnanimous. It exists also at a level where laughter and tears, whether singly or simultaneously, are no longer apposite responses. These six figures are something new in literature, so new that a critic may legitimately refuse to try to find a formula for it. The book is a continuous revelation on a level rarely touched by the novelist.

In conception, however, it is quite simple. Six characters, three men and three women, tell in alternate monologue their stories from childhood to middle age. The whole is written in the present tense, the response of the monologist accompanying every event as it happens, the awake character who regards and the somnambulist character who acts being indissolubly attached and yet separate. Seen by this passionate observer all action, all emotion, all change becomes a series of pictures. . . . Mrs. Woolf's conception of life in this book is a pessimistic one lightened only by the supersensual pleasures of the contemplating self. 'All these things happen in a second and last forever.' 'If there are no stories, what end can there be, or what beginnings? Life is not susceptible to the treatment we give it when we try to tell it.' (Incidentally this has not prevented her from trying to tell it.) 'But now I made the contribution of maturity to childhood's intuitions – satiety and doom; the sense of what is unescapable in our lot; death; the knowledge of limitations; how life is more obdurate than one had thought it.' And in a description of a meeting of all the six figures: 'We saw for a moment laid out among us the body of the complete human being whom we have failed to be, but at the same time, cannot forget.' It is in intellectual formulations such as these that the grief of Mrs. Woolf's ideal observers finds its keenest edge. That grief is very keen, but it is not a grief that can be solved by tears; it is hostile to them.

Nothing is stranger in modern literature, and nothing probably could tell us more about it, than this hostility to tears, the mark at which once even the greatest writers aimed. All that one can do is to note it. The modern writer, no matter how passionately or deeply he may feel, is never concerned with the tears in things. D.H. Lawrence was a man who felt and wrote with conspicuous passion; George Eliot, let us say, was a woman who felt and wrote not with conspicuous passion; yet in her calm way she tapped the fount of tears, whereas D.H. Lawrence, while arousing many emotions in our breasts, quite ignored this immemorial source of relief. In spite of all his anti-intellectualism he was more penetrated by what he himself called the virus of intellect than George Eliot, though she was as powerfully resolved to be intellectual, as he to be 'instinctive'. Indeed almost all modern novelists are more intellectual in a certain sense than any of their predecessors of fifty years ago: in the sense that the intellect conditions their emotional responses more decisively, making those responses less naive and immediately satisfying. More deliberate and unsure, also, however; for it is difficult to achieve, where the intellect is in part control, any effort possessing the simple inevitability of a burst of tears. This may partly account for the sense of emotional frustration, of indefinite postponement, which so many modern novels produce. It may account, for instance, for Lawrence's equivocal operation on us. The old catharsis was definitely impossible; the new one was difficult to find. In *The Waves* a new catharsis has been found. Its art is at once modern and complete.

The great step forward that Mrs. Woolf made in *The Waves* is reflected also in the style. *Mrs Dalloway* was a wonderful piece of writing, but its grace had a touch of hesitation, even of fussiness, with all those clauses and sentences ending in 'ing'. But the passage describing Clarissa sewing the silk dress is one of the finest in the book, and may serve for a test of comparison:

> So on a summer's day waves collect, overbalance, and fall; collect and fall; and the whole world seems to be saying 'that is all' more and more ponderously, until even the heart in the body which lies in the sun on the beach says too, That is all. Fear no more, says the heart. Fear no more, says the heart committing its burden to some sea, which sighs collectively for all sorrows and renews, begins, collects, lets fall. And the body alone listens to the passing bee; the wave breaking; the dog barking, far away barking and barking.

How different the rhythm of that is from that of the passages I have quoted from *The Waves*. It is a fluttering rhythm, a rhythm in which a thousand almost imperceptible hesitations are concealed. In *The Waves* this prose has put away all hesitation, and cuts out images and thoughts in one sweep. It is impatiently, almost violently immediate. What it recalls most strongly is Rilke's superb prose, which was a sort of inspired shorthand. And one imagines that it has changed in this astonishing way because Mrs. Woolf is dealing directly now with immediate and essential truths of experience. The result is an authentic and unique masterpiece, which is bound to have an influence on the mind of this generation.[47] □

CHAPTER TWO

The 1930s and 40s: Summing Up

THIS CHAPTER covers the period after the publication of *The Waves* in the 1930s to Woolf's death in 1941 and beyond to the critical aftermath of the 1940s. One major extract dominates this chapter: Erich Auerbach's impressive reading of a section of *To the Lighthouse* with which he closes his classic critical work on representation and narrative in western literature from Homer to the twentieth century. *Mimesis: The Representation of Reality in Western Literature* (1946) was first published in English in 1956 and remains one of the most important, stimulating, and highly influential, points of reference for Woolf studies. I will outline and illustrate with briefer extracts what of significance for readings of *To the Lighthouse* and *The Waves* precedes Auerbach. In this period of 'summing up' (a popular choice of title for last chapters on Woolf),[1] which began before, but was galvanised by, her death, a number of book-length studies of Woolf appeared, as well as shorter pieces, some of which have had lasting influence. In 1931 Floris Delattre, author of one of the first books on Woolf (1932),[2] published a short article on Woolf and Bergson.[3] We will return to the influence of Bergson in the next chapter, but it is worth noting that Delattre's succinct and intelligent introduction to these ideas was available alongside contemporary anglophone criticism which does not often reach the same intellectual ground.

1931 also saw the publication of a short but perceptive essay on Woolf by William Empson, who puts her work in the highest company:

■ Shakespeare was like Nature; we have been saying it for three centuries. There were more echoes in his work than he knew; he wrote from his Preconsciousness; any work in hand formed a world he was living in, so that he could find his way about in it as if by habit; any of his stones may have been made bread, and repay turning. Novelists have seldom been called Nature in this sense . . . the same claim might be made for Mrs Woolf. □

We have already noted his comments here on the importance of Woolf's feminist criticism, and his references to Shakespeare imply that he has conferred on Woolf the status of her own ideal in *A Room of One's Own*: Shakespeare's sister. In commenting on the 'complex working of . . . symbols' in *To the Lighthouse*, Empson suggests that its 'poetical attitude to language . . . would gain by an annotated edition'. But he is moved towards some reservations by Woolf's 'impressionism'. This can be a confusing term, and seems to have been favoured by critics in this period over the one more directly connected with Bloomsbury aesthetics: 'post-impressionism'. But it is a kind 'impressionism', presumably derived from their reading of Woolf's 'luminous halo' imagery in 'Modern Fiction', that these critics seem to privilege:

■ The Lighthouse becomes a symbol of energies at the basis of human life, which support and exclude the understanding; Mrs Ramsay sets herself going like the Lighthouse to sustain her party, and it is for this reason that the pulse is like a flame. Or one may say that the Lighthouse has at times been the symbol of reason and male power of setting large-scale things in order (for it is in sight of the Lighthouse that Mr Bankes and Mr Tansley go and talk politics on the terrace after dinner, as if they had gone on to the bridge of the ship to take up their bearings), and it is then with a sort of feminist triumph that it becomes a symbol of Mrs Ramsay. . . . The end of *To the Lighthouse* . . . leaves one remembering the whole book, partly by the unifying and mystifying effect of the symbol, chiefly because there is nobody left at the end about whose future behaviour you feel immediately curious. . . . The impressionist method, the attempt to convey directly your own attitude to things, how you connect one thing with another, is in a sense fallacious; it tries to substitute for telling a story, as the main centre of interest, what is in fact one of the by-products of telling a story; it tries to correlate sensations rather than the impulses that make the sensations interesting; even tries to define the impulse by an accumulation of the sensations it suggested to the author. Even those delicate interconnections on which the impressionist method depends . . . need a story to make them intelligible, and even if Shakespeare (since I have dragged him in) could afford to abandon himself to these delicious correspondences he had first to get a strong and obvious story which would be elective on the stage. I think myself, at any rate, that Mrs Woolf's most memorable successes come when she is sticking most closely to her plot. . . . So many of her images, glittering and searching as they are, spreading out their wealth of feeling, as if split, in the mind, give one just that sense of waste that is given by life itself; '. . . the great revelation perhaps never did come. Instead, there were little daily miracles, illuminations, matches struck unexpectedly in the dark'.

'How far that little candle sheds its beams'; but still it is the business of art to provide candelabra, to aggregate its matches into a lighthouse of many candlepower. If only (one finds oneself feeling in re-reading these novels), if only these dissolved units of understanding had been co-ordinated into a system; if only, perhaps, there was an index, showing what had been compared with what; if only these materials for the metaphysical conceit, poured out so lavishly, had been concentrated into crystals of poetry that could be remembered, how much safer one would feel.[4] □

Empson's is a much more generous view of Woolf's 'impressionism' than that of M.C. Bradbrook, also appearing under the banner of *Scrutiny*. Bradbrook likens Woolf to a fastidious, 'myopic', painter capable of fine detail but with no overall sense of design – infatuated with technique, she has no 'statement' to make. 'Woolf refuses to be pinned down . . . and consequently she is debarred from narrative technique, since this implies a schema of values, or even from direct presentation of powerful feelings or major situations.'[5] Woolf's writing so focuses on the present moment that it remains outside narrative progression, and therefore seems without historical awareness and without a sense of value (moral or aesthetic). This indictment was to be followed by the notorious, and even more savage attacks on Woolf's work from the *Scrutiny* quarter, first by Q.D. Leavis, in her coruscating 1938 review of *Three Guineas* (a little of which goes a long way: for example, Mrs Woolf's 'most cherished project of all' in this *anti*-fascist tract let us remember, 'is to uproot criticism root and branch in the Nazi manner'), and then by F.R. Leavis, its editor, in his 1942 article, 'After *To the Lighthouse*':

■ The envelope enclosing her dramatised sensibilities may be 'semi-transparent' but it seems to shut out all the ranges of experience accompanying those kinds of preoccupation, volitional and moral, with an external world which are not felt primarily as preoccupation with one's consciousness of it. The preoccupation with intimating 'significance' in fine shades of consciousness, together with the unremitting play of visual imagery, of 'beautiful' writing and the lack of moral interest and interest in action, give the effect of something closely akin to a sophisticated aestheticism.[6] □

The Leavises' class-based attack on Woolf's work is weakened by inflammatory hyperbole, but has, nevertheless, left a lasting legacy, which (with the exception of a television broadcast by Tom Paulin)[7] rarely manages to match their vitriol, and also includes some more measured and interesting discussion of Woolf and class. Important questions have been raised concerning the representation of working-class people in

To the Lighthouse and their near total exclusion from representation in *The Waves*. But it has been for later feminist critics to develop this debate.[8] Paradoxically, the most ugly and undignified of contentions in Woolf criticism since the *Scrutiny* attack was the 'heated and personal debate'[9] in the 1980s between the feminist scholar, Jane Marcus, who sees Woolf as a full-blooded Marxist, and Quentin Bell who insists that 'Woolf wasn't a feminist and she wasn't political.'[10]

The novelist Winifred Holtby's early study, *Virginia Woolf: A Critical Memoir* (1932),[11] offers an account of Woolf's background, including reference to the influence of her experiences in the women's movement and her views on the working class, as well as a survey of her work, closing with *The Waves*. Holtby, who in an earlier and interesting chapter looks at cinematography and *Jacob's Room*, focuses on Mrs Ramsay (who 'is the lighthouse') in her discussion of *To the Lighthouse* which, echoing Woolf's famous imagery, she defines as '. . . a ghost story. Its characters move in a radiant, half-transparent atmosphere, as though already suffused into the spiritual world.'[12] Her discussion of *The Waves* begins by acknowledging that its composition coincided with that of Woolf's controversial, political, essay (now known as 'Memories of a Working Women's Guild')[13] which formed the introduction to Margaret Llewelyn Davies' collection, *Life As We Have Known It*, by Co-Operative Working Women (1931). Holtby's conclusion, that this essay marks Woolf's 'furthest excursion into political writing' while *The Waves*, on the other hand, 'is the most delicate, complex and aesthetically pure piece of writing that she has yet produced',[14] anticipates an enduring distinction in Woolf criticism between the political and the aesthetic in her work, particularly in connection with *The Waves*. Reconciliation between these opposites becomes, as we shall see, an important task for many later critics.

Woolf, who was acquainted with Holtby,[15] did not cherish the growing critical attention her work was attracting at this time: 'I'm threatened with 3 more books upon me: Holtby has induced another publisher to print her follies . . .'.[16] She later confides to her diary that Holtby's book 'doesn't cause me a single tremor'[17] (although she writes to Ethel Smythe that a high temperature made her 'roar with laughter' at it).[18] But, writing to Hugh Walpole, she senses a premature obituary in all this: 'No I've not read Miss Holtby: Prof Delattre (in French) almost did for me; I suppose Winifred has merely added another tombstone. She is the daughter of a Yorkshire farmer and learnt to read, I'm told, while minding the pigs – hence her passion for me.'[19]

Claire Sprague blames E.M. Forster, the author of the next brief extract, for the criticism that 'became virulent in the mouth of F.R. Leavis'. She continues, 'Although E.M. Forster concludes that she escapes "the Palace of Art" . . . his essay as a whole nevertheless reflects the view that Mrs Woolf lived in an ivory tower during the politically left-oriented 30s, that she was remote from reality (though at times a shrill feminist), ignorant of the class struggle, and in William Troy's words, "as acutely refined and aristocratic" as Henry James.'[20] This seems a little hard on Forster's tribute, which movingly concludes:

■ ... she gave acute pleasure in new ways, she pushed the light of the English language a little further against darkness. Those are facts. The epitaph of such an artist cannot be written by the vulgar-minded or by the lugubrious. They will try, indeed they have already tried, but their words make no sense. It is wiser, it is safer, to regard her career as a triumphant one. She triumphed over what are primly called 'difficulties', and she also triumphed in the positive sense: she brought in the spoils. And sometimes it is as a row of little silver cups that I see her work gleaming. 'These trophies,' the inscription runs, 'were won by the mind from matter, its enemy and its friend.' □

In celebrating Woolf's love of writing, her professional dedication – 'She liked writing with an intensity which few writers have attained, or even desired' – Forster points to the sensuous vitality of her prose, 'where we can taste really new bread, and touch real dahlias'. In surveying her writing, he significantly points up the dualism at work in *To the Lighthouse* and *The Waves*. He goes on to set out his views on her flaws: her poeticism and her feminism.

■ *To the Lighthouse* is in three movements. It has been called a novel in sonata form, and certainly the slow central section, conveying the passing of time, does demand a musical analogy. We have, when reading it, the rare pleasure of inhabiting two worlds at once, a pleasure only art can give: the world where a little boy wants to go to a lighthouse but never manages it until, with changed emotions, he goes there as a young man; and the world where there is pattern, and this world is emphasised by passing much of the observation through the mind of Lily Briscoe, who is a painter. Then comes *The Waves*. Pattern here is supreme – indeed it is italicised. And between the motions of the sun and the waters, which preface each section, stretch, without interruption, conversation, words in inverted commas. It is a strange conversation, for the six characters, Bernard, Neville, Louis, Susan, Jinny, Rhoda, seldom address one another, and it is even possible to regard them ... as different facets of one single person. Yet they do not conduct internal monologues, they are in touch amongst themselves, and they all touch the character who never speaks, Percival. At the end, most perfectly balancing their scheme, Bernard, the would-be novelist, sums up, and the pattern fades out. *The Waves* is an extraordinary achievement ... It is trembling on the edge. A little less – and it would lose its poetry. A little more – and it would be over into the abyss, and be dull and arty. It is her greatest book, though *To the Lighthouse* is my favourite. . . . After this survey, we can state her problem. Like most novelists worth reading, she strays from the fictional norm. She dreams, designs, jokes, invokes, observes details, but she does not tell a story or weave a plot, and – can she create character? That is her problem's centre. . . . This is her great difficulty. Holding on with one hand to poetry, she stretches and stretches to grasp things which are best gained by letting go of poetry. She would not let go, and I think she was quite right, though critics who like a novel to be a novel will disagree. . . . As soon as we understand the nature of her equipment, we shall see that as regards human beings she did as well as she could. Belonging to the world of poetry, but fascinated by another world, she is always stretching out from her enchanted tree and snatching bits from the flux of daily life as they float past, and out of these bits she builds novels. . . . So that is her problem. She is a poet, who wants to write something as near to a novel as possible. . . . She was not confined to sensations and intellectualism. She was a social creature, with an outlook both warm and shrewd. But it was a peculiar outlook, and we can best get at it by looking at a very peculiar side of her: her feminism.

Feminism inspired one of the most brilliant of her books – the charming and persuasive *A Room of One's Own* . . . But feminism is also responsible for the worst of her books – the cantankerous *Three Guineas* – and for the less successful streaks in *Orlando*. There are spots of it all over her work, and it was constantly in her mind. She was convinced that society is man-made, that the chief occupations of men are else shedding of blood, the making of money, the giving of orders, and the wearing of uniforms, and that none of these occupations is admirable. . . . She declined to co-operate, in theory, and sometimes in fact. She refused to sit on committees or to sign appeals, on the ground that women must not condone this tragic male-made mess, or accept the crumbs of power which men throw them occasionally from their hideous feast. Like Lysistrata, she withdrew.

In my judgment there is something old-fashioned about this extreme feminism . . . However, I speak as a man here, and as an elderly one. The best judges of her feminism are neither elderly men nor even elderly women, but young women.[21] □

Forster may consider Woolf's feminism an unfortunate blemish on her work, but at least he acknowledges its significance and admits to his own inadequacy as its judge. David Daiches, offering 'rather a restricted view of her achievements',[22] in his 1942 book, is, like most of his contemporaries, enchanted by Woolf's luminous imagery, particularly in *To the*

Lighthouse which he sensitively explores in a chapter entitled 'The Semi-Transparent Envelope'. He understands *The Waves* as a corrective to this novel: 'Virginia Woolf seems to have felt, after *To the Lighthouse*, that in her attempt to present the "transparent envelope" of experience she had not done justice to the reality and significance of individual characters . . . And so in *The Waves* she bases the whole work on the carefully organised impression of a limited number of characters. . . . The result is a curiously artificial piece of work.'[23] Joan Bennett, in *Virginia Woolf: Her Art as a Novelist* (1945), also cites the famous 'Look within . . .' passage, and dissents from the Bradbrook view, but is mystified by Woolf's dualistic representation: 'the interludes in *The Waves* and the central movement in *To the Lighthouse* are not wholly satisfactory' because 'they interrupt the mood of the narrative' and 'disturb readers' "willing suspension of disbelief"'.[24] Bernard Blackstone, on the other hand, is one of the first commentators to acknowledge 'the element of comedy' in Woolf's fiction, particularly in *To the Lighthouse*.[25]

Let us turn now to Auerbach, who is possibly responsible for ensuring Woolf's place on most academic reading lists even during the post-war years of canon-making which excluded so many of her fellow women writers, and for securing the reputation of *To the Lighthouse* as a (if not *the*) major twentieth-century work of fiction. 'What is significant', according to Rachel Bowlby, in Auerbach's elevation of Woolf ('not in keeping with its time') is 'that not only is [his] decisive novel written by a woman, but the passage in question makes a woman's daydreams the paradigm for modernist conceptions of fragment, detail and randomness.'[26] By devoting his final chapter, 'The Brown Stocking', to this novel in a work which surveys western literature beginning with Homer, Auerbach may be thought to have contributed to a certain approach to liberal humanist education, implicitly rejected in Woolf's text itself, and latterly caricatured as 'Plato to Nato' or 'Beowulf to Virginia Woolf'. But this A-to-Z linear approach to cultural development, satirised so effectively in the account of Mr Ramsay's 'splendid mind' in *To the Lighthouse*, is a methodology that Auerbach himself rejects. He in fact makes the point that 'modern philologists' (himself included) share the very 'technique' of 'modern writers' (Woolf's in particular) that his final chapter explores: 'interpretation of a few passages . . . can be made to yield more, and more decisive, information . . . than would a systematic and chronological treatment. Indeed, the present book may be cited as an illustration.' It is his lucid and stimulating analysis of this technique that marks out Auerbach's contribution. His sophisticated discussion of Woolf's writing in terms of point-of-view, narrative voice, time, interior and exterior consciousness, epistemology and fragmentation, proceeds from a simple, but perceptive, question: 'Who is speaking in this paragraph?' What follows is a magnificent example of close critical reading that illuminates Woolf's prose and resonates in a number of wider cultural and political spheres. Auerbach begins by reproducing 'the fifth section of part 1' of *To the Lighthouse* which I omit for reasons of space.[27]

■ Mrs. Ramsay's very first remark is twice interrupted: first by the visual impression she receives of William Bankes and Lily Briscoe passing by together, and then, after a few intervening words serving the progress of the exterior occurrence, by the impression which the two persons passing by have left in her: the charm of Lily's Chinese eyes, which it is not for every man to see – whereupon she finishes her sentence and also allows her consciousness to dwell for a moment on the measuring of the stocking: we may yet go to the lighthouse, and so I must make sure the stocking is long enough. At this point there flashes into her mind the idea which has been prepared by her reflection on Lily's Chinese eyes (William and Lily ought to marry) – an admirable idea, she loves making matches. Smiling, she begins measuring the stocking. But the boy, in his stubborn and jealous love of her, refuses to stand still. How can she see whether the stocking is the right length if the boy keeps fidgeting about? What is the matter with James, her youngest, her darling? She looks up. Her eye falls on the room – and a long parenthesis begins. From the shabby chairs of which Andrew, her eldest son, said the other day that their entrails were all over the floor, her thoughts wander on, probing the objects and the people of her environment. The shabby furniture . . . but still good enough for up here; the advantages of the summer place; so cheap, so good for the children, for her husband; easily fitted up with a few old pieces of furniture, some pictures and books. Books – it is ages since she has had time to read books, even the books which have been dedicated to her (here the lighthouse flashes in for a second, as a place where one can't send such erudite volumes as some of those lying about the room). Then the house again: if the family would only be a little more careful. But of course, Andrew brings in crabs he wants to dissect; the other children gather seaweed, shells, stones; and she has to let them. All the children are gifted, each in a different way. But naturally, the house gets shabbier as a result (here the parenthesis is interrupted for a moment; she holds the stocking against James's leg); everything goes to ruin. If only the doors weren't always left open. See, everything is getting spoiled, even that Cashmere shawl on the picture frame. The doors are always left open; they are open again now. She listens: Yes, they are all open. The window on the landing is open too; she opened it herself. Windows must be open, doors closed. Why is it that no one can get that into his head? If you go to the maids' rooms at night, you will find all the windows closed. Only the Swiss maid always keeps her window open. She needs fresh air. Yesterday she looked out of the window with tears in her eyes and said: At home the mountains are so beautiful. Mrs. Ramsay knew that 'at home' the girl's father was dying. Mrs. Ramsay had just been trying to teach her how to make beds, how to open windows. She had been talking away and had scolded the girl too. But then she had stopped talking (comparison with a bird folding its wings after flying in sunlight). She had stopped talking, for there was nothing one could say; he has cancer of the throat. At this point, remembering how she had stood there, how the girl had said at home the mountains were so beautiful – and there was no hope left – a sudden tense exasperation arises in her (exasperation with the cruel meaninglessness of a life whose continuance she is nevertheless striving with all her powers to abet, support, and secure). Her exasperation flows out into the exterior action. The parenthesis suddenly closes (it cannot have taken up more than a few seconds; just now she was still smiling over the thought of a marriage between Mr. Bankes and Lily Briscoe), and she says sharply to James: Stand still. Don't be so tiresome.

This is the first major parenthesis. The second starts a little later, after the stocking has been measured and found to be still much too short. It starts with the paragraph which begins and ends with the motif, 'never did anybody look so sad'.

Who is speaking in this paragraph? Who is looking at Mrs. Ramsay here, who concludes that never did anybody look so sad? Who is expressing these doubtful, obscure suppositions? – about the tear which – perhaps – forms and falls in the dark, about the water swaying this way and that, receiving it, and then returning to rest? There is no one near the window in the room but Mrs. Ramsay and James. It cannot be either of them, nor the 'people' who begin to speak in the next paragraph. Perhaps it is the author. However, if that be so, the author certainly does not speak like one who has a knowledge of his characters – in this case, of Mrs. Ramsay – and who, out of his knowledge, can describe their personality and momentary state of mind objectively and with certainty. Virginia Woolf wrote this paragraph. She did not identify it through grammatical and typographical devices as the speech or thought of a third person. One is obliged to assume that it contains direct statements of her own. But she does not seem to bear in mind that she is the author and hence ought to know how matters stand with her characters. The person speaking here, whoever it is, acts the part of one who has only an impression of Mrs. Ramsay, who looks at her face and renders the impression received, but is doubtful of its proper interpretation. 'Never did anybody look so sad' is not an objective statement. In rendering the shock received by one looking at Mrs. Ramsay's face, it verges upon a realm beyond reality. And in the ensuing passage the speakers no longer seem to be human beings at all but spirits between heaven and earth, nameless spirits capable of penetrating the depths of the human soul, capable too of knowing something about it, but not of attaining clarity as to what is in process there, with the result that what they report has a doubtful ring, comparable in a way to those 'certain airs, detached from the body of the wind,' which in a later passage (2,2) move about the house at night, 'questioning and wondering.' However that may be, here too we are not dealing with objective utterances on the part of the author in respect to one of the characters. No one is certain of anything here: it is all mere supposition, glances cast by one person upon another whose enigma he cannot solve.

This continues in the following paragraph. Suppositions as to the meaning of Mrs. Ramsay's expression are made and discussed. But the level of tone descends slightly, from the poetic and non-real to the practical and earthly; and now a speaker is introduced: 'People said.' People wonder whether some recollection of an unhappy occurrence in her earlier life is hidden behind her radiant beauty. There have been rumors to that effect. But perhaps the rumors are wrong: nothing of this is to be learned directly from her; she is silent when such things come up in conversation. But supposing she has never experienced anything of the sort herself, she yet knows everything even without experience. The simplicity and genuineness of her being unfailingly light upon the truth of things, and, falsely perhaps, delight, ease, sustain.

Is it still 'people' who are speaking here? We might almost be tempted to doubt it, for the last words sound almost too personal and thoughtful for the gossip of 'people'. And immediately afterward, suddenly and unexpectedly, an entirely new speaker, a new scene, and a new time are introduced. We find Mr. Bankes at the telephone talking to Mrs. Ramsay, who has called him to tell him about a train connection, evidently with reference to a journey they are planning to make together. The paragraph about the tear had already taken us out of the room where Mrs. Ramsay and James are sitting by the window; it had transported us to an undefinable scene beyond the realm of reality. The paragraph in which the rumors are discussed has a concretely earthly but not clearly identified scene. Now we find ourselves in a precisely determined place, but far away from the summer house – in London, in Mr. Bankes's house. The time is not stated ('once'), but apparently the telephone conversation took place long (perhaps as much as several years) before this particular sojourn in the house on the island. But what Mr. Bankes says over the telephone is in perfect continuity with the preceding paragraph. Again not objectively but in the form of the impression received by a specific person at a specific moment, it as it were sums up all that precedes – the scene with the Swiss maid, the hidden sadness in Mrs. Ramsay's beautiful face, what people think about her, and the impression she makes: Nature has but little clay like that of which she molded her. Did Mr. Bankes really say that to her over the telephone? Or did he only want to say it when he heard her voice, which moved him deeply, and it came into his mind how strange it was to be talking over the telephone with this wonderful woman, so like a Greek goddess? The sentence is enclosed in quotation marks, so one would suppose that he really spoke it. But this is not certain, for the first words of his soliloquy, which follows, are likewise enclosed in quotation marks. In any case, he quickly gets hold of himself, for he answers in a matter-of-fact way that he will catch the 10:30 at Euston.

But his emotion does not die away so quickly. As he puts down the receiver and walks across the room to the window in order to watch the work on a new building across the way – apparently his usual and characteristic procedure when he wants to relax and let his thoughts wander freely – he continues to be preoccupied with Mrs. Ramsay. There is always something strange about her, something that does not quite go with her beauty (as for instance telephoning); she has no awareness of her beauty, or at most only a childish awareness; her dress and her actions show that at times. She is constantly getting involved in everyday realities which are hard to reconcile with the harmony of her face. In his methodical way he tries to explain her incongruities to himself. He puts forward some conjectures but cannot make up his mind. Meanwhile his momentary impressions of the work on the new building keep crowding in. Finally he gives it up. With the somewhat impatient, determined matter-of-factness of a methodical and scientific worker (which he is) he shakes off the insoluble problem 'Mrs. Ramsay'. He knows no solution (the repetition of 'he did not know' symbolizes his impatient shaking it off). He has to get back to his work.

Here the second long interruption comes to an end and we are taken back to the room where Mrs. Ramsay and James are. The exterior occurrence is brought to a close with the kiss on James's forehead and the resumption of the cutting out of pictures. But here too we have only an exterior change. A scene previously abandoned reappears, suddenly and with as little transition as if it had never been left, as though the long interruption were only a glance which someone (who?) has cast from it into the depths of time. But the theme (Mrs. Ramsay, her beauty, the enigma of her character, her absoluteness, which nevertheless always exercises itself in the relativity and ambiguity of life, in what does not become her beauty) carries over directly from the last phase of the interruption (that is, Mr. Bankes's fruitless reflections) into the situation in which we now find Mrs. Ramsay: 'with her head outlined absurdly by the gilt frame' etc. – for once again what is around her is not suited to her, is 'something incongruous'. And the kiss she gives her little boy, the words she speaks to him, although they are a genuine gift of life, which James accepts as the most natural and simple truth, are yet heavy with unsolved mystery.

Our analysis of the passage yields a number of distinguishing stylistic characteristics, which we shall now attempt to formulate.

The writer as narrator of objective facts has almost completely vanished; almost everything stated appears by way of reflection in the consciousness of the dramatic personae. When it is a question of the house, for example, or of the Swiss maid, we are not given the objective information which Virginia Woolf possesses regarding these objects of her creative imagination but what Mrs. Ramsay thinks or feels about them at a particular moment. Similarly we are not taken into Virginia Woolf's confidence and allowed to share her knowledge of Mrs. Ramsay's character; we are given her character as it is reflected in and as it affects various figures in the novel: the nameless spirits which assume certain things about a tear, the people who wonder about her, and Mr. Bankes. In our passage this goes so far that there actually seems to be no viewpoint at all outside the novel from which the people and events within it are observed, any more than there seems to be an objective reality apart from what is in the consciousness of the characters. Remnants of such a reality survive at best in brief references to the exterior frame of the action, such as 'said Mrs. Ramsay, raising her eyes . . .' or 'said Mr. Bankes once, hearing her voice'. The last paragraph ('Knitting her reddish-brown hairy stocking . . .') might perhaps also be mentioned in this connection. But this is already somewhat doubtful. The occurrence is described objectively, but as for its interpretation, the tone indicates that the author looks at Mrs. Ramsay not with knowing but with doubting and questioning eyes – even as some character in the novel would see her in the situation in which she is described, would hear her speak the words given.

The devices employed in this instance (and by a number of contemporary writers as well) to express the contents of the consciousness of the dramatic personae have been analysed and described syntactically. Some of them have been named (*erlebte Rede*, stream of consciousness, *monologue intérieur* are examples). Yet these stylistic forms, especially the *erlebte Rede*, were used in literature much earlier too, but not for the same aesthetic purpose. And in addition to them there are other possibilities – hardly definable in terms of syntax – of obscuring and even obliterating the impression of an objective reality completely known to the author; possibilities, that is, dependent not on form but on intonation and context. A case in point is the passage under discussion, where the author at times achieves the intended effect by representing herself to be someone who doubts, wonders, hesitates, as though the truth about her characters were not better known to her than it is to them or to the reader. It is all, then, a matter of the author's attitude toward the reality of the world he represents. And this attitude differs entirely from that of outlooks who interpret the actions, situations, and characters of their personages with objective assurance, as was the general practice in earlier times. Goethe or Keller, Dickens or Meredith, Balzac or Zola told us out of their certain knowledge what their characters did, what they felt and thought while doing it, and how their actions and thoughts were to be interpreted. They knew everything about their characters. To be sure, in past periods too we were frequently told about the subjective reactions of the characters in a novel or story; at times even in the form of *erlebte Rede*, although more frequently as a monologue, and of course in most instances with an introductory phrase something like 'it seemed to him that . . .' or 'at this moment he felt that . . .' or the like. Yet in such cases there was hardly ever any attempt to render the flow and the play of consciousness adrift in the current of changing impressions (as is done in our text both for Mrs. Ramsay and for Mr. Bankes); instead, the content of the individual's consciousness was rationally limited to things connected with the particular incident being related or the particular situation being described. . . . And what is still more important: the author, with his knowledge of an objective truth, never abdicated his position as the final and governing authority. Again, earlier writers, especially from the end of the nineteenth century on, had produced narrative works which on the whole undertook to give us an extremely subjective, individualistic, and often eccentrically aberrant impression of reality, and which neither sought nor were able to ascertain anything objective or generally valid in regard to it. Sometimes such works took the form of first-person novels; sometimes they did not. As an example of the latter case I mention Huysmans's novel *A rebours*. But all that too is basically different from the modern procedure here described on the basis of Virginia Woolf's text, although the latter, it is true, evolved from the former. The essential characteristic of the technique represented by Virginia Woolf is that we are given not merely one person whose consciousness (that is, the impressions it receives) is rendered, but many persons, with frequent shifts from one to the other – in our text, Mrs. Ramsay, 'people,' Mr. Bankes, in brief interludes James, the Swiss maid in a flash-back, and the nameless ones who speculate over a tear. The multiplicity of persons suggests that we are here after all confronted with an endeavor to investigate an objective reality, that is, specifically, the 'real' Mrs. Ramsay. She is, to be sure, an enigma and such she basically remains, but she is as it were encircled by the content of all the various consciousnesses directed upon her (including her own); there is an attempt to approach her from many sides as closely as human possibilities of perception and expression can succeed in doing. The design of a close approach to objective reality by means of numerous subjective impressions received by various individuals (and at various times) is important in the modern technique which we are here examining. It basically differentiates it from the unipersonal subjectivism which allows only a single and generally a very unusual person to make himself heard and admits only that one person's way of looking at reality. In terms of literary history, to be sure, there are close connections between the two methods of representing consciousness – the unipersonal subjective method and the multipersonal method with synthesis as its aim. The latter developed from the former, and there are works in which the two overlap, so that we can watch the development. This is especially the case in Marcel Proust's great novel. We shall return to it later.

Another stylistic peculiarity to be observed in our text – though one that is closely and necessarily connected with the 'multipersonal representation of consciousness' just discussed – has to do with the treatment of time. That there is something peculiar about the treatment of time in modern narrative literature is nothing new; several studies have been published on the subject. These were primarily attempts to establish a connection between the pertinent phenomena and contemporary philosophical doctrines or trends – undoubtedly a justifiable undertaking and useful for an appreciation of the community of interests and inner purposes shown in the activity of many of our contemporaries. We shall begin by describing the procedure with reference to our present example. We remarked earlier that the act of measuring the length of the stocking and the speaking of the words related to it must have taken much less time than an attentive reader who tries not to miss anything will require to read the passage – even if we assume that a brief pause intervened between the measuring and the kiss of reconciliation on James's forehead. However, the time the narration takes is not devoted to the occurrence itself (which is rendered rather tersely) but to interludes. Two long excursuses are inserted, whose relations in time to the occurrence which frames them seem to be entirely different. The first excursus, a representation of what goes on in Mrs. Ramsay's mind while she measures the stocking (more precisely, between the first absent-minded and the second sharp order to James to hold his leg still) belongs in time to the framing occurrence, and it is only the representation of it which takes a greater number of seconds and even minutes than the measuring – the reason being that the road taken by consciousness is sometimes traversed far more quickly than language is able to render it, if we want to make ourselves intelligible to a third person, and that is the intention here. What goes on in Mrs. Ramsay's mind in itself contains nothing enigmatic; these are ideas which arise from her daily life and may well be called normal – her secret lies deeper, and it is only when the switch from the open windows to the Swiss maid's words comes, that something happens which lifts the veil a little. On the whole, however, the mirroring of Mrs. Ramsay's consciousness is much more easily comprehensible than the sort of thing we get in such cases from other authors (James Joyce, for example). But simple and trivial as are the ideas which arise one after the other in Mrs. Ramsay's consciousness, they are at the same time essential and significant. They amount to a synthesis of the intricacies of life in which her incomparable beauty has been caught, in which it at once manifests and conceals itself. Of course, writers of earlier periods too occasionally devoted some time and a few sentences to telling the reader what at a specific moment passed through their characters' minds – but for such a purpose they would hardly have chosen so accidental an occasion as Mrs. Ramsay's looking up, so that, quite involuntarily, her eyes fall on the furniture. Nor would it have occurred to them to render the continuous rumination of consciousness in its natural and purposeless freedom. And finally they would not have inserted the entire process between two exterior occurrences so close together in time as the two warnings to James to keep still (both of which, after all, take place while she is on the point of holding the unfinished stocking to his leg); so that, in a surprising fashion unknown to earlier periods, a sharp contrast results between the brief span of time occupied by the exterior event and the dreamlike wealth of a process of consciousness which traverses a whole subjective universe. These are the characteristic and distinctively new features of the technique: a chance occasion releasing processes of consciousness; a natural and even, if you will, a naturalistic rendering of those processes in their peculiar freedom, which is neither restrained by a purpose nor directed by a specific subject of thought; elaboration of the contrast between 'exterior' and 'interior' time. The three have in common what they reveal of the author's attitude: he submits, much more than was done in earlier realistic works, to the random contingency of real phenomena; and even though he winnows and stylises the material of the real world – as of course he cannot help doing – he does not proceed rationalistically, nor with a view to bringing a continuity of exterior events to a planned conclusion. In Virginia Woolf's case the exterior events have actually lost their hegemony, they serve to release and interpret inner events, whereas before her time (and still today in many instances) inner movements preponderantly function to prepare and motivate significant exterior happenings. This too is apparent in the randomness and contingency of the exterior occasion (looking up because James does not keep his foot still), which releases the much more significant inner process.

The temporal relation between the second excursus and the framing occurrence is of a different sort: its content (the passage on the tear, the things people think about Mrs. Ramsay, the telephone conversation with Mr. Bankes and his reflections while watching the building of the new hotel) is not a part of the framing occurrence either in terms of time or of place. Other times and places are in question; it is an excursus of the same type as the story of the origin of Odysseus' scar, which was discussed in the first chapter of this book. Even from that, however, it is different in structure. In the Homer passage the excursus was linked to the scar which Euryclea touches with her hands, and although the moment at which the touching of the scar occurs is one of high and dramatic tension, the scene nevertheless immediately shifts to another clear and luminous present, and this present seems actually designed to cut off the dramatic tension and cause the entire foot-washing scene to be temporarily forgotten. In Virginia Woolf's passage, there is no question of any tension. Nothing of importance in a dramatic sense takes place; the problem is the length of the stocking. The point of departure for the excursus is Mrs. Ramsay's facial expression: 'never did anybody look so sad'. In fact several excursuses start from here; three, to be exact. And all three differ in time and place, differ too in definiteness of time and place, the first being situated quite vaguely, the second somewhat more definitely, and the third with comparative precision. Yet none of them is so exactly situated in time as the successive episodes of the story of Odysseus' youth, for even in the case of the telephone scene we have only an inexact indication of when it occurred. As a result it becomes possible to accomplish the shifting of the scene away from the window-nook much more unnoticeably and smoothly than the changing of scene and time in the episode of the scar. In the passage on the tear the reader may still be in doubt as to whether there has been any shift at all. The nameless speakers may have entered the room and be looking at Mrs. Ramsay. In the second paragraph this interpretation is no longer possible, but the 'people' whose gossip is reproduced are still looking at Mrs. Ramsay's face – not here and now, at the summer-house window, but it is still the same face and has the same expression. And even in the third part, where the face is no longer physically seen (for Mr. Bankes is talking to Mrs. Ramsay over the telephone), it is nonetheless present to his inner vision; so that not for an instant does the theme (the solution of the enigma Mrs. Ramsay), and even the moment when the problem is formulated (the expression of her face while she measures the length of the stocking), vanish from the reader's memory. In terms of the exterior event the three parts of the excursus have nothing to do with one another. They have no common and externally coherent development, as have the episodes of Odysseus' youth which are related with reference to the origin of the scar; they are connected only by the one thing they have in common – looking at Mrs. Ramsay, and more specifically at the Mrs. Ramsay who, with an unfathomable expression of sadness behind her radiant beauty, concludes that the stocking is still much too short. It is only this common focus which connects the otherwise totally different parts of the excursus; but the connection is strong enough to deprive them of the independent 'present' which the episode of the scar possesses. They are nothing but attempts to interpret 'never did anybody look so sad'; they carry on this theme, which itself carries on after they conclude: there has been no change of theme at all. In contrast, the scene in which Euryclea recognises Odysseus is interrupted and divided into two parts by the excursus on the origin of the scar. In our passage, there is no such clear distinction between two exterior occurrences and between two presents. However insignificant as an exterior event the framing occurrence (the measuring of the stocking) may be, the picture of Mrs. Ramsay's face which arises from it remains present throughout the excursus; the excursus itself is nothing but a background for that picture, which seems as it were to open into the depths of time – just as the first excursus, released by Mrs. Ramsay's unintentional glance at the furniture, was an opening of the picture into the depths of consciousness.

The two excursuses, then, are not as different as they at first appeared. It is not so very important that the first, so far as time is concerned (and place too), runs its course within the framing occurrence, while the second conjures up other times and places. The times and places of the second are not independent; they serve only the polyphonic treatment of the image which releases it; as a matter of fact, they impress us (as does the interior time of the first excursus) like an occurrence in the consciousness of some observer (to be sure, he is not identified) who might see Mrs. Ramsay at the described moment and whose meditation upon the unsolved enigma of her personality might contain memories of what others (people, Mr. Bankes) say and think about her. In both excursuses we are dealing with attempts to fathom a more genuine, a deeper, and indeed a more real reality; in both cases the incident which releases the excursus appears accidental and is poor in content; in both cases it makes little difference whether the excursuses employ only the consciousness-content, and hence only interior time, or whether they also employ exterior shifts of time. After all, the process of consciousness in the first excursus likewise includes shifts of time and scene, especially the episode with the Swiss maid. The important point is that an insignificant exterior occurrence releases ideas and chains of ideas which cut loose from the present of the exterior occurrence and range freely through the depths of time. It is as though an apparently simple text revealed its proper content only in the commentary on it, a simple musical theme only in the development-section. This enables us also to understand the close relation between the treatment of time and the 'multi-personal representation of consciousness' discussed earlier. The ideas arising in consciousness are not tied to the present of the exterior occurrence which releases them. Virginia Woolf's peculiar technique, as exemplified in our text, consists in the fact that the exterior objective reality of the momentary present which the author directly reports and which appears as established fact – in our instance the measuring of the stocking – is nothing but an occasion (although perhaps not an entirely accidental one). The stress is placed entirely on what the occasion releases, things which are not seen directly but by reflection, which are not tied to the present of the framing occurrence which releases them.

Here it is only natural that we should recall Proust's work. He was the first to carry this sort of thing through consistently; and his entire technique is bound up with a recovery of lost realities in remembrance, a recovery released by some externally insignificant and apparently accidental occurrence. . . . Now with Proust, a narrating 'I' is preserved throughout. It is not, to be sure, an author observing from without but a person involved in the action and pervading it with the distinctive flavor of his being, so that one might feel tempted to class Proust's novel among the products of the unipersonal subjectivism which we discussed earlier. So to class it would not be wrong but it would be inadequate. It would fail to account completely for the structure of Proust's novel. . . . Proust aims at objectivity, he wants to bring out the essence of events: he strives to attain this goal by accepting the guidance of his own consciousness – not, however, of his consciousness as it happens to be at any particular moment but as it remembers things. A consciousness in which remembrance causes past realities to arise, which has long since left behind the states in which it found itself when those realities occurred as a present, sees and arranges that content in a way very different from the purely individual and subjective. Freed from its various earlier involvements, consciousness views its own past layers and their content in perspective; it keeps confronting them with one another, emancipating them from their exterior temporal continuity as well as from the narrow meanings they seemed to have when they were bound to a particular present. There is to be noted in this a fusion of the modern concept of interior time with the neo-Platonic idea that the true prototype of a given subject is to be found in the soul of the artist; in this case, of an artist who, present in the subject itself, has detached himself from it as observer and thus comes face to face with his own past. . . . The distinctive characteristics of the realistic novel of the era between the two great wars . . . – multipersonal representation of consciousness, time strata, disintegration of the continuity of exterior events, shifting of the narrative view-point (all of which are interrelated and difficult to separate) – seem to us indicative of a striving for certain objectives, of certain tendencies and needs on the part of both authors and public. These objectives, tendencies, and needs are numerous; they seem in part to be mutually contradictory; yet they form so much one whole that when we undertake to describe them analytically, we are in constant danger of unwittingly passing from one to another.

Let us begin with a tendency which is particularly striking in our text from Virginia Woolf. She holds to minor, unimpressive, random events: measuring the stocking, a fragment of a conversation with the maid, a telephone call. Great changes, exterior turning points, let alone catastrophes, do not occur; and though elsewhere in *To the Lighthouse* such things are mentioned, it is hastily, without preparation or context, incidentally, and as it were only for the sake of information. The same tendency is to be observed in other and very different writers, such as Proust or Hamsun. . . . Now many writers present minor happenings, which are insignificant as exterior factors in a person's destiny, for their own sake or rather as points of departure for the development of motifs, for a penetration which opens up new perspectives into a milieu or a consciousness or the given historical setting. They have discarded presenting the story of their characters with any claim to exterior completeness, in chronological order, and with the emphasis on important exterior turning points of destiny. James Joyce's tremendous novel – an encyclopedic work, a mirror of Dublin, of Ireland, a mirror too of Europe and its millennia – has for its frame the externally insignificant course of a day in the lives of a schoolteacher and an advertising broker. It takes up less than twenty-four hours in their lives – just as *To the Lighthouse* describes portions of two days widely separated in time. (There is here also, as we must not fail to observe, a similarity to Dante's Comedy.) Proust presents individual days and hours from different periods, but the exterior events which are the determining factors in the destinies of the novel's characters during the intervening lapses of time are mentioned only incidentally, in retrospect or anticipation. The ends the narrator has in mind are not to be seen in them; often the reader has to supplement them. . . . This shift of emphasis expresses something that we might call a transfer of confidence: the great exterior turning points and blows of fate are granted less importance; they are credited with less power of yielding decisive information concerning the subject; on the other hand there is confidence that in any random fragment plucked from the course of a life at any time the totality of its fate is contained and can be portrayed. There is greater confidence in syntheses gained through full exploitation of an everyday occurrence than in a chronologically well-ordered total treatment which accompanies the subject from beginning to end, attempts not to omit anything externally important, and emphasizes the great turning points of destiny. It is possible to compare this technique of modern writers with that of certain modern philologists who hold that the interpretation of a few passages from *Hamlet*, *Phèdre*, or *Faust* can be made to yield more, and more decisive, information about Shakespeare, Racine, or Goethe and their times than would a systematic and chronological treatment of their lives and works. Indeed, the present book may be cited as an illustration. I could never have written anything in the nature of a history of European realism; the material would have swamped me; I should have had to enter into hopeless discussions concerning the delimitation of the various periods and the allocation of the various writers to them, and above all concerning the definition of the concept realism. . . . As opposed to this I see the possibility of success and profit in a method which consists in letting myself be guided by a few motifs which I have worked out gradually and without a specific purpose, and in trying them out on a series of texts which have become familiar and vital to me in the course of my philological activity; for I am convinced that these basic motifs in the history of the representation of reality – provided I have seen them correctly – must be demonstrable in any random realistic text. But to return to those modern writers who prefer the exploitation of random everyday events, contained within a few hours and days, to the complete and chronological representation of a total exterior continuum – they too (more or less consciously) are guided by the consideration that it is a hopeless venture to try to be really complete within the total exterior continuum and yet to make what is essential stand out. Then too they hesitate to impose upon life, which is their subject, an order which it does not possess in itself. He who represents the course of a human life, or a sequence of events extending over a prolonged period of time, and represents it from beginning to end, must prune and isolate arbitrarily. Life has always long since begun, and it is always still going on. And the people whose story the author is telling experience much more than he can ever hope to tell. But the things that happen to a few individuals in the course of a few minutes, hours, or possibly even days – these one can hope to report with reasonable completeness. . . . We are constantly endeavouring to give meaning and order to our lives in the past, the present, and the future, to our surroundings, the world in which we live; with the result that our lives appear in our own conception as total entities – which to be sure are always changing, more or less radically, more or less rapidly, depending on the extent to which we are obliged, inclined, and able to assimilate the onrush of new experience. These are the forms of order and interpretation which the modern writers here under discussion attempt to grasp in the random moment – not one order and one interpretation, but many, which may either be those of different persons or of the same person at different times; so that overlapping, complementing, and contradiction yield something that we might call a synthesised cosmic view or at least a challenge to the reader's will to interpretative synthesis.

Here we have returned once again to the reflection of multiple consciousnesses. It is easy to understand that such a technique had to develop gradually and that it did so precisely during the decades of the First World War period and after. The widening of man's horizon, and the increase of his experiences, knowledge, ideas, and possible forms of existence, which began in the sixteenth century, continued through the nineteenth at an ever faster tempo – with such a tremendous acceleration since the beginning of the twentieth that synthetic and objective attempts at interpretation are produced and demolished every instant. The tremendous tempo of the changes proved the more confusing because they could not be surveyed as a whole. They occurred simultaneously in many separate departments of science, technology, and economics, with the result that no one – not even those who were leaders in the separate departments – could foresee or evaluate the resulting overall situations. Furthermore, the changes did not produce the same effects in all places, so that the differences of attainment between the various social strata of one and the same people and between different peoples came to be – if not greater – at least more noticeable. . . . In all parts of the world crises of adjustment arose; they increased in number and coalesced. They led to the upheavals which we have not weathered yet. In Europe this violent clash of the most heterogeneous ways of life and kinds of endeavor undermined not only those religious, philosophical, ethical, and economic principles which were part of the traditional heritage and which, despite many earlier shocks, had maintained their position of authority through slow adaptation and transformation; nor yet only the ideas of the Enlightenment, the ideas of democracy and liberalism which had been revolutionary in the eighteenth century and were still so during the first half of the nineteenth; it undermined even the new revolutionary forces of socialism, whose origins did not go back beyond the heyday of the capitalist system. These forces threatened to split up and disintegrate. They lost their unity and clear definition through the formation of numerous mutually hostile groups, through strange alliances which some of these groups effected with non-socialist ideologies, through the capitulation of most of them during the First World War, and finally through the propensity on the part of many of their most radical advocates for changing over into the camp of their most extreme enemies. Otherwise too there was an increasingly strong factionalism – at times crystallising around important poets, philosophers, and scholars, but in the majority of cases pseudo-scientific, syncretistic, and primitive. The temptation to entrust oneself to a sect which solved all problems with a single formula, whose power of suggestion imposed solidarity, and which ostracized everything which would not fit in and submit – this temptation was so great that, with many people, fascism hardly had to employ force when the time came for it to spread through the countries of old European culture, absorbing the smaller sects.

As recently as the nineteenth century, and even at the beginning of the twentieth, so much clearly formulable and recognized community of thought and feeling remained in those countries that a writer engaged in representing reality had reliable criteria at hand by which to organize it. At least, within the range of contemporary movements, he could discern certain specific trends; he could delimit opposing attitudes and ways of life with a certain degree of clarity. To be sure, this had long since begun to grow increasingly difficult. Flaubert (to confine ourselves to realistic writers) already suffered from the lack of valid foundations for his work; and the subsequent increasing predilection for ruthlessly subjectivistic perspectives is another symptom. At the time of the First World War and after – in a Europe unsure of itself, overflowing with unsettled ideologies and ways of life, and pregnant with disaster – certain writers distinguished by instinct and insight find a method which dissolves reality into multiple and multi-valent reflections of consciousness. That this method should have been developed at this time is not hard to understand.

But the method is not only a symptom of the confusion and helplessness, not only a mirror of the decline of our world. There is, to be sure, a good deal to be said for such a view. There is in all these works a certain atmosphere of universal doom: especially in *Ulysses*, with its mocking odi-et-amo hodgepodge of the European tradition, with its blatant and painful cynicism, and its uninterpretable symbolism – for even the most painstaking analysis can hardly emerge with anything more than an appreciation of the multiple enmeshment of the motifs but with nothing of the purpose and meaning of the work itself. And most of the other novels which employ multiple reflection of consciousness also leave the reader with an impression of hopelessness. There is often something confusing, something hazy about them, something hostile to the reality which they represent. We not infrequently find a turning away from the practical will to live, or delight in portraying it under its most brutal forms. There is hatred of culture and civilisation, brought out by means of the subtlest stylistic devices which culture and civilisation have developed, and often a radical and fanatical urge to destroy. Common to almost all of these novels is haziness, vague indefinability of meaning: precisely the kind of un-interpretable symbolism which is also to be encountered in other forms of art of the same period.

But something entirely different takes place here too. Let us turn again to the text which was our starting-point. It breathes an air of vague and hopeless sadness. We never come to learn what Mrs. Ramsay's situation really is. Only the sadness, the vanity of her beau-ty and vital force emerge from the depths of secrecy. Even when we have read the whole novel, the meaning of the relationship between the planned trip to the lighthouse and the actual trip many years later remains unexpressed, enigmatic, only dimly to be conjectured, as does the content of Lily Briscoe's concluding vision which enables her to finish her painting with one stroke of the brush. It is one of the few books of this type which are filled with good and genuine love but also, in its feminine way, with irony, amorphous sadness, and doubt of life. Yet what realistic depth is achieved in every individual occur-rence, for example the measuring of the stocking! Aspects of the occurrence come to the fore, and links to other occurrences, which, before this time, had hardly been sensed, which had never been clear-ly seen and attended to, and yet they are determining factors in our real lives. What takes place here in Virginia Woolf's novel is precisely what was attempted everywhere in works of this kind (although not everywhere with the same insight and mastery) – that is, to put the emphasis on the random occurrence, to exploit it not in the service of a planned continuity of action but in itself. And in the process some-thing new and elemental appeared: nothing less than the wealth of reality and depth of life in every moment to which we surrender our-selves without prejudice. To be sure, what happens in that moment – be it outer or inner processes – concerns in a very personal way the individuals who live in it, but it also (and for that very reason) concerns the elementary things which men in general have in common. It is precisely the random moment which is comparatively independent of the controversial and unstable orders over which men fight and despair; it passes unaffected by them, as daily life. The more it is exploited, the more the elementary things which our lives have in common come to light. The more numerous, varied, and simple the people are who appear as subjects of such random moments, the more effectively must what they have in common shine forth. In this un-prejudiced and exploratory type of representation we cannot but see to what an extent – below the surface conflicts – the differences between men's ways of life and forms of thought have already lessened. The strata of societies and their different ways of life have become inextricably mingled. . . . Beneath the conflicts, and also through them, an economic and cultural levering process is taking place. It is still a long way to a common life of mankind on earth, but the goal begins to be visible. And it is most concretely visible now in the unprejudiced, precise, interior and exterior representation of the random moment in the lives of different people. So the complicated process of dissolution which led to fragmentation of the exterior action, to reflection of consciousness, and to stratification of time seems to be tending toward a very simple solution. Perhaps it will be too simple to please those who, despite all its dangers and catastrophes, admire and love our epoch for the sake of its abundance of life and the incomparable historical vantage point which it affords. But they are few in number, and probably they will not live to see much more than the first forewarnings of the approaching unification and simplification.[28] □

CHAPTER THREE

The 1950s and 60s: Unifying Strategies – Myth, Philosophy, Psychology

THIS PERIOD sees the consolidation of Woolf's reputation as a major writer and the expansion of critical attention, which developed in two ways: firstly in attempts to account for the whole *œuvre*, out of which *To the Lighthouse*, *Mrs Dalloway* and *The Waves* emerge as the most popular and most significant works; and secondly, in attempts at detailed analytical readings of particular works, where these novels again receive a deal of attention. (*The Waves*, if slightly less written about than *To the Lighthouse*, is usually considered Woolf's highest achievement.) Common to both projects was the desire to come up with a unifying way of understanding Woolf's work – whether by looking for a totalising Woolfian philosophy evident throughout the *œuvre*, or by scrutinising individual works in terms of a unifying philosophical, mythic, psychoanalytic or psychological approach. In 1953 selections from Woolf's diary were published in *A Writer's Diary* which had considerable impact on such attempts to account for her achievement.[1] Further information about Woolf's background and circumstances also began to appear: Noel Annan published a biography of her father, Leslie Stephen, in 1951,[2] and J.K. Johnstone's *The Bloomsbury Group: A Study of E.M. Forster, Lytton Strachey, Virginia Woolf, and Their Circle* was published in 1954.[3]

In the same year appeared a thoroughgoing academic study of Woolf's writing and philosophy by James Hafley, *The Glass Roof: Virginia Woolf as Novelist*, which was in turn surpassed by Jean Guiguet's monumental work extracted below. Hafley focuses on the unifying figures of Mrs Ramsay in *To the Lighthouse*, and Bernard in *The Waves*. He quotes approvingly John Graham's invocation of T.S. Eliot's famous phrase to describe the symbolic function of the lighthouse as 'a vital synthesis of time and eternity: an *objective correlative* for Mrs Ramsay's vision, after whose death it is her meaning.'[4] Hafley's assessment of the 'cosmic' rather than 'limited social background' for the characters of *The Waves* has been an enduring one in criticism of the novel.[5] So too has an occupation with the symbolism of Woolf's novels,[6] although, as Su Reid points out, the 1970s marked a move away from the orthodox critical tendency 'to impose complex symbolic meanings onto the novels'.[7] Woolf's significance as a writer was given academic confirmation by the spring 1956 number of *Modern Fiction Studies* which was devoted to Woolf's work and included a ten-page checklist of selected criticism. She is also prominent in a number of studies of the modern novel and of psychological fiction. I will briefly discuss some of these studies before turning to the four main extracts of the chapter, which exemplify a number of the approaches outlined above: Joseph Blotner's (1956) essay, offering a mythic and Freudian analysis of *To the Lighthouse*; Shiv Kumar's (1962) study of Bergsonism and modern fiction; extracts on *To the Lighthouse* and *The Waves* from Guiguet's classic study of Woolf's *œuvre* (1962); and Frank McConnell's (1968) essay on romanticism and phenomenology in *The Waves*.

Arnold Kettle 'continued the Leavisite tradition from another angle', according to Suzanne Raitt, 'by complaining that *To the Lighthouse* was "not about anything very interesting or important",'[8] but his assessment, in *An Introduction to the English Novel*, lacks the Leavisite vitriol, and is in places complimentary as well as controversial on some critical orthodoxies. Having cited the 'Look within . . .' passage, for example, Kettle rejects as cultural tool the usual 'symbolic' approach to Woolf's writing. He continues with mixed evaluation:

■ Virginia Woolf may justly be regarded as a finer, more truly artistic writer than any of the Edwardian novelists we have discussed. But that is not the only thing to be said. What is lacking in *To the Lighthouse* is a basic conflict, a framework of human effort. What does Lily Briscoe's vision really amount to? □

Kettle enlists D.S. Savage's criticism of Woolf that 'it is a typical feature of the characters of her novels to be altogether lacking in the capacity for discriminating within experience'.[9] But, 'what is positive in Virginia Woolf's achievement', Kettle adds, 'is her expression of discontent with the dreary flatness of so much naturalistic writing and her reassertion of the luminousness of life'.[10] D.H. Lawrence, however, is implicitly the measure of such vitalism.

Walter Allen's *The English Novel: A Short Critical History* (1954) offers a much more troubling account of Woolf's work. But even here there are some promising observations on aspects of her writing which later critics were to explore more fruitfully and more sympathetically. Allen cites the passages on 1910 and 'Look within . . .',[11] but also points to similarities between Woolf's prose and that of Walter Pater,[12] the topic of a recent book by Perry Meisel, as we shall see. He looks, like many of his contemporaries, for symbolic unity in the fiction, finding 'a powerful unifying factor [in] the lighthouse itself', yet doesn't approve of the 'prose-poetry' in *The Waves* and *To the Lighthouse*. But it is Allen's most unsympathetic and chauvinist statement that paradoxically anticipates later feminist interpretations of Woolf's 'feminine' writing practice:

■ **At present, the reaction against her work is probably at its greatest, and I must admit to sharing it. Much of her fiction seems marred by portentousness, and I cannot escape the feeling that from time to time the exercise of sensibility has become an end in itself. Nor do the moments of revelation and illumination always seem illuminative in any very real sense; but rather a succession of short, sharp female gasps of ecstasy; an impression intensified by Mrs Woolf's use of the semi-colon where the comma is ordinarily enough.[13]** □

Allen connects here Woolf's actual sentence structure with the inscription of feminine sexual pleasure, and in so doing anticipates recent French feminist theories of '*écriture féminine*' which will be discussed in a later chapter. He also reflects Woolf's own considerations of 'the psychological sentence of the feminine gender' which she ascribes to Dorothy Richardson, and which she describes as 'more elastic than the old, capable of stretching to the extreme, of suspending the frailest particles, of enveloping the vaguest shapes. . . . It is a woman's sentence, but only in the sense that it is used by a woman to describe a woman's mind by a writer who is neither proud nor afraid of anything that she may discover in the psychology of her sex.'[14] The unwitting feminist closes his account of Woolf with grudging and faint praise – 'All the same, it is difficult not to believe that the future will see her as an indubitable minor master in the novel.' – before turning his thoughts to James Joyce 'whose talents are so much greater'.[15]

Joseph L. Blotner, in his article, 'Mythic Patterns in *To the Lighthouse*', is also concerned with feminine, and even feminist (which he subdues), aspects of the novel. He reads it in terms of Freudian and Jungian theories and the myth of Persephone. His focus, as for so many of his contemporaries, is the unifying power of Mrs Ramsay. Usually understood as a positive, benign presence, Mrs Ramsay was also 'singled out . . . for a blistering attack' by Glenn Pederson two years after Blotner's homage.[16] The interest in deep mythic resolution to literary texts is symptomatic of a certain strand in modernist criticism influenced by Eliot's, Yeats' and Joyce's use of myth. Eliot's famous review of *Ulysses* underlines the unifying power of the new 'mythical method' for these writers, and is worth recalling here: 'It is simply a way of controlling, of ordering, of giving a shape and a significance to the immense panorama of futility and anarchy which is contemporary history. Psychology . . . ethnology, and *The Golden Bough* have concurred to make possible what was impossible even a few years ago. Instead of the narrative method, we may now use the mythical method.'[17] But Blotner is careful, in outlining his own critical methodology, to show that he is using myth and psychoanalytic theories as tools of reading, he is not locating or uncovering them in Woolf's text. The following extract will make for helpful comparison with later feminist uses of Freud (such as Rachel Bowlby's which appears later in this guide) for interpreting *To the Lighthouse*.

■ The impulses and convictions which gave birth to *Three Guineas* and *A Room of One's Own* carried over into Virginia Woolf's fiction. Their most powerful expression is found in *To the Lighthouse*. But something, probably her strict and demanding artistic conscience, prevented their appearance in the form of the intellectual and argumentative feminism found in the first two books. In this novel Virginia Woolf's concept of woman's role in life is crystallised in the character of Mrs Ramsay, whose attributes are those of major female figures in pagan myth. The most useful myth for interpreting the novel is that of the Primordial Goddess, who 'is threefold in relation to Zeus: mother (Rhea), wife (Demeter), and daughter (Persephone)'. One of the major sources of the myth is the Homeric 'Hymn to Demeter', in which the poet compares Rhea with her daughter Demeter, and makes it clear that Demeter and her daughter Persephone 'are to be thought of as a *double figure,* one half of which is the ideal complement of the other'.[18] This double figure is that of the Kore, the primordial maiden, who is also a mother. Also useful in interpreting the novel is the Oedipus myth. . . . This method is used from the outside, so to speak. It is not an interior approach asserting that myth was present at the conception and execution of the work; it rather asserts that myth may be brought to the work at its reading. It is like laying a colored transparency over a sheet covered with a maze of hues to reveal the orderly pattern which otherwise resides within them unperceived. Thus, in *To the Lighthouse* the myths of Oedipus and the Kore, superimposed momentarily upon the novel, provide a framework within whose boundaries and by virtue of whose spatial ordering the symbolic people, passages, and phrases of the book can be seen to assume a relationship to each other which illuminates their reciprocal functions and meanings. But since one key may open several doors in a house while leaving several more still locked, the mythic approach will not be urged as a Rosetta Stone for fathoming all the meanings of *To the Lighthouse*. However, this interpretation has several advantages. It shows that this is not, as has often been asserted, a novel which is poetic but plotless.[19] The poetry is certainly there but so is the plot, if one reads the novel with all its striking parallels against these myths which are so strong in plot. . . . The reappearance of Persephone has its symbolic equivalent in the novel in the return of the force which Mrs Ramsay represented. Mrs McNab receives orders to have the house restored. The predominant activity in the last section of the book is the expedition to the Lighthouse, upon which Mr Ramsay is determined almost as if it were a rite of propitiation toward Mrs Ramsay's spirit. And clearly, her spirit has a profound effect upon Lily. In this, Virginia Woolf may have been influenced by *A Passage to India*, the novel of her intimate friend E.M. Forster. This book, which she felt represented Forster in 'his prime',[20] appeared three years before *To the Lighthouse*. The central female figure in Forster's novel is Mrs Moore, an old Englishwoman. Through her influence, felt returning after her death, some of the wounds inflicted during the conflict between the British and the Indians in Chandrapore are healed. Earlier in *To the Lighthouse*, Mrs Ramsay has performed an act symbolic of Demeter's role in the rescue of Persephone. Going to the nursery, she has covered the boar's skull which has kept her daughter Cam awake until eleven o'clock at night – covered the skull with her own green shawl. The symbol of death is banished and obliterated by the symbol of fertility. In Lily's first night in the house after her return, she reflects that 'peace had come' (213). If the guests were to go down to the darkened beach, 'They would see then night flowing down in purple; his head crowned; his sceptre jewelled; and how in his eyes a child might look' (213). This dark and kingly deity, whose symbol had earlier frightened a child from sleep, has now been disarmed. The feminine principle, the Kore, has triumphed over the dark underworld with her release from it.

As the day passes, Lily invokes Mrs Ramsay, fruitlessly at first. But then she feels her imminence. '"Mrs Ramsay! Mrs Ramsay!" she repeated. She owed it all to her' (241). At times Lily's longing is so intense that

> she called out silently, to that essence which sat by the boat, that abstract one made of her, that woman in grey, as if to abuse her for having gone, and then having gone, come back again. It had seemed so safe, thinking of her. Ghost, air, nothingness, a thing you could play with easily and safely at any time of day or night, she had been that, and then suddenly she put her hand out and wrung the heart thus. (266)

. . . As the boat reaches the Lighthouse and the rapport is achieved between James, Cam, and Mr Ramsay, Lily completes her picture, becomes, in this individual work, fruitful as an artist. Just as Mrs Ramsay's spirit has been the force which brings about the consummation of the trip to the Lighthouse, so her spirit brings about Lily's epiphany. In that famous passage, 'With a sudden intensity, as if she saw it clear for a second, she drew a line there, in the centre. It was done; it was finished. Yes, she thought, laying down her brush in extreme fatigue, I have had my vision' (310). The return of Persephone is thus twofold. Mrs Ramsay, in the Persephone aspect of the Kore, has returned as an almost palpable presence to the Isle of Skye from which she had been snatched by death. Persephone has also returned through Lily's final achievement of the artistic vision and triumph denied her ten years earlier.[21] As clear as the existence of the relationship between Mrs Ramsay and Lily is the function of this relationship: 'Demeter and Kore, mother and daughter, extend the feminine consciousness both upwards and downwards. They add an "older and younger", "stronger and weaker" dimension to it and widen out the narrowly limited conscious mind bound in space and time, giving it intimations of a greater and more comprehensive personality which has a share in the eternal course of things' (Jung, p. 225). Both the mother-figure and the daughter-figure are united in that they are artists – the one in paints and the other in human relationships – and in that they are bound to each other by psychic bonds which remain firm even beyond death. Demeter has effected the liberation of Persephone.

Sigmund Freud's interpretation of the Oedipus myth is almost as famous as the myth itself. This pattern, Freud says, dramatized in the legend of the Greek youth who unwittingly kills his father, marries and begets children with his mother, and then blinds himself in atonement, is fundamental in human experience. It is so basic that 'the beginnings of religion, ethics, society, and art meet in the Oedipus complex'. We are moved by Sophocles' play, Freud says, by the consciousness that Oedipus' fate 'might have been our own. . . . It may be that we were all destined to divert our first sexual impulses toward our mothers, and our first impulses of hatred and violence toward our fathers; our dreams convince us that we were.'[22]

That the relationship between James, Mrs Ramsay, and Mr Ramsay reflects this pattern is so clear as to be almost unmistakable. The intense adoration which James cherishes for his mother has its opposite in an equally strong hatred for his father, 'casting ridicule upon his wife, who was ten thousand times better in every way than he was (James thought) . . .' (10). Virginia Woolf says of Mr Ramsay that 'his son hated him' (57). This emotion is thoroughgoing: 'Had there been an axe handy, or a poker, any weapon that would have gashed a hole in his father's breast and killed him, there and then,

James would have seized it' (10). Mrs Ramsay is solicitous and fearful for James as Jocasta might have been for the young Oedipus: 'what demon possessed him, her youngest, her cherished?' (43).

James's jealousy and feelings of rivalry with his father are intensified by his perhaps unconscious knowledge of the sexual aspect of the relationship between his parents. He is made acutely aware of it in the episode early in the novel in which Mr Ramsay comes to his wife for the sympathy and reassurance he demands. The imagery used to describe this action is patently sexual. James, standing between his mother's knees, feels her seem 'to raise herself with an effort, and at once to pour erect into the air a rain of energy . . . and into this fountain and spray of life, the fatal sterility of the male plunged itself, like a beak of brass, barren and bare' (58). Then James feels shut out when, the demand complied with, 'Mrs Ramsay seemed to fold herself together, one petal closed in another, and the whole fabric fell in exhaustion upon itself, so that she had only strength enough to move her finger, in exquisite abandonment to exhaustion . . . while there throbbed through her, like a pulse in a spring which has expanded to its full width and now gently ceases to beat, the rapture of successful creation' (60–1).

Into the third section of the novel, across the space of ten years, James carries these same emotions undiminished in intensity. Of his mother he thinks, 'She alone spoke the truth; to her alone could he speak it' (278). Contemplating his father, James realizes that 'He had always kept this old symbol of taking a knife and striking his father to the heart' (273). The pattern is so strong that now James and his father compete in another triangle in which Cam has been substituted for Mrs Ramsay. The two children have made a compact to resist their father's tyranny, but James feels that he will lose to him again just as he had before. As Mr Ramsay begins to win Cam over, James acknowledges his defeat. '"Yes," thought James pitilessly . . . "now she will give way. I shall be left to fight the tyrant alone"' (250). An instant later, the antecedent of the present experience is dredged up out of the recesses of his memory: 'There was a flash of blue, he remembered, and then somebody sitting with him laughed, surrendered, and he was very angry. It must have been his mother, he thought, sitting on a low chair, with his father standing over her' (251).

Freud writes of the ambivalence the child feels toward his father, the conflict between tenderness and hostility. He concludes that unless the child is successful in repressing the sexual love for the mother and hostility for the father, while concomitantly allowing the natural affection for the father to grow, neurosis will be the result. Significantly, at the end of the finally accomplished journey to the Lighthouse, James experiences his rapport with Mr Ramsay. Cam addresses herself silently to James: 'You've got it at last. For she knew that this was what James had been wanting . . . He was so pleased that he was not going to let anybody share a grain of his pleasure. His father had praised him' (306).

The Oedipus myth is consonant with the Persephone myth in its application to *To the Lighthouse* and both are reflections of fundamental patterns of human experience. The two old antagonists testify to this judgment of their importance, Freud to the former and Jung to the latter. Appropriately, the symbol for one section of the novel, 'The Window', is female, and that for another section, 'The Lighthouse', is male. Exalting the feminine principle in life over the masculine, Virginia Woolf built her novel around a character embodying the life-giving role of the female. In opposition, she shows the male, both in the father and son aspect, as death-bearing – arid, sterile, hateful, and 'fatal' (58). The female principle in life is exalted in all its aspects of love which are opposed to the harsh and critical aspects of the male principle, of fertility with its pattern of triumph over death in rebirth. What, then, becomes of the single obvious central symbol, the Lighthouse? Its use is simply this: in its stability, its essential constancy despite cyclical change which is not really change at all, this symbol refers to Mrs Ramsay herself. This meaning is revealed to the reader explicitly: Mrs Ramsay 'looked up over her knitting and met the third stroke and it seemed to her like her own eyes meeting her own eyes, searching as she alone could search into her mind and heart . . . She praised herself – in praising the light, without vanity, for she was stern, she was searching, she was beautiful like that light' (97). And just as there are three persons combined in the Primordial Goddess, so there are three strokes to the Lighthouse beam, and 'the long steady stroke, the last of the three . . . was her stroke . . .' (96).

As Mrs Ramsay gives love, stability, and fruitfulness to her family and those in her orbit, so the female force should always function. It serves to ameliorate or mitigate the effects of male violence, hate, and destructiveness. And should the physical embodiment of this force pay her debt to the world of shades, this is not an ever-enduring loss, for it returns through those whom it has made fruitful and thus drawn into the rebirth pattern. Or it may be sought, found, and embraced as, in their separate ways, James, Cam, and Mr Ramsay experience it at the end of their ritual and symbolic voyage to the Lighthouse.[23] □

At the same time as the symbolism and mythic potential of Woolf's text were being explored for unity and resolution, investigations of her stream-of-consciousness technique were also under way. Woolf is prominently discussed in a number of books appearing in the mid-1950s devoted to the 'psychological' or 'stream-of consciousness' novel.[24]

I have reproduced extracts from Shiv Kumar's later (1962) work, *Bergson and the Stream of Consciousness Novel*, since it consolidates many of the earlier accounts and makes the case for Bergsonian readings in a cogent, and insightful argument. Bergsonism became a very influential factor in readings of Woolf's work, particularly in the characterisation of the Woolfian 'moment', and there are several other works to pursue in this strand of criticism.[25] But Kumar's study remains a very helpful introduction. While not every one would agree with his claim that 'all her literary experiments as a novelist can be explained in terms of Bergson's *la durée*', the parallel remains strong in much work on Woolf.[26] Before reading Kumar, it would be helpful to summarise Bergson's theory of *la durée*. Briefly, it may be defined as subjective, psychological, non-spatial, time.[27] True time is understood as impenetrable and seamlessly continuous *flux* (a key term), and to exist only within, subjectively: 'Outside ourselves we should find only space, and consequently nothing but simultaneities.'[28] Bergson speaks of 'two different selves . . . one of which is . . . the external projection of the other, its spatial and, so to speak, social representation'; but the more 'fundamental' of which is connected to *la durée* and is therefore 'free'. It is reached 'by deep introspection'. Bergson emphasises that only in 'rare moments' do we have access to *la durée* and to our true selves, and that only in such moments may we 'act freely'.[29] Bergson's 'rare moments' of introspection seem to resemble Woolf's; and his suggestion of an inner illumination casting its 'colourless shadow' into the external world may also inform Woolf's 'luminous halo' imagery.[30] But despite this resemblance, critics were to become wary of fully equating the two. Tony Inglis, for example, in 1977 notes that for some time in Woolf studies 'pondered reading and critical accounts [have] tended to show that Woolf's novels are better read as weapons against flux than as inert surrenders to it'. He continues:

■ From Empson onward it had been possible to take for granted Woolf's *dynamic* use of the stream-of-consciousness convention; Daiches and Auerbach had shown how she *used* reverie, rather than simply reducing experience to reverie. Savage's impatient and reductive accounts . . . are coloured and unduly sharpened by an anxiety over indeterminacy and the lack of absolutes that, a generation later, has been substantially overcome – we swim in the waves of flux instead of drowning in them.[31] □

In the following extract, Kumar compares Woolf's writing with that of contemporaries such as Joyce and Proust and with the earlier work of Sterne. He makes some helpful distinctions between the latter's experimentalism and Woolf's. This is followed by analysis of *To the Lighthouse* and *The Waves* in terms of *la durée*.

- 'And all our intuitions mock
  The formal logic of the clock.'
  (W. H. Auden: *New Year Letter*)

Of all the stream of consciousness novelists, Virginia Woolf alone seems to have presented a consistent and comprehensive treatment of time. Time with her is almost a mode of perception, a filter which distils all phenomena before they are apprehended in their true significance and relationship. Her characters, like those of Proust, are 'monsters occupying a place in Time infinitely more important than the restricted one reserved for them in space'.[32] Her protest against the Edwardian novel was, in fact, a revolt against the tyranny of chronological time that is 'matter' in favour of *la durée*, that is 'spirit'. This also explains why she considers Joyce and other contemporary novelists of the time-school to be 'spiritualists' as against the 'materialism' of Galsworthy, Bennett and Wells. All her literary experiments as a novelist can be explained in terms of Bergson's *la durée*. In fact, it is possible to trace her development from the point of view of her progressive awareness of the various aspects of psychological time.

Time has always been one of the most baffling problems for the novelist. It is, says Henry James, 'that side of the novelist's effort – the side of most difficulty and thereby of most dignity – which consists in giving the sense of duration, of the lapse and accumulation of time. This is altogether to my view the stiffest problem that the artist in fiction has to tackle.'[33] It was towards this problem that Virginia Woolf addressed her main efforts as a novelist. Her various literary experiments are, in fact, directed towards finding a suitable medium which could render most appropriately this elusive 'sense of duration'.

However, before interpreting her work in terms of Bergson's durational flux, it may be interesting to compare her with Sterne who had conducted similar experiments with time and evolved a highly fluid and indeterminate type of narrative. In her essay on 'The Sentimental Journey', Virginia Woolf presents him as 'the forerunner of the moderns'. 'No writing', she says, 'seems to flow more exactly into the very folds and creases of the individual mind, to express its changing moods, to answer its slightest whim and impulse . . . *the utmost fluidity exists.*'[34]

Sterne is undoubtedly the first time-novelist who had, as early as 1760, anticipated some of the fictional experiments of James Joyce, Virginia Woolf and Dorothy Richardson. He was the first to revolt against the rigours of chronological sequence of time. This is how the narrator in *Tristram Shandy* presents the qualitative aspect of time which can never be assessed in terms of such statistical terms as minutes, hours, months and years. This theme forms the subject of a discussion between Mr. Shandy and Uncle Toby: '. . . my father . . . was pre-determined in his mind to give my Uncle Toby a clear account of the matter by a metaphysical dissertation upon the subject of duration and its simple modes', and after these preliminary remarks Mr. Shandy proceeds to give a more elaborate description of 'duration' and the succession of ideas after the manner of John Locke.

> . . . in our computations of time, we are so used to minutes, hours, weeks, and months – and of clocks (I wish there was not a clock in the kingdom) to measure out their several portions to us. . . . Now, whether we observe it or no, continued my father, in every sound man's head there is a regular succession of ideas of one sort or other, which follow each other in train . . . [35]

Although dressed in a humorous garb, this passage appropriately brings out the importance of inner duration to a psychological novelist whose primary intention should be faithfully to render the 'regular succession of ideas'. But Sterne's approach to duration being Lockean, he can conceive psychic phenomena only as discrete elements capable of being arranged in juxtaposition alongside of each other in a homogeneous medium which is nothing else than space. The metaphor employed by Mr. Shandy in describing Locke's theory of ideas is that of a train.[36] This conception of duration is obviously atomistic and retains under the guise of continuity the whole apparatus of numerical multiplicity. We are, therefore, still far from Bergson's concept of duration as a medium in which all psychic states permeate one another in a qualitative process, like notes in a musical phrase.[37]

To understand Virginia Woolf's treatment of la durée in her novels, it would be necessary to note the difference between Locke's spatial analysis of duration and Bergson's presentation of it as a qualitative process of creative evolution. It could, therefore, be remarked that just as Locke is the informing spirit behind Tristram Shandy, so might Bergson have been the philosophic inspiration behind Virginia Woolf's realisation of la durée. Quite instinctively, she employs metaphors which unlike Sterne's, do not suggest a process of quantitative assemblage, but, like Bergson's, present duration as a ceaseless succession of qualitative changes. . . . Time being one of the most significant aspects of the work of Virginia Woolf, it should be possible to trace her development as a novelist in terms of her gradual swing from a traditional view of time to Bergson's durée. . . . To the Lighthouse, unlike Mrs. Dalloway, is limited to the space of ten years. In the three sections of the novel, we have three corresponding aspects of time represented symbolically. In the first section entitled, 'The Window', covering about two-thirds of the entire narrative, Virginia Woolf describes an intense human experience in a mere cross-section of a September evening from six o'clock to supper time. Therefore, whereas the clock covers only a couple of hours, it is only through *la durée* that we are enabled to participate in the inner experience of various characters. In Mrs. Ramsay time becomes a symbol of inner expansion because she fills it with love, hope and understanding; Mr. Ramsay's inordinate egotism, on the other hand, contracts time; to James it is synonymous with 'tomorrow' and the promise of a visit to the lighthouse; to Lily Briscoe time is a symbolic process of the intaking of sensory impressions and memories. *La durée*, as suggested in this novel, is a living organism. It is a qualitative process and not an assemblage of discrete moments of experience. '. . . how life', says Mrs. Ramsay, 'from being made up of little separate incidents which one lived one by one, became curled and whole like a wave which bore one up with it . . .'[38]

The second section, 'Time Passes', brings into contrast with the inner duration, the flow of external time – ten years. Events, after Mrs. Ramsay's death, assume a different aspect altogether. They are announced, rather unceremoniously, within bracketed interpolations, beginning with Mrs. Ramsay's death 'the night before'; Prue Ramsay's marriage and death a year later in child-birth; Andrew Ramsay's death by shell-explosion; the publication of Carmichael's poems, etc. In the march of these events and seasons, imponderable flow of external time, 'night and day, month and year ran shapelessly together',[39] and thus time unrelated to Mrs. Ramsay becomes a confused rout. *La durée*, Virginia Woolf indirectly suggests, is not a medium of time-mensuration but almost a mode of perception with its own aesthetic values. When the memory of Mrs. Ramsay, after an interval of ten years, re-emerges in the mind of Lily Briscoe (third section), the former again begins to inspire her values in the minds of those who remember, love and respect her. She becomes like Albertine 'a mighty goddess of Time'.[40]

The Ramsays' summer house is not an inanimate structure in three spatial dimensions, but like Proust's Combray church exists also in the fourth dimension – *la durée*. It becomes a durational link between the past and future, reassuming its significant role with the return of Lily Briscoe 'one late evening in September'. It symbolizes the point from which Lily Briscoe can 'tunnel' back into the past in remembrance of Mrs. Ramsay, and Mr. Ramsay, together with James and Cam, can sail into the future on their expedition to the lighthouse. But these arbitrary segments of time, the past, present and future, merge into each other to form *durée réelle* when, on the one hand the party lands on the lighthouse and, on the other Lily Briscoe, in a moment of sudden revelation, realizes her vision. Lily Briscoe's painting seems to be designed on a durational pattern, since it derives its aesthetic validity from a qualitative interpenetration of the past, present and future.

> 'He has landed' . . . 'It is finished.'
>
> Quickly, as if she were recalled by something over there, she turned to her canvas. There it was – her picture . . . she looked at her canvas; it was blurred. *With a sudden intensity,* as if she saw it clear for a second, *she drew a line there, in the centre. It was done;* it was finished. Yes, she thought, laying down her brush in extreme fatigue, I have had my vision.[41]

'He has landed . . . It is finished', and so is also finished the period of anxious travail in discovering the most appropriate blendings of colours, and in solving 'the question . . . of some relation between those masses'.[42] Then arrives the moment of illumination, and with a bold stroke Lily Briscoe draws a line in the centre. This definitive stroke symbolizes a sudden intuitive realization of the qualitative blending into each other of the mechanically separated segments of time. Not the present moment of experience, but only its recapitulation after an interval, can reveal its true essence by releasing it from the cramping influence of the immediate circumstances. Lily Briscoe could not have realized her vision earlier in the first section, because the personal presence of Mrs. Ramsay would have been an embarrassing distraction, disabling her from conceiving the picture in its true perspective. Ten years had to pass, the proposed expedition to the lighthouse had to materialise, before the final vision could dawn within her consciousness. . . .[43] *The Waves* . . . cannot be classified with any of her earlier or later novels. Exquisite in lyrical composition, rich in poetic imagery, this novel attempts to communicate an almost inexpressible fluid impulse behind all human experience. Its basic intent can again be analysed in terms of durational flux. Here Virginia Woolf has tried to project time on two different levels: the normal lifespan and the diurnal movement of the sun. On the former level, she treats life in a pseudo-biographical method employed earlier in *Jacob's Room*; and on the latter level she presents, through such symbols as the rise and decline of the sun and waves, a single day's duration as already shown in *Mrs. Dalloway*. Each phase of the lives of the six characters in the novel corresponds to each of the nine progressive phases of the sun. But these arbitrary divisions should not be taken literally to imply that Virginia Woolf accepts the theory of the Eleatic School and accordingly, presents personality as an assemblage of immobile spatial units. These lunar sections, slicing into bits and thus attempting to regulate life's inner flow, merely expose, as mentioned earlier, the restrictive nature of language and any formal schematization of fluid reality. '. . . how tired I am of phrases,' says Bernard, 'that come down beautifully with all their feet on the ground! Also, how I distrust neat designs of life that are drawn upon half-sheets of notepaper. . . . What delights me then is the confusion, the height, the indifference and the fury. Great clouds always changing, and movement . . .'[44] Virginia Woolf, therefore, has to strain hard after creating a sense of fluidity through an appropriate use of words, similes and metaphors. All the six characters often seem to fade into one another (as they 'flow and change')[45] forming, as it were, a larger self into which its components are always merging in a process of qualitative transformation. If Virginia Woolf resorts to the device of 'substantive parts'[46] it is only by way of concession to the demands of intelligibility and communication. The world in which Bernard and his friends transmit their innermost feelings in soliloquised musings is not governed by the clock, its seasons and climates obey other laws, its pulsations are 'measured' only by *la durée* which, in Bernard's own words, is a process of 'the eternal renewal, the incessant rise and fall and fall and rise again'.[47]

The clock which contracts our impulses and sensations is again referred to, in *The Waves*, as an antithesis to *la durée* which is a symbol of inner expansion.

> Yes, but suddenly one hears a clock tick. We who had been immersed in this world became aware of another. It is painful. It was Neville who changed our time. He, who had been thinking with the unlimited time of the mind, which stretches in a flash from Shakespeare to ourselves, poked the fire and began to live by that other clock which marks the approach of a particular person. The wide and dignified sweep of his mind contracted. He became on the alert . . . I noted how he touched a cushion. *From the myriads of mankind and all time past he had chosen one person one moment in particular.*[48]

This is a typical Bergsonian passage in which Virginia Woolf tries to suggest how necessity or action, by focusing the mind on a fixed point of interest ('poked the fire', 'touched a cushion') immobilizes its free movement backward and forward in *la durée*. The link with 'all time past' is broken, the mind shrinks, is impoverished of its infinite richness and assumes the threadbare vesture of the present moment, a mathematical instant in the ceaseless flow of time. . . . 'Movement and change are the essence of our being', writes Virginia Woolf in her essay on Montaigne, 'rigidity is death; conformity is death.'[49]

By immersing herself in her characters' streams of consciousness,

Virginia Woolf experiences under the frozen surface of their conventional ego, a state of perpetual flux of which her novels are the most faithful representations. Like Bergson, she conceives thinking as a 'continual and continuous change of inward direction'.[50] 'How fast the stream flows', says Bernard in *The Waves*, 'from January to December! We are swept by the torrent of things grown so familiar that they cast no shadow. We float, we float . . .'[51] along this stream of consciousness backward and forward in time.

In the task of representing this fluid reality, a novelist is more happily placed than a metaphysician, since the former, without having to construct it in terms of immutable concepts, is able to suggest it symbolically by employing a suitable method of narrative. In contemporary fiction, the stream of consciousness method of characterisation constitutes such an effort to represent symbolically the dynamic aspect of human personality.[52] . . . The most emphatic assertion of flux as the ultimate reality forms the theme of one of Louis's soliloquies in which he compares it with the continuous rhythmic movement of a waltz . . .:

'I am conscious of flux . . . *It is like a waltz tune*, eddying in and out. The waitresses, balancing trays, swing in and out, round and round . . . *Where then is the break in this continuity?* What the fissure through which one sees disaster? *The circle is unbroken; the harmony complete.* Here is the central rhythm; here the common mainspring. I watch it expand, contract; and then expand again.'[53]

This *pulsation éternelle*, in a typical Bergsonian sense, is the creative impulse behind the work of Virginia Woolf. Bernard feels in his dreamy state like 'one carried beneath the surface of a stream.'[54] 'The tree alone resisted', he says in a later soliloquy, '*our eternal flux*. For I changed and changed; was Hamlet, was Shelley, was the hero, whose name I now forget, of a novel by Dostoevsky; was for a whole term, incredibly, Napoleon. . . .'[55] Any attempt to regulate this 'eternal flux', superimpose an arbitrary design, would be a distortion of reality, for it is a mistake, says Bernard, '*this extreme precision, this orderly and military progress; a convenience, a lie.* There is always deep below it, even when we arrive punctually at the appointed time with our white waistcoats and polite formalities, a rushing stream of broken dreams . . .'[56]

This stream of inner flux flows through all characters, through Mr. Ramsay who is 'always changing,'[57] through Bernard who is always tormented by 'the horrible activity of the mind's eye',[58] through Neville who knows 'the person is always changing'.[59] The moment Lily Briscoe loses 'consciousness of outer things, and her name and her personality and her appearance, and whether Mr. Carmichael was there or not, her mind kept throwing up from its depths, scenes, and names, and sayings, and memories and ideas, like a fountain spurting over . . .'[60]

She experiences this sensation of inner flux more consciously when she had

> let the flowers fall from her basket . . . screwing up her eyes and standing back as if to look at her picture, which she was not touching, however, with all her faculties in a trance, frozen over superficially but moving underneath with extreme speed.[61]

That in rendering such a metaphorical description of the inner flux, Virginia Woolf suggests a close parallelism with Bergson, may be seen from the following extract:

> There is, beneath these sharply cut crystals and this frozen surface, a continuous flux which is not comparable to any flux I have ever seen.[62]

> (*An Introduction to Metaphysics*)

Another Bergsonian metaphor that occurs frequently in the work of Virginia Woolf likens this inner stream to the swelling of a tune. The melody, according to Bergson, represents perfectly this process of psychic movement:

> Il y a simplement la mélodie continue de notre vie intérieure – mélodie qui se poursuit et se poursuivra, indivisible, du commencement à la fin de notre existence consciente. Notre personnalité est cela même.[63]

In this continuous movement of inner life there are no pauses; perceptions, memories and sensations roll on, as it were, in laval flow, recreating self in eternally new forms. Life, as Virginia Woolf conceives it, is not a predetermined and precisely patterned thing. Since its determining aspect is *la durée*, it has no spatial symmetry or cohesion about it. It is, as she affirms in a famous passage, 'not a series of gig lamps symmetrically arranged; life is a luminous halo, a semitransparent envelope surrounding us from the beginning of consciousness to the end'.[64] Such a statement, obviously, implies the supremacy of intuition and flux over logic and determinism.

It matters little whether Virginia Woolf was directly acquainted with Bergson's work or not, nor is it important to assess in this direction her indebtedness to such earlier novelists as Proust, James Joyce and Dorothy Richardson. To attempt to analyse in precise terms the composition of literary genius and resolve it into its components, is a task that has often led literary criticism into bypaths. Our intention in this chapter has been merely to indicate that the basic issues involved in Virginia Woolf's literary theory and practice, particularly her use of the stream of consciousness, are of a philosophical nature and can be most adequately explained in terms of Bergson's view of time and personality. In its rich poetic imagery, tone and rhythmic flow of sentences, and intuitive perception of reality as flux, her work parallels in a remarkable manner the style and philosophic thought of Bergson.[65] □

Jean Guiguet's 'magisterial' study of Woolf's œuvre became the standard work of reference in Woolf criticism. It did much to establish her importance as a writer after the ravages of some of the earlier assessments we have sampled from the 'Bloomsbury baiters'.[66] But in putting forward a powerful philosophically based interpretation of her entire œuvre, drawing heavily on Sartrean existentialism, and ignoring the 'more materialist aspects' of her work (as John Mepham points out in his helpful discussion of Guiguet's influence),[67] Guiguet also reinforced earlier stereotypes of Woolf as an intensely subjective and otherworldly writer: 'To exist, for Virginia Woolf, meant experiencing that dizziness on the ridge between two abysses of the unknown, the self and the non-self.' He places her work quite firmly in a number of philosophical and aesthetic contexts, while claiming that Woolf could not be allied to any one of these exclusively: 'Bergsonians, relativists, empiricists, associationists, idealists, existentialists, may each in turn claim her as an adept: she belongs to none of these schools, and she participates in all of them. She has no pretensions to abstract thought: her domain is life, not ideology.' [68] Most importantly, Guiguet sets the agenda in psychobiographical readings by making, for the first time, extensive use of *A Writer's Diary* in analysis of the fiction. In the following extract are a short sample of his reading of *To the Lighthouse*, in which he focuses on the connected symbolism of the lighthouse and Mrs Ramsay, and a more extensive discussion of *The Waves*. As well as Woolf's diary, Guiguet also cites the famous passage from 'Modern Fiction', and in a highly influential analysis of this in relation to *The Waves*, directs critical attention to 'The Moment: Summer's Night' as a paradigm for understanding the Woolfian moment (the essay is a special focus, for example, in Harvena Richter's later philosophical study of Woolf).[69] The extract concludes with his countering of Daiches's negative assessment of *The Waves*.

■ The lighthouse that shines out at night, in the offing from the island where the Ramsays are spending their holidays with a group of friends, is the vanishing point, both material and symbolic, towards which all the lines of *To the Lighthouse* converge. . . . That Mrs Ramsay has usurped the place belonging to her husband is a point to which I shall return. What interests us here is rather the way in which the central character dominates the book. Behind the account of Mrs Ramsay's day we find no analysis of her feelings, no generalized interpretation of her attitudes; she is not the centre toward which all elements converge, as was the case with *Mrs Dalloway*, in order to define her and strengthen her autonomous personality in face of the conflicts that divide her and the contradictory impressions that she arouses around her. On the contrary, by a kind of centrifugal process, Mrs Ramsay radiates through the book, impregnating all the other characters. And it is the relations that emanate from her personality, rather than the personality that emanates from these relations, that becomes the focus of interest in the book. . . . Freed from the requirements of cohesion involved in the working out of a single character, she finds herself closer to the 'purely psychological' conception of D.H. Lawrence.[70] . . . It is not surprising to find Arnold Bennett condemning [the] second part.[71] There is no doubt that the virtuosity of these pages emphasises their strangeness. Yet they are neither irrelevant ornament nor a purely technical device. Their aim is precisely to set in the very centre of the book, in a significant fashion, the essential, ambiguous protagonist: Time-Duration. Whereas under the aspect of Duration it plays its role in the two other sections, discreetly merged into the consciousness of the dramatic personae, in this second part, under the aspect of Time, it achieves its inhuman task as cosmic agent.

No doubt Virginia Woolf implicitly admits a heterogeneity, the dangers of which she did not minimize: 'The lyric portions of *To the Lighthouse* are collected in the 10-year lapse and don't interfere with the text so much as usual.' But declaring in the next sentence that the book fetched its circle pretty completely this time, she asserts thereby that its heterogeneity, far from interrupting the line of the work, is an integral part of it. Without contesting that the dual nature of the tone is evidence of a duality in the author's personality, what has been called (by R. Las Vergnas) her androgynousness, I should like to suggest that *To the Lighthouse*, by its structure, its movement, as also by its essential subject, attempts to resolve that duality, and that *The Waves* only develops and carries to the limits of their potential the resources of style and composition which are exploited here. . . . Having taken *The Waves* as an example for my study of the genesis of a work, I shall refer the reader to that analysis for all that concerns the circumstances of its composition and the relations that may be established between that point in Virginia Woolf's work and her personality, her inmost preoccupations, her artistic purpose.[72] In the following pages I shall merely study *The Waves* in the light of what has already been said, supplementing this however with certain passages from the Diary directly referring to the form or content of the book.

Although *The Waves* is classified among the novels and described as such on its cover, it would be rash and futile to approach it without defining the term more precisely. From the beginning, even before she has formed more than a vague suggestion of the work, Virginia Woolf describes it as 'a new kind of play, prose yet poetry, a novel and a play'. A little later, she drops the word novel and speaks of a 'play-poem'.[73] We read elsewhere of a 'serious, mystical poetical work',[74] and an 'abstract mystical eyeless book'.[75] This must be our starting-point, rather than the label 'novel' attached primarily for commercial reasons to *The Waves*. . . . Before seeking a fuller definition in *The Waves* itself, we may turn to the sketch *The Moment: Summer's Night*[76] in which certain phrases formulate in brief abstract fashion the essential lines of the complex whole we are striving to grasp: '. . . everybody believes that the present is something, seeks out the different elements in this situation in order to compose the truth of it, the whole of it.'[77] This is the postulate that must be accepted before venturing on *The Waves*, and without which the book has no meaning. 'To begin with: it [the present moment] is largely composed of visual and of sense impressions.' [78] The words 'I see', 'I hear', 'Look', in the opening lines of *The Waves* fling pure sensations at the reader; but more than this, they are incantatory formulae which awaken his sensibility to the world of impressions into which he is entering. True, we immediately recognize the 'myriad impressions' received by the mind 'from all sides . . . an incessant shower of innumerable atoms' which, as early as 1919, Virginia Woolf had declared it the novelist's task to convey 'with as little mixture of the alien and external as possible'.[79] But this was the first time she was going to follow literally, in a novel, her own critical suggestion and to concentrate unremittingly and uncompromisingly on rendering life as she had conceived it: 'a luminous halo, a semi-transparent envelope surrounding us from the beginning of consciousness to the end.'[80] Moreover, the 1919 formulation is a general one; it expresses an intuition without, however, analysing it. The phrases are often quoted, on account of their concentration and their startling newness at the time. But they are only a point of departure; I have quoted them in order to stress the unity of Virginia Woolf's thought. We must return to *The Moment* to follow that thought to the final stages of its development.

'But this moment is also composed of a sense that the legs of the chair are sinking through the centre of the earth, passing through the rich garden earth; they sink, weighted down.'[81] Sense impressions were the surface of the moment; here we have its depth, its relation with the rest of the universe, its roots in the darkness. That rich garden soil, that centre of the earth with which the moment brings us into contact, are all those forms of reality which, through the different layers of the concrete, lead us to the heart and essence of things. And our participation in this essence, our rootedness, is fate itself weighing us down.

Finally, the moment includes a third component, of a different nature: 'Here in the centre is a knot of consciousness; a nucleus divided up into four heads, eight legs, eight arms, and four separate bodies.'[82] The other elements, whether peripheral or central, were detached and, so to speak, unsupported; they made up the multiplicity, the heterogeneity, the discontinuity of the moment. Perhaps this is the world of *Jacob's Room*, circumscribing a void in which something could be sensed, something had to be postulated: that something was the third element of the moment, this integrating power, this nucleus of consciousness. It may seem surprising that Virginia Woolf took so long to make so simple a discovery. But then its simplicity is only apparent. What is this consciousness? It is one and yet manifold; and it has always haunted Virginia Woolf. Remember that Septimus Smith was Clarissa Dalloway's 'double'; and the inextricable multiplicity of *Orlando* may be only an arabesque scribbled in the margin of the research that led up to *The Waves*. These separate consciousnesses, which, released from the prison of single bodies to which centuries of rationalist and pragmatic thought had confined them, are fused in the moment, are to be the central element in *The Waves*. And inversely, the succession of moments that makes up the book organize themselves around these consciousnesses, while merging with them to become their very substance.[83] That dateless morning in the garden of their childhood means for each of the six protagonists what he is for and through the other five, as well as what he is for and through himself. On this first layer all later experience will settle; their shared years at school, their meetings in youth and in maturity. And even in the inevitable separation imposed upon them by their individual destinies, the six consciousnesses will constantly adhere to one another. If each of them becomes a centre: Susan on her farm, Rhoda in her solitude, Jinny in her sensual adventures, Neville amongst his books, Louis at his office and Bernard in his social life, one or other of the rest is constantly appearing as though to ensure a relief or to make a contribution.

Naturally, this synthesis attains perfection on the two occasions when the six friends meet. On the first, when they are saying goodbye to Percival, the latter – a mythical figure through his silence, a symbol through his name – becomes the kingpin of this multiple consciousness. The others' love for him is the catalytic agent that gives rise to this perfect moment, 'the thing we have made, that globes itself here . . .'. To tell the content of 'this globe whose walls are made of Percival'[84] one would have to quote the whole page. The moment holds all human things, all space, the happiness of a secluded life, of ordinary life, of fields and seasons, of the future which is still to be created and which they will create. This richness justifies Bernard's phrase: 'The moment was all; the moment was enough.'[85]

Does Percival's death mean the disintegration of this multiple consciousness? Does it bring to an end the eager quest which, through him, they all pursued? The twenty-fifth year, his departure and his death are perhaps only one and the same event. To measure the extent of this catastrophe, listen to Bernard, who has a gift for words, some twenty years after, at their final gathering:

> It was different once. . . . Once we could break the current as we chose. How many telephone calls, how many post cards, are now needed to cut this hole through which we come together, united, at Hampton Court? How swift life runs from January to December! We are all swept on by the torrent of things grown so familiar that they cast no shade; we make no comparisons; think scarcely ever of I or of you; and in this unconsciousness attain the utmost freedom from friction and part the weeds that grow over the mouths of sunken channels.[86]

Once, that's to say in their youth, when Percival was alive and their communion was a living thing, their intermingled consciousnesses, made keen by mutual contact, could grasp the profound reality of the universe and of life. Each in his own way and according to his individual tendencies, but stimulated and enriched by the differences between them, they went from one moment to the next, and each moment was fullness and knowledge and shared rebirth. The here-and-now, which was a miracle, has become a routine: it has been consciousness, voice and communion; it has become unconsciousness, silence and solitude.[87]

Yet, for all the note of despair in this last moment, recovered against all reason by an act of will which is also an act of faith, Bernard – and doubtless the others too, since he is their mouth-piece – refuses to abdicate, and turns defeat into victory. From the universal which has swept him away and broken his impetus, he takes fresh impetus. Since everything goes too fast for the moments to expand, since life now consists of actions and events, to fit oneself into the new rhythm is the only possible solution; by accepting and willing it, one can dispel its evil power, subjugate it, recover the initiative, become central once again: the quest assumes its other aspect, that of a fight; the first was turned towards life, the second faces death: 'Against you

I will fling myself, unvanquished and unyielding, O Death!'[88]

Hitherto, by analysing the blended voices and the content of that poetic utterance which unfolds the single substance of which the speakers are made, I have in some sort followed the path traced by the novel. However, if I quoted its final phrase, it was only on account of its forcefulness. Actually I have not yet considered the final section, the long monologue in which Bernard sums things up.

Bernard, indeed, has always loved words and stories, and by dint of turning everything, himself included, into words and stories, he has even anticipated, as it were, his ultimate role: 'I conceive myself called upon to provide, some winter's night, a meaning for all my observations – a line that runs from one to another, a summing up that completes.'[89] Yet, even if there was a slight affectation about his voice, if it tended rather more than the rest to be abstract and prosaic, it was not essentially different: it was just a man's voice. And yet he is not heard in the sixth section, nor is Rhoda. Neither the one who has the gift of communication, Bernard, the sociable, talkative one, nor the other who, on the contrary, has no gift for making contact, Rhoda, the timid, lonely one, takes part in this song of life. Rhoda's abstention is due no doubt to her being too deeply and intimately involved with her own inner reality to break the silence essential to her being, even by some inward melody. But Bernard? Must it be admitted that his voice was too clear and too shrill? That he would have lapsed from the intense level of the moment and, seduced by his evil genius, would have talked about life instead of expressing it? Thus it is quite natural that when the time comes to sum up and explain he, who was mute in the sphere of life and action, becomes the narrator, enabled, through words, to make solid what is in process of becoming, to circumscribe people and things; enabled by means of phrases to shape life into groups and sequences and constructions. Yet we must not forget that Bernard repeatedly doubts himself: 'But what are stories? Toys I twist, bubbles I blow, one ring passing through another. And sometimes I begin to doubt if there are stories.' Age and experience have increased his doubts, which have even become a negative certainty by that winter evening when he renders his account: 'Of story, of design I do not see a trace then.' Thanks to this doubt which, perhaps, destroys something essential to Bernard but which brings him closer, in extremis, to his friends, his voice follows quite naturally on the other voices: his summing-up sounds no jarring note, and is all the more truthful for it. . . . Many critics,[90] while recognising the merits of the book, have none the less condemned it, claiming that the convention on which it is based is as rigid, and moreover as remote from reality, as the realistic conventions that Virginia Woolf rejected and sought to replace. The comparison suggested by Daiches between the mask theory of Yeats and O'Neill and the voices of *The Waves* is interesting.[91] Yet it is difficult to accept it, save as shedding special light on the art of Virginia Woolf, revealing therein certain expressionist features. Still less can we extend the mask theory to criticism of the whole of her work, even by ricochet as does Daiches at the close of his study of a book which he evidently does not like:

> [The mask] is itself so rigid and inflexible that unless you have seen its meaning beforehand you can never be persuaded of it by watching the mask. The mask is most effective as a means of communication between those who have the same insights. But Virginia Woolf *in her novels* tried to convey unique insights.[92] (My italics)

If a certain community of vision is undoubtedly necessary for the understanding of *The Waves*, we must not forget that to bring us to the meaning concealed within their stylized form, Virginia Woolf's masks have at their disposal all the resources of poetry. And all things considered, the only reproach that can be levelled at *The Waves, A Novel*, is that it is neither the 'novel' that it promises nor even the 'lyrical novel' that Delattre saw in it, but that 'play-poem' which Virginia Woolf had longed to write.[93] □

The last extract in this chapter takes a close look at the poetic fabric of this 'play-poem', *The Waves*, and offers some sensitive intertextual readings with the romantic poetry that imbues its pages. But the main focus of Frank D. McConnell's essay on *The Waves* is an examination of 'the world of things'. This phenomenological reading is important in several respects: reasserting a more dualistic understanding of Woolf's writing, McConnell draws attention to the significance of the object, material (but not political) world in her text, and counters the many mystical readings of *The Waves* by pointing to Woolf's ambivalent diary entry on the subject. He also draws on a story by Woolf, 'Evening Over Sussex', for this phenomenological reading. McConnell significantly counters assessments such as Guiguet's which suggest that there is ultimately a single unifying voice – usually Bernard's – in *The Waves*, again opening up dualism and differences in the text. Finally, he likens *The Waves* to the work of the 'new French novelists': Nathalie Sarraute and Alain Robbe-Grillet. This is a pivotal essay, then, in Woolf studies for so many reasons, and it provides a fitting bridge to many of the debates which occupy the remaining chapters of this guide:

■ . . . The terrible ambiguity, Coleridgean in origin, implied by the autonomy of the creative mind, the fear that what seems an imaginative transfiguration of the world of matter may in the end be only the vaudeville trick Edward Bostetter calls it: ventriloquism.[94]

Virginia Woolf, writing about Shelley in 1927, at about the time she envisioned the novel that was to become *The Waves*, seems to have been aware of this distinctively romantic problem:

> He loved the clouds and the mountains and the rivers more passionately than any other man loved them; but at the foot of the mountain he always saw a ruined cottage; there were criminals in chains, hoeing up the weeds in the pavement of St. Peters Square; there was an old woman shaking with ague on the banks of the lovely Thames. . . . The most ethereal of poets was the most practical of men.[95]

It is an odd conflation of Shelley with Wordsworth and with Virginia Woolf herself; for certainly the 'ruined cottage' is an unconscious reminiscence of *The Excursion*, and the old woman on the banks of the Thames seems remarkably like the grimly prophetic figure, 'a tall quivering shape, like a funnel, like a rusty pump, like a wind-beaten tree for ever barren of leaves,' Peter Walsh encounters in *Mrs. Dalloway*.[96] But as an evaluation of Shelley it is enlightened, accurate, and, for the era of the 'New Criticism', courageously generous. And by one of those tricks which literary history seems delighted to play on authors, it ironically anticipates the critical fate of Virginia Woolf's own work, particularly her strangest and richest novel, *The Waves*. For while criticism, both enthusiastic and dyslogistic, of Virginia Woolf has taken it more or less for granted that she is 'the most ethereal of novelists,' indications have been rare – if indeed there have been any – that she is also 'the most practical of women': that the aestheticism of her 'stream of consciousness' includes the qualifying and fulfilling counter-movement toward things in their blind phenomenalism, a countermovement which is an essential energy of the profoundest romantic and modern literature.

The reasons for Virginia Woolf's reputation as ethereal are, of course, both apparent and inevitable, with a perverse kind of inevitability. The very violence with which she inveighed against a double critical standard for women writers, and her vast scorn for the characterisation of herself as 'lady novelist,' have insured for her an enduring attractiveness to people who hold precisely the values she contemned: a hypersensitive feminist apartheid, a concern for the obsessively 'mystical' element in literature, and a kind of narrative introspectionism which has less to do with the mainstream of twentieth-century fiction than with the neurasthenia of the suffragette who insists on the vote but swoons at the editorial page. The inaccuracy of such a view finally results in the domesticated 'Mrs. Woolf' of a book like Dorothy Brewster's *Virginia Woolf*,[97] a mixture of the tough-minded narrator with her own heroines, a book much like one that would result if one were to take as the final authoritative voice in *The Rape of the Lock* Belinda rather than Pope; or the Virginia Woolf-guru of N.C. Thakur's *The Symbolism of Virginia Woolf*, which in an access of mystagogy identifies as analogues for *The Waves* the Persian mystic Malauna Rumi, the Christian Trinity, the Hindu Trimurti, a misreading of Shelley's 'Hymn to Intellectual Beauty', and the sayings of Buddha – in a single page.[98]

It is finally 'mysticism', as a kind of exalted subjectivity, which is the *ignis fatuus* for Virginia Woolf's commentators, and particularly for commentators on *The Waves*. For *The Waves*, as both Miss Brewster and Mr. Thakur inform us, was the novel which the author called her 'abstract mystical eyeless book', her 'playpoem'. The reference is to a 1928 entry in Virginia Woolf's diary, one of the earliest pertaining to *The Waves*, at that time still to be called *The Moths*. But the passage, read more carefully, puts a significant bias on the aura of 'mysticism'. Virginia Woolf writes '. . . I must come to terms with these mystical feelings.'[99] It was, in fact, in one sense precisely the 'coming to terms' with the mystical feelings that accounted for the long and complex growth of the book and its transformation from *The Moths* to *The Waves*. An earlier entry, from 1927, in Virginia Woolf's diary explains the relevance of the first title as she again mentions 'the play-poem idea; the idea of some continuous stream, not solely of human thought, but of the ship, the night, etc., all flowing together: intersected by the arrival of the bright moths.'[100] She obviously thought of this book as the *chef d'oeuvre* of her distinctive fictional talents, and obviously identified the initial impulse of its writing as a quasi-mystical revelation of what the completed whole would be like – the prophetic 'fin in a waste of waters' which finds its way into Bernard's Roman vision. But in the very writing of the book, in the 'coming to terms' with its subjectivist origin, it seems to have grown into something which Virginia Woolf herself could not have recognised at the beginning, something both tougher and more profoundly relevant to her own best gifts than the triumph of affectiveness the book has often been thought to be – something whose insignia is in fact the difference between the bright and evanescent moths who were first to 'intersect' the book's plot and the inhuman, terrifying neutral waves which have the last inarticulate 'word' in the final novel and give their ambiguous benediction to the human sense of a personal immortality.

'Coming to terms' with mysticism – at least in the English imaginative mainstream – is precisely a matter of translation, which implies necessarily eradication of the full subjective flower of mysticism, of writing it down, turning contemplation into verbalisation, vision into version. From Walter Hilton's medieval *Scale of Perfection*, which in making the mystic's way a ladder refuses to leave out the lower rungs of unrefined experience, to Wesley's 'methodising' of the Evangelical Inner Light; and from the Red Cross knight's descent from the mount of vision to the self-conscious and quizzical apocalypse of *Prometheus Unbound*, the massive common-placing bias of the English mainstream is clear: a mainstream to which Virginia Woolf irrevocably belongs, as her earliest diary entries indicate, with their unflattering comparison of Christina Rossetti to the Byron of *Don Juan*.[101]

One of the most important 'translations' of the mystic into the fictive is the passage already referred to, describing Bernard's experience in Rome:

> These moments of escape are not to be despised. They come too seldom. Tahiti becomes possible. Leaning over this parapet I see far out a waste of water. A fin turns. This bare visual impression is unattached to any line of reason, it springs up as one might see the fin of a porpoise on the horizon. Visual impressions often communicate thus briefly statements that we shall in time to come uncover and coax into words. I note under F., therefore, 'Fin in a waste of waters.' I, who am perpetually making notes in the margin of my mind for some final statement, make this mark, waiting for some winter's evening.[102]

There is something remarkably Wordsworthian about this passage, not only in the gratuitousness with which the vision, the moment of escape, comes, but also in its spareness, the deliberate and nearly abstract simplicity of it. What gives it its peculiar force, however, is the determination of Bernard to 'coax into words' the phenomenon whose irrational, unawaited appearance defeats his present effort at description. The fin, he says, springs up sullenly, like a fin in a waste of waters.[103] And with the romantic phrasemaker's characteristic faith in his own failures, he duly notes the phenomenon in his mental chapbook for later working into the story he is trying to make of his life and the lives of his friends.

It is, in fact, precisely the befuddlement of the vision which makes it important to Bernard. For if the vision of the fin in a waste of waters is a 'moment of escape,' the escape is *from* words themselves, with their implicit 'plotting' of human life and with their pretensions to causality and coherence. Bernard simultaneously welcomes and forestalls the defeat of his language since this defeat, by revealing a tension between word and world, insures his liberation from the possible 'mysticism', or absolute subjectivity, of his perpetual story-telling. He is the most pretentious and self-conscious of catalogers, noting this purely phenomenological and non-human revelation under 'F' for 'fin'; but it is just this pretension, anxious to take risks with experience yet willing to be made absurd by the experience itself, which is his imaginative salvation.

Is there a story to tell at all? asks Bernard a moment before he has the vision of the fin. Confronted with the teeming and massively undifferentiated sight of a Roman street, he realises that he could isolate any figure or grouping within range and 'make it a story': '. . . But why impose my arbitrary design? Why stress this and shape that and twist up little figures like the toys men sell in trays in the street? Why select this, out of all that – one detail?' (p. 306) It is a question directly relevant, not only to the internal coherence of *The Waves* and, indeed, of all fiction, but to the specific situation in which Bernard finds himself. For his Roman monologue is, among other things, his first speech after the death of Percival, the strange, mute seventh figure about whom the other six characters of *The Waves* weave so much of their discourse. . . . If Percival's death is a rupture in the hopes and sensibilities of the other characters, it is equally a rupture in the serial organisation of their monologues: a delicate and highly subtle instance of imitative form. In the manner of serial music, each set of monologues by the six characters begins with a speech by Bernard and runs through the speeches of the other five before Bernard initiates a new 'movement'. But at the beginning of the fifth large section of the novel, the section introducing the news of Percival's death, Bernard for the first and only time does not begin the series. . . . Throughout the fifth and sixth sections, Bernard does not appear, and the order of speakers is Neville – Rhoda – Louis – Susan – Jinny – and again Neville. Six speakers, but no Bernard. With that kind of mathematical aesthetic puzzlement which is common to *The Waves* and serial music, we can ask whether Bernard when he begins section six with his Italian monologue is initiating a new series or ending the previous one; whether he is reacting to Percival's death or continuing (subsisting) in Percival's absence; whether, in fact, this most articulate of the six has overcome or been overcome by the sheer datum of the body's end. The narrative placement of his voyage to Rome imposes on the reader the same kind of casuistry he imposes upon himself in his crucial vision of the fin. And in forcing us to ask, with and about Bernard and his friends, Is there a story? or, Does the form hold? – the book also forces us to question, again with Bernard, the subjectivity which is its own inmost structure.

All this, of course, depends upon Percival, the silent, physically impressive character whose nearly Sartrean role in *The Waves* is to be present and to be seen by the others. 'But look,' says Neville, seeing

Percival in the school chapel, 'he flicks his hand to the back of his neck. For such gestures one falls hopelessly in love for a lifetime' (p. 199). And the lonely Louis, in his vision of fields and grass and sky, sees that 'Percival destroys it, as he blunders off, crushing the grasses, with the small fry trotting subservient after him. Yet it is Percival I need; for it is Percival who inspires poetry' (p. 202). As the figure who is, resplendently, *there*, both conscious and yet definitely the object of all the other consciousnesses in the book, Percival is necessarily the inspirer of poetry as transaction between the inner and outer worlds. He is also necessarily mute since the fullness of his presence in his own body is a plenum of self-consciousness which does not require the kind of speech the others constantly perform: their continual effort at pontification, or bridge-building between consciousness and experience.[104] Neville notes this essential 'in-himselfness' of Percival at the crucial dinner party in section four of *The Waves*. 'Without Percival,' he says, 'there is no solidity. We are silhouettes, hollow phantoms moving mistily without a background' (p. 259). And Bernard, least affected yet most perceptive about Percival, puts the matter in the precise terms, not only of the characters' experience but of the book's own highly self-conscious structure:

'Here is Percival,' said Bernard, 'smoothing his hair, not from vanity (he does not look in the glass), but to propitiate the god of decency. He is conventional; he is a hero. The little boys trooped after him across the playing-fields. They blew their noses as he blew his nose, but unsuccessfully, for he is Percival. Now, when he is about to leave us, to go to India, all these trifles come together. He is a hero.' (p. 260)

Much in the manner of the window-turned-mirror in the first chapter of *To the Lighthouse*, Percival by his presence organises the other six into a 'party' in the fourth section of *The Waves*, and again organises them – this time by his absence – in the final gathering in section eight. For the unity he represents, the impossible – for the six and for the book itself – full transaction between subject and object, is a unity no less primary in its negation than in its assertion. Susan realises this when she addresses the dead Percival:

'You have gone across the court, further and further, drawing finer and finer the thread between us. But you exist somewhere. Something of you remains. A judge. That is, if I discover a new vein in myself I shall submit it to you privately. I shall ask, "What is your verdict?" You shall remain the arbiter' (p. 283).

Percival is a 'hero' of acclimatization, of that at-homeness in both the world of things and the world of self-awareness whose loss is the creative trauma of the Romantic imagination. He represents in his self-containment, his absolute visibility, the sense which the other characters can never quite attain or resign themselves to, the sense that 'I am (rather than I have) this body' which implies that 'I am of (as well as in) this world.' Bernard's summing-up of the final gathering of the six at Hampton Court is, in this context, an immensely poignant coda to the book's career: 'We saw for a moment laid out among us the body of the complete human being whom we have failed to be, but at the same time, cannot forget' (p. 369). For the body is at once the body of the dead Percival, impossible of attainment for these modern children, the stunted corpses of each one's potential self, and of course the shattered and diminishing continuity of the six sensibilities taken as a single *gestalt*.

That the six speaking characters do form a kind of *gestalt*, not only in their common relationship to Percival, but in their sustained effort to see clearly the world around them and each other, has long been commonplace of commentary on *The Waves*. But we must not confuse the *gestalt*-narrative with either lyricism or allegory; we must not assume, with Jean Guiguet, that the monologues of *The Waves* are a sustained single voice only factitiously differentiated by character names,[105] or, with Dorothy Brewster, that the six characters are a code for different aspects of a single massive human personality. Both interpretations, which end by more or less totally 'subjectivizing' the book, fail to take account of the range of complexity and phenomenological subtlety of the grouping of the six.

Perhaps the most useful commentary on the organisation of *The Waves* is Virginia Woolf's brief sketch, 'Evening Over Sussex: Reflections in a Motor Car', published posthumously in *The Death of the Moth*. In this remarkable performance, Virginia Woolf not only projects a set of six 'personalities' – six separate yet complementary reactions to the world of things – but explicitly links them to the central Romantic and modern problem of breaking out of the subjective into a real resonance with the phenomenal: the selves are 'six little pocket knives with which to cut up the body of a whale' (p. 8); and although she may not have had Melville in mind at the time, the 'whale' involved is obviously of the same mysterious objectivity, terrible in its purity, as Moby Dick. . . . But more important than these striking parallels of mood is the light thrown by 'Evening Over Sussex' on the basic phenomenological impulse of *The Waves*, which, as I have tried to indicate, is a compelling effort to subvert the subjective or the comfortably 'mystical.' For as it is the discomfort – highly Wordsworthian or Shelleyan – of the first self at the intransigence of the non-human world which necessitates the procession of 'selves', so Neville's crucial version in the first chapter of the man with his throat cut seems to 'begin' the movement of the novel. The version must be quoted at length:

> His blood gurgled down the gutter. His jowl was white as a dead codfish. I shall call this structure, this rigidity, 'death among the apple trees' for ever. There were the floating, pale-grey clouds; and the immitigable tree; the implacable tree with its greaved silver bark. The ripple of my life was unavailing. I was unable to pass by. There was an obstacle. 'I cannot surmount this unintelligible obstacle,' I said. And the others passed on. But we are doomed, all of us by the apple trees, by the immitigable tree which we cannot pass. (p. 191)

The tone of this passage is inescapably related to one of the most important apprehensions of things in the English language, Wordsworth's despairing sight of the *Intimations Ode*:

> – But there's a Tree, of many one,
> A single Field which I have looked upon,
> Both of them speak of something that is gone:
> The Pansy at my feet
> Doth the same tale repeat:
> Whither is fled the visionary gleam?
> Where is it now, the glory and the dream?
> (II. 51–7)

The doom is, of course, the doom of consciousness-in-the-body, the 'dying animal' of Yeats or the 'ghost in the machine' of Gilbert Ryle. And this is the essential context for the italicised passages describing the waves, the house, and the birds at the beginning of each chapter. For these passages are not simply, as Joan Bennett and others have described them, compelling prose-poems paralleling human life with the cycle of the day and of nature. They are, on the other hand, deliberate and highly effective attempts to present a phenomenal world without the intervention of human consciousness, a world of blind things which stands as a perpetual challenge to the attempts of the six monologists to seize, translate, and 'realize' their world. And although full of lyrical and 'anthropomorphic' metaphors, it is difficult not to see in these passages an anticipation of the concerns and predispositions of contemporary novelists like Alain Robbe-Grillet and Nathalie Sarraute:

The sun fell in sharp wedges inside the room. Whatever the light touched became dowered with a fanatical existence. A plate was like a white lake. A knife looked like a dagger of ice. Suddenly tumblers revealed themselves upheld by streaks of light. . . . The veins on the glaze of the china, the grain of the wood, the fibres of the matting became more and more finely engraved. Everything was without shadow. (p. 251)

The sense of preternatural (or preconscious) clarity, the way in which the precision with which things appear actually jeopardises their stability as 'this' thing – everything Robbe-Grillet most desires for the so-called 'new novel' is there, and profoundly assimilated to the central theme of *The Waves*. In fact, the obvious parallel between the 'day' of these descriptions and the lives of the characters may well be quite too obvious. The connection is such a ready commonplace that the ease with which we adopt it may be a deliberately planted instance of our own willingness to assume an overeasy mastery of the universe of things. Certainly the very end of the book is disturbingly ambiguous: Bernard's final ecstatic resolve to assert the human, to fling himself, 'unvanquished and unyielding' against death itself is followed by the chilling line: 'The waves broke on the shore' (p. 383). To ask whether this is an affirmation or a denial of Bernard's resolve is nugatory: it is simply and sublimely irrelevant to Bernard, as Bernard to it, and therein lies its enormous power. For the 'nature' of the italicised passages is neither the anthropomorphic and sympathetic nature of the pastoral nor its malevolent but equally anthropomorphic contrary in a view like Gloucester's: 'As flies to wanton boys, are we to th' Gods;/ They kill us for their sport.' It is rather the nature of sublime and self-sufficient *un*humanity which finds articulation in the dirge from *Cymbeline* (an important 'hidden theme' for both *Mrs. Dalloway* and *The Waves*), in Shelley's confrontation with Mont Blanc, or in Sartre's conception of the forbidding and impenetrable *être-en-soi*.

Each of the characters, in lifelong quest of a fully articulate existence, reflects in one way or another the inherent tension between the words of subjective consciousness and the irrecoverable otherness of both things and other people. Only Bernard, in a moment of vision near the end of his final summing-up, achieves a perception which 'redeems' him and his five friends precisely by bringing the terms of their failure to full consciousness: 'For one day as I leant over a gate that led into a field, the rhythm stopped: the rhymes and the hummings, the nonsense and the poetry. A space was cleared in my mind. I saw through the thick leaves of habit. Leaning over the gate I regretted so much litter, so much accomplishment and separation, for one cannot cross London to see a friend, life being so full of engagements' (p. 373). As the life of intrasubjectivity, 'so full of engagements,' grows finally to the proportions where it chokes off the possibility of even the most minimal actions, Bernard momentarily shunts off personality and sees 'the world without a self':

> But how describe the world seen without a self? There are no words. Blue, red even they distract, even they hide with thickness instead of letting the light through. How describe or say anything in articulate words again? . . . (p. 376)[106]

It is a vision of absolute phenomenality, where 'there are no words' or, in Bernard's earlier terms, 'there is no story.'[107] And as such it is not an absolutely beautiful vision, since 'beauty' is a product of the affective consciousness.[108] 'Loveliness' and 'blindness' return together as the vision fades and becomes habitual – literally as it again becomes a vision subject to the use of language. But what is most startling about this passage is what Bernard does see in his moment of enlightenment. What 'the old nurse' (who may very well be a reminiscence of the foster-mother Nature of the *Intimations Ode*) *shows* Bernard is precisely the world of the italicised chapter-heads, 'the house, the garden, and the waves breaking' – precisely, that is, the world of unobserved, nonconscious things in the full ambivalence of its relationship to the characters of *The Waves* so that in a moment of almost perfect representative form, Bernard simultaneously breaks out of subjectivity into a phenomenological perception, and breaks into *The Waves* in its inmost narrative structure. Her lyrical tough-mindedness will not allow Virginia Woolf to take the way either of aestheticism or of 'objectivism,' but insists even here that narrative form and formless world mutually condition each other. The way out and the way in, like the way up and the way down, are one and the same.

Finally, what *The Waves* gives us is something very like the world of Jorge Luis Borges' fable, 'Tlön, Uqbar, Orbis Tertius', where an attempt to project a fictive, totally Berkeleyan and subjective world ends by taking over and transforming the 'real' world. Virginia Woolf's mystical and eyeless book achieves a subjectivity so total and so self-conscious that it finally becomes a radical criticism of 'mysticism' and of the subjective eye itself in the face of sheer phenomenalism. It is a kind of Hegelian paradox of 'purity' whereby the subjective carries itself through a mirror reversal, entering a new and strange style of the insuperably nonhuman and 'other':

> People go on passing they go on passing against the spires of the church and the plates of ham sandwiches. The streamers of my consciousness waver out and are perpetually torn and distressed by their disorder. I cannot therefore concentrate on my dinner.

'I would take a tenner. The case is handsome; but it blocks up the hall.' They dive and plunge like guillemots whose feathers are slippery with oil. (*The Waves*, p. 240)

Soon unfortunately time will no longer be master. Wrapped in their aura of doubt and error, this day's events, however insignificant they may be, will in a few seconds begin their task, gradually encroaching upon the ideal order, cunningly introducing an occasional inversion, a discrepancy, a confusion, a warp, in order to accomplish their work: a day in early winter without plan, without direction, incomprehensible and monstrous.[109]

The first passage is Louis's monologue in a London restaurant; the second is Robbe-Grillet's description of a day in a French café. The remarkable resemblance between these passages, from novels normally assumed to represent polar schools of contemporary literature,[110] is an index not only of the substantiality of a 'modern tradition' of narrative but also of the profound contemporaneity of Virginia Woolf's greatest novel. Far from being the *sui generis* masterpiece of a hyper-aesthetic 'lady novelist', *The Waves* is a tough-minded and sobering examination of the chances for the shaping intellect to shape meaningfully at all. And far from being a 'dead end' for fiction,[111] it is a novel whose penetration to the roots of a distinctly modern and crucially humanistic problem is human and humanising as few other books can claim to be.[112] □

CHAPTER FOUR

The 1970s and 80s: Diverging Approaches – Androgyny, Art, Feminism

THIS PERIOD marks an escalation in Woolf studies, and a move away from the critical emphasis on symbolic and philosophic unity or synthesis. In the first part of the period (the 1970s) much of the groundwork was done for the major developments in feminist criticism that followed in the 1980s and 90s. If previously Woolf's writing was thought to lack conflict, this term now becomes prominent in critics' vocabulary, along with dynamism, opposition and difference. James's discovery, in *To the Lighthouse*, that 'nothing was simply one thing',[1] is taken to heart; so too Woolf's dualistic model of good writing as 'granite and rainbow',[2] combining fact and fiction, the prosaic and the poetic,[3] and of the best writers as 'androgynous': 'Perhaps a mind that is purely masculine cannot create, any more than a mind that is purely feminine. . . . Coleridge . . . meant, perhaps, that the androgynous mind is resonant and porous; that it transmits emotion without impediment; that it is naturally creative, incandescent and undivided.'[4] This is not to say that criticism of *To the Lighthouse* and *The Waves* adopts a new consensus, finding ambivalence, where once harmony was the goal, for this is also a period of increasing conflicts and differences of opinion and approach in the criticism itself. An important question in the androgyny debate, for example, might be whether Woolf's vision of androgyny means gender synthesis or the perpetuation of difference – or the creation of a third position beyond the binary: it has not been settled. Increasing critical interest in this debate, and in more analytical approaches to form and aesthetics, made *To the Lighthouse* the most important, most discussed and analysed, of Woolf's texts. The focus here seems to shift and sharpen from vague, mystical, reveries on the mother/wife, Mrs Ramsay and her symbolic relationship to the lighthouse, to close critical, and sometimes feminist, assessments of the painter, Lily Briscoe and her closing vision.[5] *The Waves*, while still the focus of much critical attention, particularly formal and aesthetic, becomes problematic for some feminist readings, although Bernard, like Lily, is posited as an exemplary figure of androgyny.

The diversity and range of criticism is by now becoming so great that it is difficult to do justice even to the most significant contributions of this time. The three main extracts I have chosen for this chapter are from impressive and influential readings of the two novels which make use of certain important spheres of influence on Woolf's work: Allen McLaurin, in *Virginia Woolf: The Echoes Enslaved* (1973), draws on the visual arts and the aesthetic theories of Roger Fry for a sophisticated analysis of Woolf's literary technique, with special focus on *To the Lighthouse*; Perry Meisel's book, *The Absent Father: Virginia Woolf and Walter Pater* (1980), is a fascinating meditation on literary influence; and Gillian Beer's essay, 'Hume, Stephen, and Elegy in *To the Lighthouse*', looks at the combining influences of the philosophical, biographical and elegiac. All three are considered turning points in criticism of Woolf, and I will indicate the important developments each has engendered in their field. While none seem, from their titles, overtly feminist in approach, the latter two, as we shall see, are significant in feminist criticism.

Before turning to the extracts, I want briefly to touch on some of the developments in formalist, androgyny-based, and feminist criticism, areas which interlock and overlap, as we shall see. Formal analysis of Woolf's fiction, building on and departing from the achievement of Auerbach, became much more sophisticated in the 1970s. Particularly recommended are two influential essays: Geoffrey H. Hartman's 'Virginia's Web',[6] which goes in fact 'beyond formalism' in its early deconstructionist approach (taken up by later critics extracted below), examining aesthetic order and disorder in *To the Lighthouse* and *Mrs Dalloway*; and J.W. Graham's, 'Point of View in *The Waves*: Some Services of the Style',[7] which puts forward an illuminating analysis of the 'gradual development' of point of view in the two holograph drafts and final version of the novel. Graham also makes use of Woolf's diary entries on her 'seminal vision'[8] of 'that fin in the waste of water' which finds its way into Bernard's 'Roman' monologue. His analysis of 'certain stylistic features' marks a convincing departure from the earlier orthodoxies of Bergsonian and stream-of-consciousness approaches: 'the rigid uniformity of the language throughout and its verbal sophistication, both . . . make [*The Waves*] unsuitable as vehicle for even one stream of consciousness, much less those of six characters.' Graham's emphasis remains on the abstract qualities of Woolf's visionary prose – 'its strange blend of fear and excitement, detachment and involvement, remoteness and intensity, impersonality and rapt absorption.'[9] Less lucid, and verging on the 'algebraic',[10] is Mitchell A. Leaska's detailed book-length formalist analysis, *Virginia Woolf's Lighthouse: A Study in Critical Method*, to catch the scientific flavour of which requires only a brief quote:

■ In so far as Lily Briscoe's use of abstract nouns is concerned, it would be tempting to say that, because the quantity is slightly above the mean value (40.7), she represents that duality of personality in which the intellectual, sensitive part abstracts experience, while the artistic, intuitive moiety senses life as concrete, specific, on the 'level of ordinary experience'.[11] □

More digestible close readings of *To the Lighthouse* and *The Waves* can be found in Hermione Lee's (1977) study of Woolf's novels.[12] Leaska's emphasis on 'duality', however, is in keeping with the new critical interest in androgyny centring on Woolf's work in the early 1970s. Inspired by the work of Carolyn Heilbrun,[13] two books on Woolf and androgyny appeared in 1973 by Alice Van Buren Kelley[14] and Nancy Topping Bazin. The feminist efficacy of Woolf's androgynous vision is heavily criticised by Elaine Showalter, in her controversial chapter, 'Virginia Woolf and the Flight into Androgyny' (of which more later), where Woolf is understood to abandon feminism in favour of mysticism,[15] a criticism which might also be levelled at Kelley and Bazin. This is how Bazin, for example, understands the closing vision of *To the Lighthouse*: 'Lily's painting symbolizes the androgynous work of art: in it an equilibrium is established between Mr and Mrs Ramsay, symbols of the evanescent and eternal aspects of reality.'[16] Madeline Moore, on the other hand, exploring a decade later, the dualism of 'the mystical and the political' in Woolf's writing, understands this vision as follows:

■ Lily joins her past yearning for a mythical mother to the ongoing process of her dedication to life as it is. . . . Woolf herself left many questions unanswered in *To the Lighthouse*. The formal poetic desire and indeed the psychological plateau which Lily reaches may indeed be something of an anticlimax because the scope of her art is still tethered to the ledges of class division.[17] □

Her attention to the materialist concerns of class politics reflects feminist criticism's encounters with Marxist theories of the late 1970s and early 1980s. An important contribution to this wider debate was the publication of Michèle Barrett's collection of Woolf's feminist essays in 1979.[18] In her 'Introduction' Barrett argues that Woolf should be understood as a materialist feminist, a view supported by a famous passage from *A Room of One's Own*:

■ Fiction, imaginative work that is, is not dropped like a pebble upon the ground, as science may be; fiction is like a spider's web, attached ever so lightly perhaps, but still attached to life at all four corners. Often the attachment is scarcely perceptible. . . . But when the web is pulled askew, hooked up at the edge, torn in the middle, one remembers that these webs are not spun in mid-air by incorporeal creatures, but are the work of suffering human beings, and are attached to grossly material things, like health and money and the houses we live in.[19] □

Woolf criticism in the 1980s was to some extent dominated by the work of one critic in particular – Jane Marcus[20] – in some sympathy with this view. But her Marxism is idiosyncratic enough to embrace even Woolf's apparent mysticism as radical:

■ As a feminist critic I had avoided the subject of Woolf's mysticism, and of *The Waves*, feeling that acknowledging her as a visionary was a trap that would allow her to be dismissed as another female crank, irrational and eccentric. I was drawn to her most anticapitalist, anti-imperialist novels, to Woolf the socialist and feminist, logical, witty, and devastating in argument.[21] □

Marcus is shown the light by Catherine Smith who 'asks us to study mysticism and feminism together.'[22] Marcus' recent, ground-breaking (and certainly less mystical) essay on *The Waves* forms the centre-piece to the final chapter of this guide.

I want now to return to an important critical work on Woolf not informed by androgyny or feminism, but still concerned with her dualism. Contradictions, the 'antitheses' of Samuel Butler in fact, are the opening inspiration to Allen McLaurin's enormously influential study of Woolf's debt to visual aesthetics: 'Butler argues that life itself is irrational, and, indeed, based on contradictions. These antitheses, especially the interpenetration of life and death, are the "granite and rainbow" of Virginia Woolf's work.' McLaurin's is a sustained analysis of repetition and rhythm in Woolf's writing, informed by the theories of Roger Fry: 'Like Roger Fry', he claims, 'Lily sees things in terms of "form" and "geometry".'[23] The most significant work on this topic before McLaurin's is probably John Hawley Roberts' perceptive 1946 article, '"Vision and Design" in Virginia Woolf'.[24] But there has been enormous critical interest in it ever since.[25] Particularly distinguished are a number of articles by Jack F. Stewart offering neoplatonic readings of light and colour in *To the Lighthouse* and *The Waves*.[26] McLaurin's study, however, sets the standard for sophisticated analyses of the painterly aspects of these novels. Feminism has made an impact in this area of criticism too.

Diane Filby Gillespie, for example, emphasises Woolf's creative and professional relationship with her sister, the artist, Vanessa Bell. 'Lily Briscoe', she suggests, 'combines the verbal and visual. Woolf often makes little distinction between art media because, like her sister, she is most interested in the creative activity itself.'[27]

In the following extract McLaurin begins by examining Lily Briscoe's painting technique with close reference to theories of Roger Fry and G.E. Moore. Clive Bell's theories, evident in such phrases below as 'formal significance', and 'emotional significance', also influence his discussion. As well as Woolf's colour references, also examines her infamous use of framing brackets.

■ Language and art gain their value by their difference from sensation, by their escape from the tyranny of immediacy. Lily Briscoe's great desire, to convey the 'jar on the nerves', is one felt by many artists:

> She must try to get hold of something that evaded her. It evaded her when she thought of Mrs Ramsay; it evaded her now when she thought of her picture. Phrases came. Visions came. Beautiful pictures. Beautiful phrases. But what she wished to get hold of was that very jar on the nerves, the thing itself before it has been made anything.[28]

Painting, we often feel, is nearer to 'sensation' than literature; it has an immediate, almost physiological impact. Literary interpretations of visual art often obstruct this non-verbal appreciation of form or colour. This accounts partly for Fry's wish to free painting from anecdotal criticism and his disparagement of such painting as was amenable to that approach. He felt that in the past, literature in England had been so dominant that it had pushed painting in a literary direction. The co-operation between himself and Virginia Woolf turns out to be, in a sense, an attempt to reverse the process, and this is particularly evident in *To the Lighthouse*. That 'jar on the nerves' which a painter can more adequately convey than an artist in words is what Virginia Woolf wishes to achieve, and the anecdotal aspect of the novel, as in most of her work, is neglected. The visual shock which Lily tries to put on to her canvas has its origin in the more general sensations of everyday life. Just as the Impressionist blur becomes Mrs Ramsay's short-sightedness, so the visual shock of a painting is related to all the other shocks which we suffer, not only visual, but to the other senses, and emotional shocks as well. The sound of a gun wakes Lily from her reverie, and echoes the 'explosion' of her thoughts. We are then given a picture of the scene as she comes round from her daydream:

> . . . until her thought which had spun quicker and quicker
> exploded of its own intensity; she felt released; a shot went off
> close at hand, and there came, flying from its fragments, fright-
> ened, effusive, tumultuous, a flock of starlings.[29]

There follows immediately afterwards another shock, and then the
calming down is expressed in visual terms again, with the settling of
the starlings on the trees. . . .[30] Later in the novel Lily is awakened
from her private thoughts by the banging of a gate, and this is related
to a blow in the face from a sprung bramble branch. The long sentence
of reverie is brought to a sudden end by the two abrupt sentences at
the end of the section. A new movement begins in the next section as
Lily gets down to the problem of her painting, but the preceding
shock is carried over in the image of a blow in the face. . . .[31] There are
similar little shocks throughout the novel, which are an attempt to
give that 'jar on the nerves' which Lily speaks of.

In view of the agreement between Roger Fry and Virginia Woolf in
their attack on photographic representation in painting and literature,
it follows that a thoughtful artist like Lily Briscoe would not be portrayed as a representational painter. Indeed in the novel she is
contrasted with Mr Paunceforte and his disciples. Mrs Ramsay notices
that 'Since Mr Paunceforte had been there, three years before, all the
pictures were like that she said, green and grey, with lemon-coloured
sailing-boats, and pink women on the beach.'[32] Like Roger Fry, Lily
sees things in terms of 'form' and 'geometry'. Mrs Ramsay is seen as
'dome shaped'[33] and in the final painting she appears as a purple
triangle. To some extent, then, Lily is an abstract artist. The act of
selection inevitably involves some degree of abstraction, but there
remains the moral problem of whether it is right to reduce a person to
a triangle. The emotional importance of form as opposed to the obvious
appeal of recognisable subject-matter, is seen in the following passage, in which Lily and William Bankes discuss the dehumanisation
of art. It might be useful here to remember Roger Fry's discussion of
this problem in *Vision and Design*:

> In such circumstances the greatest object of art becomes of no more
> significance than any casual piece of matter; a man's head is no
> more and no less important than a pumpkin, or, rather, these
> things may be so or not according to the rhythm that obsesses the
> artist and crystallises his vision. Since it is the habitual practice of
> the artist to be on the lookout for these peculiar arrangements of
> objects that arouse the creative vision, and become material for cre-
> ative contemplation, he is liable to look at all objects from this
> point of view. . . . It is irrelevant to ask him, while he is looking

with this generalised and all-embracing vision, about the nature of the objects which compose it.[34]

In the following discussion Lily speaks for precisely this habitual vision of the artist:

Nothing could be cooler and quieter. Taking out a penknife, Mr Bankes tapped the canvas with the bone handle. What did she wish to indicate by the triangular purple shape, 'just there?' he asked.

It was Mrs Ramsay reading to James, she said, She knew his objection – that no one could tell it for a human shape. But she had made no attempt at likeness, she said. For what reason had she introduced them then? he asked. Why indeed? – except that if there, in that corner, it was bright, here, in this, she felt the need of darkness. Simple, obvious, commonplace, as it was, Mr Bankes was interested. Mother and child then – objects of universal veneration, and in this case the mother was famous for her beauty – might be reduced, he pondered, to a purple shadow without irreverence.[35]

William Bankes is one of those people who, in Fry's terms, would say of a landscape 'What a nice place' instead of 'What a good picture'. William's other criteria, the unaesthetic ones of size and monetary value, are also very much those which Roger Fry constantly rejected:

The truth was that all his prejudices were on the other side, he explained. The largest picture in his drawing-room, which painters had praised, and valued at a higher price than he had given for it, was of the cherry trees in blossom on the banks of the Kennet.[36]

William also brings into the discussion irrelevant private emotional associations: 'He had spent his honeymoon on the banks of the Kennet, he said. Lily must come and see that picture, he said.'[37] The kind of abstraction that Lily is concerned with is very different from the scientific examination which he is used to. Her abstraction can only be conveyed in paint, it can only be expressed with her paint-brush:

But now – he turned, with his glasses raised to the scientific exam-ination of her canvas. The question being one of the relations of masses, of lights and shadows, which, to be honest, he had never considered before, he would like to have it explained – what then did she wish to make of it? And he indicated the scene before them. She looked. She could not show him what she wished to make of it, could not see it even herself, without a brush in her hand.[38]

It is only in the actual making of the work of art that she realises what she wants to 'say'. Mrs Ramsay's distinguished presence and Lily's affection for her are very important in the novel, but Lily as painter must select only the formal visual aspects of her experience, and so Mrs Ramsay becomes a purple triangle. The equivalent problem for Virginia Woolf herself was the transmutation of her knowledge of her mother and father into the characters of Mr and Mrs Ramsay. The careful balancing which we can see in their portrayal gives them a formal significance which is more generally valid than a straight auto-biography or biography would be. There is a careful selection and abstraction here which is emotionally significant.

. . . Colour as a physiological effect cannot be captured in litera-ture; but . . . this aspect of colour is only a small part of its significance even in visual art. Only by moving away from sensation, only by the establishment of a relation or by the use of a colour word can there be any meaning. . . . In *To the Lighthouse*, as we might expect in a novel concerned with painting, the use of colour is quite distinctive. I think it can be shown that there is a range of colour in a kind of scale here, similar to the 'keyboard' of metaphor in *Mrs Dalloway*.

In *To the Lighthouse*, 'white', the absence of colour, symbolises just that – the uncolourful, definite meaning of science and abstract thought. William Bankes seems to be clothed in a white scientific coat [39] and Lily Briscoe thinks of his work in terms of sections of potatoes.[40] Mr Ramsay's work on 'subject and object' she sees as a 'white scrubbed table'.[41]

The next colour group as we move along the scale is that of red and brown. David Daiches rightly points out that there is 'colour symbol-ism running right through the book'. He goes on to say that:

Red and brown appear to be the colours of individuality and ego-tism, while blue and green are the colours of impersonality. Mr Ramsay, until the very end of the book, is represented as an ego-tist, and his colour is red or brown; Lily is the impersonal artist, and her colour is blue; Mrs Ramsay stands somewhere between, and her colour is purple.[42]

This is to some extent valid, and might be supported by the passage in which Mrs Ramsay imagines James dressed in a judge's red gown.[43] Here, red is connected with the public world of men and the profes-sions. The red-brown stocking which Mrs Ramsay is knitting for the lighthouse-keeper's son puts her philanthropic gesture into the same general area of meaning. But this is already something much vaguer than Daiches suggests – we are drifting away from his 'individuality and egotism'. The use of red-brown, in contrast to the use of white, is deliberately blurred, it covers a wider area of half-meaning.

As we move along the scale, the use of colour becomes less 'literary' in the traditional way. Colour is used to convey something which can be described vaguely as an emotional equivalence, a subtle relation which is not logical. As we pointed out earlier, Roger Fry describes the physiological effect of colour as being less important in painting than the establishment of a relation. We can see this sort of emotional relation established in the equivalence which is made between the ashen ship which leaves behind a purple patch of oil[44] and Mrs Ramsay, whose grey clothes are mentioned[45] and who becomes a purple triangle in Lily's painting.

In her use of yellow in the novel, Virginia Woolf is trying to come close to the 'pure' colour of a painting – colour without any literary meaning. This is very much Carmichael's colour. His beard is white with a streak of yellow. There is again a relation established, like that between Mrs Ramsay and the ship, for earlier in the novel James colours a white shirt yellow.[46] Yellow is a positive avoidance of logical meaning, in contrast with white, which is a negative lack of colour. In the scale we have been constructing then, yellow and white are the extreme terms. Carmichael is a poet and an opium addict, the embodiment of 'things in themselves', of autonomy, and this rubs off on to the colour with which he is associated. Yellow means simply yellow, it represents the quality of colour which cannot be translated into other terms. G.E. Moore makes this point in *Principia Ethica*, and by coincidence his example is the same:

> Consider yellow, for example. We may try to define it, by describing its physical equivalent; we may state what kind of light-vibrations must stimulate the normal eye, in order that we may perceive it. But a moment's reflection is sufficient to show that those light-vibrations are not themselves what we mean by yellow. *They* are not what we perceive. Indeed we should never have been able to discover their existence, unless we had first been struck by the patent difference of quality between the different colours. The most we can be entitled to say of those vibrations is that they are what corresponds in space to the yellow which we actually perceive.[47]

Blue, Daiches sees as 'impersonality'. Once again, as with his discussion of 'red', his definition is too limiting. Certainly, impersonality might be included in the meaning, but blue also indicates 'distance' and 'space', which are more general than the purely literary idea of impersonality. As we shall see in the subsequent discussion, Virginia Woolf is trying to create spatial effects in the novel. In its formal sense, the blue is that which we see on the distant horizon. This is impersonal, but it does not *mean* impersonal. Blue is used in the novel to give the spatial, pictorial effect, in conjunction with the literary spaces of the sea, history, the eyes of another person, and so on. The people in the novel have blue eyes, except Carmichael, whose are green, that is, a mixture of autonomous yellow and 'distant' blue.

As we saw earlier, the idea of the frame is of some importance in the aesthetics of Roger Fry and Virginia Woolf. It can convert the every-day scene into a rudimentary work of art. Mrs Ramsay's head is framed in this way by a picture frame hanging behind her and so becomes something to contemplate, like a picture:

> Knitting her reddish-brown hairy stocking, with her head out-lined absurdly by the gilt frame, the green shawl which she had tossed over the edge of the frame, and the authenticated master-piece by Michael Angelo, Mrs Ramsay smoothed out what had been harsh in her manner a moment before, raised his head, and kissed her little boy on the forehead. 'Let's find another picture to cut out,' she said.[48]

This frame, or any work of art, no matter how exalted, helps us to recapture the imaginative power which many children possess. Mrs Ramsay, who is outlined here by the picture frame, is also, for Lily painting her garden, framed by the window. She is no longer simply Mrs Ramsay, she is cut off from the practical world and transfigured into something like a painting of the Mother and Child. This process of framing, of taking objects out of the stream of everyday 'practical' life, is described earlier in the novel from a child's point of view. As with the 'impressionism' in the novel, the artistic imagination is seen in its 'everyday' round. James cuts out pictures of commonplace objects and invests them with an emotional significance. . . . Virginia Woolf attempts more specifically in the novel to simulate certain spatial aspects of visual art. This has sometimes been attempted in the past by the use of typographical devices, but it is difficult to fuse the two arts in this way. In *To the Lighthouse* the use of square and round brackets cannot be described simply as a typographical device, although this is certainly part of it. Virginia Woolf uses parentheses as something more than a mere device in the novel, for the whole form can be seen as a parenthesis. The first and last sections, being parallel, form brackets around the central section, 'Time Passes'. Throughout the novel smaller parentheses mirror this overall pattern; the book is made up of 'curves and arabesques flourishing round a centre of complete emptiness'.[49] Within the 'emptiness' of the central section, there are various parentheses which give a sense of the mere contingency of human life. The death of Andrew Ramsay is given in this way: '[A shell exploded. Twenty or thirty young men were blown up in France, among them Andrew Ramsay, whose death, mercifully, was instantaneous.]'[50] Even the fact of Mrs Ramsay's death is conveyed in a parenthesis, quite casually, as if she were only a very minor character in whom we had little interest: '[Mr Ramsay stumbling along a passage stretched his arms out one dark morning, but, Mrs Ramsay having died rather suddenly the night before, he stretched his arms out. They remained empty.]'[51] The effect is partly one of irony, which is intensified by the fact that the parenthesis equates these deaths with a candle blown out: '[Here Mr Carmichael, who was reading Virgil, blew out his candle. It was past midnight.]'[52] The square brackets are essentially vertical, like the lighthouse itself, or the tree which Lily would move to the middle of the painting. Seeing the novel as a whole shape, the thin central section is like a vertical line, as well as being an empty space bracketed by the first and last sections.

The other dominant shape in *To the Lighthouse* is the arabesque, which is described by the rounded brackets. The word 'arabesque' appears frequently throughout the novel, as it does in Roger Fry's criticism. Much of the movement of the novel is curved. The boat slices a curve in the bay, and the ball describes an arc when the children are playing catches. There is recurrent mention of beak and scimitar shapes.[53] The curve is linked with the scythe of Father Time and also with the indirect method of achieving the truth, but a further intention is to make the novel approximate as nearly as possible to the visual effect of a painting.

We have suggested that space is indicated by the use of blue, and that parenthesis, the picture frame, and the looking-glass hold a 'world hollowed out'. Lily's method of working is described as 'tunnelling her way into her picture, into the past'.[54] This is close to the 'tunnelling' which Virginia Woolf describes in her own diary, and is strikingly similar to that phrase of Seurat's which Fry was fond of quoting: 'hollowing out a canvas'. This creation of space, this 'framing' in order to cut off the picture space from ordinary space, is the basis of all painting.[55] □

Rather than the extremely well-documented influences of Woolf's contemporaries, Perry Meisel's study, in the spirit of Harold Bloom's notion of the 'anxiety of influence', speculates on the unacknowledged influence of her predecessor in literary aesthetics, Walter Pater. This is a splendid book, not only for its thesis on Woolf, but for its excellent discussion of nineteenth-century aesthetics. Meisel develops ideas similar to those of Hartman's, in 'Virginia's Web', in his analysis of subjectivity and the webs and systems of language. He is particularly illuminating on constructions of the self – individual and collective – in *The Waves*. Repetition, as for McLaurin, is important here. In the following extract, Meisel's argument is informed by Pater's ideas in the 'Conclusion' to *The Renaissance* (1873). Meisel is unusual in considering *To the Lighthouse* a more abstract work than *The Waves*, and it is his discussion of the latter that I have reproduced more fully. The extract opens, however, with a stimulating analysis of repetition in *To the Lighthouse*.

■ Lily is burdened with that view of experience she wishes to be free of: 'as if she were caught up in one of those habitual currents which after a certain time forms experience in the mind, so that one repeats words without being aware any longer who originally spoke them' (*TL*, 246). Indeed, Mrs. Ramsay is herself a victim of this same uneasy experience in which 'one repeats words' that are neither one's own nor anyone else's one can specify:

> It will end. It will end, she said. It will come, it will come, when suddenly she added, We are in the hands of the Lord.
>
> But instantly she was annoyed with herself for saying that. Who had said it? not she; she had been trapped into saying something she did not mean. She looked up over her knitting . . . searching as she alone could search into her mind and heart, purifying out of existence that lie, any lie. (*TL*, 101)

Mrs. Ramsay's desire to 'purify . . . out of existence that lie, any lie' is, of course, as impossible an ideal as Pater's – and Woolf's – to purge away all that is not properly the individual's, since all three are wishes to purify an existence whose very intelligibility is founded upon the residue or impurity of the trace. Hence Mrs. Ramsay is denied the priority and immediate relation to life that everyone in the novel wishes to assign to her as a means of accounting for her power to organise and compose. Like the rest or us, she, too, must be situated within a 'cobweb of allusions'.

What is gained in this loss, however, is a kind of supra-Paterian art in which systematicity itself is musically and semantically exploited thanks to the very thing that dooms original perception – repetition:

> She was not inventing; she was only trying to smooth out something she had been given years ago folded up; something she had seen. For in the rough and tumble of daily life, with all those

> children about, all those visitors, one had constantly a sense of
> repetition – of one thing falling where another had fallen, and so
> setting up an echo which chimed in the air and made it full of
> vibrations. (*TL*, 305)

From one point of view the sign of our belatedness as creatures who
come to exist within systems erected before our individual births,
repetition now becomes the compensatory principle of Woolf's art – 'of
one thing falling where another had fallen, and so setting up an echo
which chimed in the air and made it full of vibrations'.

Ironically, *To the Lighthouse* is a far more abstract account of the way
the self is situated in the common life than *The Waves* (1931), Woolf's
apparently most oblique achievement. Here she is exceedingly concrete: 'the streets are laced together with telegraph wires. . . . London
is now veiled' (*W*, 66). 'My mind hums,' says Bernard of the subliminal
and structuring murmur of language itself, 'with its veil of words for
everything' (*W*, 127). Sensation, too, is a network of 'membranes,
webs of nerve' (*W*, 146). And in school, remembers Rhoda, 'we sit
herded together under maps of the entire world' (*W*, 35). Indeed, at
the reunion late in the novel, Jinny, too, remembers school in terms of
'maps' and 'geography' (*W*, 135), in terms of the territorial classifica-
tions one must learn as a child. And, again as in *Mrs. Dalloway*, these
global co-ordinates also function graphically as the 'line' of connection
between people: 'How strange,' says Bernard, 'to feel the line that is
spun from us lengthening its fine filament across the misty spaces of
the intervening world. . . . Between us is this line' (*W*, 95).

Along with maps comes the figure of the text, too: 'we decipher the
hieroglyphs written on other people's faces,' says Jinny, largely
because the 'common fund of experience' (*W*, 190) provides those
grammars by which we may learn to read the languages of everyday
life. Indeed, Louis's somewhat guilty reflections about the life of the
businessman nonetheless express how the 'I' is a function of what is
held in common, and how self and system help to strengthen and
determine one another:

> Clear-cut and unequivocal am I too. Yet a vast inheritance of expe-
> rience is packed in me. I have lived thousands of years. . . . I, now
> a duke, now Plato, companion of Socrates; the tramp of dark men
> and yellow men migrating east, west, north and south; the eternal
> procession, women going with attaché cases down the Strand as
> they went once with pitchers to the Nile; all the furled and close-
> packed leaves of my many-folded life are now summed in my
> name; incised cleanly and barely on the sheet. . . . I have helped by
> my assiduity and decision to score those lines on the map there by

which the different parts of the world are laced together.
(*W*, 181–82)

Using the figures of language and of colonial settlement coterminously, Bernard even reminds us that 'one cannot despise these phrases laid like Roman roads across the tumult of our lives, since they compel us to walk in step like civilised people with the slow and measured tread of policemen though one may be humming any nonsense under one's breath at the same time' (*W*, 284). And, in a dance episode resonant with Symbolist precedent, Jinny uses the figure of the figure, of the building, and of the fabric to say how 'we are swept now into this large figure; it holds us together; we cannot step outside its sinuous, its hesitating, its abrupt, its perfectly encircling walls. Our bodies, his hard, mine flowing, are pressed together within its body; it holds us together; and then lengthening out, in smooth, in sinuous folds, rolls us between it, on and on' (*W*, 111).

Indeed, the descriptions of infancy at the start of the novel, like those in 'A Sketch of the Past', find the child emerging into a world of pre-existent systems out of which he will be fashioned. 'I am all fibre. All tremors shake me' (W, 10), says the yet-unformed Louis. 'I dance. I ripple,' says Jinny. 'I am thrown over you like a net of light' (*W*, 12). In fact, as children, the six friends 'melt into each other with phrases. We are edged with mist,' says Bernard of the emerging nets on the periphery of childhood vision. 'We make an unsubstantial territory' (*W*, 14–15).

The self, in other words, is not yet mapped and pinioned to a spot in the landscape. Indeed, the landscape itself has yet to be grasped as such by the child: 'There is an order in this world,' says Neville; 'there are distinctions, there are differences in this world upon whose verge I step' (*W*, 20). Thus the child emerges into a world of 'differences' by which order will be constituted, much as the primary level of meaning in the book's section prologues, and the level from which all other meaning is built, is the rather Paterian 'difference' between 'light' and 'shadow' (*W*, 119).

'Thus,' says Neville, 'we spin round us infinitely fine filaments and construct a system. Plato and Shakespeare are included, also quite obscure people, people of no importance whatsoever' (*W*, 194). Of course, the 'system' is largely given rather than created, and often the 'lines twist and intersect . . . round us, wrapping us about' (*W*, 194). Stable selfhood means a disentanglement and co-ordination of these 'lines' so that 'now,' according to Neville, 'this room' – this particular self – 'seems to me central. . . . Here we are centred' (*W*, 194).

The opposite of selfhood, of course, is shapelessness and fragmentation. 'I am broken into separate pieces,' says Rhoda in fear; 'I am no longer one' (*W*, 114), even though a moment earlier she is 'fixed' by the 'immense pressure' of 'the weight of centuries' (*W*, 114). 'Everything,' says Neville, 'must be done to rebuke the horror of deformity' (*W*, 196).

Selfhood proper, on the other hand, is a specular achievement, as Jinny well knows:

> So I skip up the stairs past them, to the next landing, where the long glass hangs and I see myself entire. I see my body and head in one now; for even in this serge frock they are one, my body and my head. Look, when I move my head I ripple all down my narrow body; even my thin legs ripple like a stalk in the wind. (*W*, 44)

Rhoda's experience of self is the same as Jinny's: 'That is my face . . . in the looking-glass behind Susan's shoulder – that face is my face' (*W*, 45). And to see identity disappear 'I will duck behind her to hide it, for I am not here. I have no face' (*W*, 45). Even late in the novel the same rhythm is repeated if Jinny sits 'before a looking-glass' (*W*, 242), Rhoda counters with the claim, 'I have no face' (*W*, 243), and attributes Jinny's 'authority' and 'fame' to the fact that she is 'embedded in a substance made of repeated moments run together' (*W*, 243).

Indeed, the rootedness of achieved selfhood represented by Jinny's 'stalk' suggests how, at times, the security of identity is so intoxicating that it can engender the illusion of a natural self as well as the conviction of autogenesis: 'My roots,' says Louis, 'go down to the depths of the world' (*W*, 10); 'I, Louis, I, who shall walk the earth these seventy years, am born entire' (*W*, 41). Hence 'identity,' as Bernard puts it in a figure reminiscent of Leslie Stephen, 'becomes robust' (*W*, 282, 286); in a Paterian figure, 'robust' identity is instead 'the crystal, the globe of life as one calls it' (*W*, 280). 'I am,' says Bernard, 'wedged into my place in the puzzle' (*W*, 236).

Without a self that is natural or autonomous – without a self beyond culture – we are left with Bernard's testimony that 'one cannot live outside the machine for more perhaps,' in a whimsical attempt at humor, 'than half an hour' (*W*, 167). The 'machine', of course, is 'the rhythm, the throb' (*W*, 165) of life itself, precisely what the dead Percival, at least according to Bernard, 'sees . . . no longer' (*W*, 165). Indeed, one section prologue suggests this 'machine' to be the very 'engine' (*W*, 117) that manufactures the order of nature itself, at least as the human eye construes it. Bernard even sums up the machine's many parts – 'intestines' and 'tongue', nature and culture compact – and includes among its primary components the body itself: 'Muscles, nerves, intestines, blood-vessels, all that makes the coil and spring of our being, the unconscious hum of the engine, as well as the dart and flicker of the tongue' (*W*, 285). Indeed, when Louis describes the 'engine' of the common life in terms of weaving and the image of 'corn', Woolf even grazes the deindividuating moments of the 'Conclusion' to *The Renaissance*: 'I feel myself woven in and out of the long summers and winters that have made the corn flow and have frozen the streams' (*W*, 220).[56] □

Intellectual origins are the topic of the closing extract for this chapter, Gillian Beer's essay, 'Hume, Stephen, and Elegy in *To the Lighthouse*', which sensitively explores the philosophical and familial influences for Woolf's meditations on subjectivity there. There are several studies looking at various aspects of Woolf's engagement with elegy, from formal to psychobiographical, many with special reference to *To the Lighthouse* and *The Waves*.[57] Beer interprets *To the Lighthouse* biographically as an elegy on Woolf's parents, but positions her discussion of Leslie Stephen's influence in wider intellectual context too. He is seen 'both as father and philosopher'.[58]

■ When my perceptions are remov'd for any time, as by sound sleep; so long am I insensible of myself, and may truly be said not to exist. And were all my perceptions remov'd by death, and cou'd I neither think, nor feel, nor see, nor love, nor hate after the dissolution of my body, I should be entirely annihilated, nor do I conceive what is farther requisite to make me a perfect non-entity.
　　　　(David Hume, *A Treatise on Human Nature*, 1736, ed. T.H. Green and T.H. Grose, Vol. I, p. 534, 1874)[59]

Father's birthday. He would have been 96, yes, today; and could have been 96, like other people one has known; but mercifully was not. His life would have entirely ended mine. What would have happened? No writing, no books; – inconceivable. I used to think of him and mother daily; but writing The Lighthouse, laid them in my mind. And now he comes back sometimes, but differently.
　　　　(Virginia Woolf, *Diary*, 28 November 1928)[60]

Several of Virginia Woolf's books compose themselves about an absence: Jacob's absence from his room, Mrs. Ramsay's in the second half of *To the Lighthouse*, and in *The Waves* Percival's in India and in death. Absence gives predominance to memory and to imagination. Absence may blur the distinction between those who are dead and those who are away. In one sense, everything is absent in fiction, since nothing can be physically there. Fiction blurs the distinction between recall and reading. It creates a form of immediate memory for the reader.

　　Writing about Hume, the philosopher he most admired, Leslie Stephen glosses his position thus:

The whole history of philosophical thought is but a history of attempts to separate the object and the subject, and each new attempt implies that the previous line of separation was erroneously drawn or partly 'fictitious'. (p. 48)[61]

In *To the Lighthouse* the fictitiousness of the separation between object and subject, the question of where to draw the line, is passionately explored, not only by the painter, Lily Briscoe, but by the entire narrative process. It is through Lily that the philosophical and artistic problem is most directly expressed and the connection between Mr. Ramsay and Hume first mooted. Near the beginning of the book, Lily asks Andrew what his father's books are about.

'Subject and object and the nature of reality,' Andrew had said. And when she said Heavens, she had no notion what that meant. 'Think of a kitchen table then,' he told her, 'when you're not there.' (p. 40)[62]

In the book's last paragraph, remembering Mrs. Ramsay, looking at the empty steps, Lily at last solves the problem of the masses in her picture to her own satisfaction:

She looked at the steps; they were empty; she looked at her canvas; it was blurred. With a sudden intensity, as if she saw it clear for a second, she drew a line there, in the centre. (p. 320)

The separation of the object and the subject, and the drawing of a line less erroneous, less 'fictitious', than in previous attempts, defines the nature of elegy in this work. Virginia Woolf attempts to honour her obligations to family history and yet freely to dispose that history. In the course of doing so, she brings into question our reliance on symbols to confer value.

Virginia Woolf's other books imply aesthetic theories and draw upon the ideas of contemporary philosophers, particularly Bertrand Russell's warning against assuming that language mirrors the structure of the world: 'Against such errors' he writes in *The Analysis of Mind* (1921), 'the only safeguard is to be able, once in a way, to discard words for a moment and contemplate facts more directly through images'.[63] That is an ideal and a difficulty which moves through Virginia Woolf's practice as a writer. Only in *To the Lighthouse*, however, is the power of philosophical thinking and its limitations openly a theme of the book. That has to do with the work's special nature as elegy. In 1925, when she was beginning *To the Lighthouse*, Virginia Woolf wrote in her diary: 'I will invent a new name for my books to supplant "novel". A new – – by Virginia Woolf. But what? Elegy?'

In elegy there is a repetition of mourning and an allaying of mourning. Elegy lets go of the past, formally transferring it into language, laying ghosts by confining them to a text and giving them its freedom. Surviving and relinquishing are both crucial to the composition of *To the Lighthouse*. Learning how to let go may be as deep a difficulty in writing and concluding a novel as it is in other experience.

The problem of achieving and of letting go is shared by mothers and artists. Mrs. Ramsay lets go through death. After her death the book continues to explore what lasts (how far indeed has she let go or will others let her go?). The novel questions the means by which we try to hold meaning and make it communicable.

> Meanwhile the mystic, the visionary, walked the beach, stirred a puddle, looked at a stone, and asked themselves 'What am I?' 'What is this?' and suddenly an answer was vouchsafed them (what it was they could not say). (pp. 203–4)

All Virginia Woolf's novels brood on death, and death, indeed, is essential to their organisation as well as their meaning. Death was her special knowledge: her mother, her sister Stella, her brother Thoby had all died prematurely. But death was also the special knowledge of her entire generation, through the obliterative experience of the first world war. The long succession of family and generation, so typically the material of the nineteenth-century *roman fleuve*, such as Thackeray's *Pendennis* and *The Virginians*, or Zola's Rougon-Macquart series, becomes the site of disruption. The continuity of the family can with greatest intensity express the problems of invasion and even extinction.

Lawrence originally imagined *The Rainbow* and *Women in Love* as one long novel to be called *The Sisters*. But when the two books eventually appeared the first was a rich genealogical sedimentation, the second was thinned, lateral, preoccupied with a single generation. The parents in *Women in Love* are enfeebled and dying; the major relationships explored in the work are chosen, not inherited. In *To the Lighthouse* Virginia Woolf still tried to hold within a single work what Lawrence had eventually had to separate: the experience of family life and culture, before and after the first world war. She held them together by separating them. 'Time Passes', like Lily's line, both joins and parts. It is one formal expression of the profound question: 'What endures?' 'Will you fade? Will you perish?', 'The very stone one kicks with one's boot will outlast Shakespeare.' 'Distant views seem to outlast by a million years (Lily thought) the gazer and to be communing already with a sky which beholds an earth entirely at rest.'

'Ah, but how long do you think it'll last?' said somebody. It was as if she had antennae trembling out from her, which, intercepting certain sentences, forced them upon her attention. This was one of them. She scented danger for her husband. A question like that would lead, almost certainly, to something being said which reminded him of his own failure. How long would he be read – he would think at once. (p. 166)

This passage brings home the other anxiety about survival which haunts the book: how long will writing last? Mr. Ramsay's ambition to be remembered as a great philosopher registers some of Woolf's ambitions and longings as an artist too. They are expressed in another mode by Lily, who must complete her picture and complete it truly, but who foresees its fate: 'It would be hung in the attics, she thought; it would be destroyed. But what did that matter? she asked herself, taking up her brush again.' (p. 320)

So the topics of the British empiricists, Locke, Hume, Berkeley – the survival of the object without a perceiver, the nature of identity and non-entity, the scepticism about substance – lie beneath the activity of the narrative. They bear on the question of how we live in our bodies and how we live in the minds of others. Hume writes of mankind in general that '. . . they are nothing but a bundle or collection of different perceptions, which succeed each other with an inconceivable rapidity, and are in a perpetual flux and movement' (p. 534).

The emphasis on perception and on 'flux and movement' is repeated in Virginia Woolf's writing. But, as I have already suggested, there was a more immediate reason for Hume's insistent and sometimes comic presence in *To the Lighthouse*.

When Hume is named in *To the Lighthouse* he is strongly identified with Mr. Ramsay's thoughts. He is first mentioned at the end of Mr. Ramsay's long meditation on the need for ordinary men and on their relation to great men (exemplified in the twin figures of Shakespeare and the 'liftman in the Tube'). The section ends with Mr. Ramsay's self-defeated questioning of his own powers. Yet, he thinks:

. . . he was for the most part happy; he had his wife; he had his children; he had promised in six weeks' time to talk 'some nonsense' to the young men of Cardiff about Locke, Hume, Berkeley, and the causes of the French Revolution. (p. 73)

His meditation had begun with the question: 'If Shakespeare had never existed . . . would the world have differed much from what it is today?' (p. 70). The apposition of empiricism and revolution ('Locke, Hume, Berkeley, and the causes of the French Revolution') suggests a possible partial answer to that question, but it is self-deprecatingly framed as 'some nonsense'. The issue remains unresolved.

Hume's name next appears interrupting, and yet almost a part of, the current of thought generated by Mrs. Ramsay in section 11 as she thinks about 'losing personality', eternity, the Lighthouse, and finds herself repeating phrases: 'Children don't forget' . . . 'It will end . . . It will come . . . We are in the hands of the Lord'.

> The insincerity slipping in among the truths roused her, annoyed her. She returned to her knitting again. How could any Lord have made this world? she asked. . . . There was no treachery too base for the world to commit; she knew that. No happiness lasted; she knew that. She knitted with firm composure, slightly pursing her lips and, without being aware of it, so stiffened and composed the lines of her face in a habit of sternness that when her husband passed, though he was chuckling at the thought that Hume, the philosopher, grown enormously fat, had stuck in a bog, he could not help noting, as he passed, the sternness at the heart of her beauty. (p. 102)

Hume, philosopher of mind, has grown so absurdly substantial that he sinks into the bog. That physical episode becomes meta-memory for Mr. Ramsay, who sees it, not having been there. The full story is reserved for section 13 when at the end:

> . . . the spell was broken. Mr. Ramsay felt free now to laugh out loud at Hume, who had stuck in a bog and an old woman rescued him on condition he said the Lord's Prayer, and chuckling to himself he strolled off to his study. (p. 116)

Hume, the sceptical philosopher, is obliged to repeat the words of faith. We remember Mrs. Ramsay's involuntary 'We are in the hands of the Lord'. Communal faith usurps the individual will. At the end of this episode (section 13) Mr. Ramsay feels comfortable: Hume has been worsted. The giant towering above his own endeavours as a philosopher proves to be a gross man subsiding. For a moment he can be held to scale, contained in anecdote. But Mr. Ramsay is himself measured by his will to worst. The narrative engages with the difficulties that Hume's work raises. And by this means, as we shall see, Virginia Woolf movingly allows to her father, Leslie Stephen, within her own work, a power of survival, recomposition, rediscovery even.

Hume's presence in the work allows her to bring sharply into focus the question of what is 'when you're not there', a topic traditional to elegy but here given greater acuity. In 1927 Bertrand Russell wrote in *The Analysis of Matter*:

I believe that matter is less material, and mind less mental, than is commonly supposed, and that, when this is realized, the difficulties raised by Berkeley largely disappear. Some of the difficulties raised by Hume, it is true, have not yet been disposed of. (p. 7)

Hume's persistence, the fact that his difficulties cannot be disposed of, makes him a necessary part of the book's exploration of substance and absence, of writing as survival.

We know that Virginia Woolf read Hume, perhaps not for the first time, in September 1920. But his importance in *To the Lighthouse* is connected with his special value for Leslie Stephen. In the process of transformation from Leslie Stephen to Mr. Ramsay, Virginia Woolf notably raises the level of creativity and attainment at which the father-figure is working, placing him in the rearward and yet within reach of major philosophers. Whereas Leslie Stephen was a doughty thinker, high populariser, and man of letters, Mr. Ramsay is a possibly major, though self-debilitated, philosopher. This raising and enlarging sustains the scale of the father in relation to the writer and at the same time allows a process of identification between writer and father in their artistic obsessions. Virginia Woolf did not acknowledge having read much of Leslie Stephen's work. But when we turn to Stephen's *History of English Thought in the Eighteenth Century* (2 vols, 1876) the congruities between the themes of that work and *To the Lighthouse* are remarkable enough, and Stephen's actual exposition of Hume and the directions in which he seeks to move beyond him are closely related to the concerns of *To the Lighthouse*. The first of these is reputation and survival.

The first sentence of Stephen's book simultaneously places Hume at a pinnacle of achievement and presents the problem of literary reputation.

Between the years of 1739 and 1752 David Hume published philosophical speculations destined, by the admission of friends and foes, to form a turning-point in the history of thought. His first book fell dead-born from the press; few of its successors had a much better fate. (p. 1)

The first section of the Introduction is entitled 'The influence of great thinkers' and it grapples with the question of how far the thinker thinks alone or as an expression of communal concerns. How does thought affect society? Stephen argues that

The soul of the nation was stirred by impulses of which Hume was but one, though by far the ablest, interpreter; or, to speak in less mystical phrase, we must admit that thousands of inferior thinkers were dealing with the same problems which occupied Hume, and though with far less acuteness or logical consistency, arriving at similar conclusions. (p. 2)

Thinking is not exclusively the province of great thinkers, nor – more strikingly – are their conclusions different from others.

In *To the Lighthouse* Mr. Bankes suggests:

We can't all be Titians and we can't all be Darwins, he said; at the same time he doubted whether you could have your Darwin and your Titian if it weren't for humble people like ourselves. (p. 114)

The relationship between 'humble people like ourselves' – or not quite like ourselves – and great art, great ideas, great events, haunts and troubles *To the Lighthouse*. It is part of the work's deepest questioning of what will survive. The question includes the questioning of the concept of 'great men', of indomitable achievement, of a world centred on human will, and extends to human memory and the material world.

Does the progress of civilisation depend upon great men? Is the lot of the average human being better now than in the time of the pharaohs? Is the lot of the average human being, however, he asked himself, the criterion by which we judge the measure of civilisation? Possibly not. Possibly the greatest good requires the existence of a slave class. The liftman in the Tube is an eternal necessity. The thought was distasteful to him. (p. 70)

Stephen, pursuing the relationship between 'great men' and the mass of thinking, writes:

Society may thus be radically altered by the influence of opinions which have apparently little bearing upon social questions. It would not be extravagant to say that Mr. Darwin's observations upon the breeds of pigeons have had a reaction upon the structure of society. (p. 12)

Abstract thought and social action seem at times in *To the Lighthouse* to be polarised between Mr. and Mrs. Ramsay, but most of the thinking in the book is sustained by the activity of laying alongside and intermelding the separate thought processes within individuals in such a way that the reader perceives the connections which the characters themselves cannot. The interpenetration of consciousnesses in language on the page allows us to think through problems of substance and absence unreservedly.

In his analysis of Hume's thought Stephen gives particular emphasis to the idea of fictionality. Stephen writes:

> The belief that anything exists outside our mind when not actually perceived, is a 'fiction' . . . Association is in the mental what gravitation is in the natural world.

(Lily's floating table is anchored by association, not gravitation, we remember.)

> . . . We can only explain mental processes of any kind by resolving them into such cases of association. Thus reality is to be found only in the ever-varying stream of feelings, bound together by custom, regarded by a 'fiction' or set of Actions as implying some permanent set of external or internal relations. . . . Chance, instead of order, must, it would seem, be the ultimate objective fact, as custom, instead of reason, is the ultimate subjective fact. (p. 44)

There are obvious connections with *To the Lighthouse* in such an emphasis on reality as an 'ever-varying stream of feelings'. 'Life', he writes in his discussion of Hume, 'is not entirely occupied in satisfying our material wants, and co-operating or struggling with our fellows. We dream as well as act. We must provide some channel for the emotions generated by contemplation of the world and of ourselves' (p. 11).

Stephen, with Hume, affirms chance and custom rather than order and reason as the basis of perception. Nevertheless, such affinities with Virginia Woolf's writing appear at a very general level and need not imply any particularly intense recall of Stephen's work or conversation. If such consonances were all, I would feel justified only in calling attention to similarity, rather than implying a process of re-reading, re-placing. However, the actual examples that Stephen selects are so crucial in the topography of *To the Lighthouse* as to suggest that Virginia Woolf's writing is meditating on problems raised in the father's text.[64] □

CHAPTER FIVE

The 1980s: Sexual/Textual Readings

For this chapter, and the final one, it becomes even more difficult to arrive at a representative selection of criticism, since in the 1980s and 90s Woolf studies, and work on *To the Lighthouse* and *The Waves*, have proliferated in so many directions. As a result obedience to linear chronology falters a little here. I have devoted this chapter to textually based, deconstructive and psychoanalytic, approaches, and the next to contextually based, historical and post-colonialist, ones. Although conveniently labelled in my chapter headings as 1980s and 1990s concerns respectively, these approaches do not, of course, obey the demarcations of the decades, nor are they the only ways of reading *To the Lighthouse* and *The Waves* to have emerged in this period. But while it would be tempting to characterise these recent efflorescences in terms of postmodernist pluralism, it may also be possible to discern the two areas outlined as not only dominant, but also sometimes theoretically conflicting, in their significant shifts of approach. The four main extracts for this chapter, by Toril Moi, Gayatri Chakravorti Spivak, Garrett Stewart and Rachel Bowlby, are all from the 1980s, but their arguments and concerns continue in much criticism of the 1990s.

My chapter heading is derived from one of the most influential works of literary criticism to emerge in the 1980s: Toril Moi's popular introduction to the theories of French feminism, *Sexual/Textual Politics: Feminist Literary Theory* (1985). Moi opens this by addressing the debates over Woolf's feminism we have seen emerging in the 1970s. In her controversial introductory sections, 'Who's afraid of Virginia Woolf? Feminist readings of Woolf', and 'Rescuing Woolf for feminist politics: some points towards an alternative reading', she takes to task Elaine Showalter for her condemnations of Woolf, while applauding the innovations of the androgyny-based critics, in order to bring in, as *deus* (more appropriately, *dea*)-*ex-machina*, the new French feminist theories of Julia Kristeva, Hélène Cixous and Luce Irigaray (broadly associated with the idea of '*écriture feminine*').[1] Moi begins with a critique of Showalter's objections to Woolf's theory of androgyny and stylistic experimentalism in *A Room of One's Own*, concluding that just like the Marxist critic Georg Lukács whose ideas Showalter draws on in her argument, Showalter betrays a dangerous totalising humanism, which is in fact at odds with her proclaimed feminism, a charge also levelled at a number of other feminist commentators on Woolf, including Michèle Barrett,[2] Jane Marcus, and Kate Millett, the title of whose earlier ground-breaking book, *Sexual Politics*, Moi revises for her own. Moi brings to her reading of Woolf's non-fiction *and* fiction, the post-structuralist (Derridean) and psycho-analytic (post-Freudian/Lacanian) inspired theories of French feminism as a way out of this impasse:

■ Showalter's traditional humanism surfaces clearly enough when she first rejects Woolf for being too subjective, too passive and for wanting to flee her female gender identity by embracing the idea of androgyny, and then goes on to reproach Doris Lessing for merging the 'feminine ego' into a greater collective consciousness in her later books (311). Both writers are similarly flawed: both have in different ways rejected the fundamental need for the individual to adopt a unified, integrated self-identity. Both Woolf and Lessing radically undermine the notion of the unitary self, the central concept of Western male humanism and one crucial to Showalter's feminism. . . . This kind of universalising humanist aesthetic leads straight to a search for the representation of strong, powerful women in literature, a search reminiscent of The Soviet Writers' Congress's demand for socialist realism in 1934. Instead of strong, happy tractor drivers and factory workers, we are now, presumably, to demand strong, happy *women* tractor drivers. . . . What feminists such as Showalter . . . fail to grasp is that the traditional humanism they represent is in effect part of patriarchal ideology. At its centre is the seamlessly unified self – either individual or collective – which is commonly called 'Man'. As Luce Irigaray or Hélène Cixous would argue, this integrated self is in fact a phallic self, constructed on the model of the self-contained, powerful phallus. Gloriously autonomous, it banishes from itself all conflict, contradiction and ambiguity. In this humanist ideology the self is the *sole author* of history and of the literary text: the humanist creator is potent, phallic and male – God in relation to his world, the author in relation to his text.[3] History or the text become nothing but the 'expression' of this unique individual: all art becomes autobiography, a mere window on to the self and the world, with no reality of its own. The text is reduced to a passive, 'feminine' reflection of an unproblematically 'given', 'masculine' world or self.

Showalter wants the literary text to yield the reader a certain security, a firm perspective from which to judge the world. Woolf, on the other hand, seems to practise what we might now call a 'deconstructive' form of writing, one that engages with and thereby exposes the duplicitous nature of discourse. In her own textual practice, Woolf exposes the way in which language refuses to be pinned down to an underlying essential meaning. According to the French philosopher Jacques Derrida, language is structured as an endless deferral of meaning, and any search for an essential, absolutely stable meaning must therefore be considered metaphysical. There is no final element, no fundamental unit, no *transcendental signified* that is meaningful *in itself* and thus escapes the ceaseless interplay of linguistic deferral and difference. The free play of signifiers will never yield a final, unified meaning that in turn might ground and explain all the others.[4] It is in the light of such textual and linguistic theory that we can read Woolf's playful shifts and changes of perspective, in both her fiction and in *Room*, as something rather more than a wilful desire to irritate the serious-minded feminist critic. Through her conscious exploitation of the sportive, sensual nature of language, Woolf rejects the metaphysical essentialism underlying patriarchal ideology, which hails God, the Father or the phallus as its transcendental signified.

But Woolf does more than practise a non-essentialist form of writing. She also reveals a deeply sceptical attitude to the male-humanist concept of an essential human identity. For what can this self-identical identity be if all meaning is a ceaseless play of difference, if *absence* as much as presence is the foundation of meaning? The humanist concept of identity is also challenged by psychoanalytic theory, which Woolf undoubtedly knew. The Hogarth Press, founded by Virginia and Leonard Woolf, published the first English translations of Freud's central works, and when Freud arrived in London in 1939 Virginia Woolf went to visit him. Freud, we are tantalizingly informed, gave her a narcissus.

For Woolf, as for Freud, unconscious drives and desires constantly exert a pressure on our conscious thoughts and actions. For psychoanalysis the human subject is a complex entity, of which the conscious mind is only a small part. Once one has accepted this view of the subject, however, it becomes impossible to argue that even our conscious wishes and feelings originate within a unified self, since we can have no knowledge of the possibly unlimited unconscious processes that shape our conscious thought. Conscious thought, then, must be seen as the 'overdetermined' manifestation of a multiplicity of structures that intersect to produce that unstable constellation the liberal humanists call the 'self'. These structures encompass not only unconscious sexual desires, fears and phobias, but also a host of conflicting material, social, political and ideological factors of which we are equally unaware. It is this highly complex network of conflicting structures, the anti-humanist would argue, that produces the subject and its experiences, rather than the other way round. This belief does not of course render the individual's experiences in any sense less real or valuable; but it does mean that such experiences cannot be understood other than through the study of their multiple determinants – determinants of which conscious thought is only one, and a potentially treacherous one at that. If a similar approach is taken to the literary text, it follows that the search for a unified individual self, or gender identity or indeed 'textual identity' in the literary work must be seen as drastically reductive.

It is in this sense that Showalter's recommendation to remain detached from the narrative strategies of the text is equivalent to not reading it at all. For it is only through an examination of the detailed strategies of the text on all its levels that we will be able to uncover some of the conflicting, contradictory elements that contribute to make it precisely *this* text, with precisely these words and this configuration. The humanist desire for a unity of vision or thought (or . . . for a 'non-contradictory perception of the world') is, in effect, a demand for a sharply reductive reading of literature – a reading that, not least in the case of an experimental writer like Woolf, can have little hope of grasping the central problems posed by pioneering modes of textual production. A 'noncontradictory perception of the world', for Lukács's Marxist opponent Bertolt Brecht, is precisely a reactionary one.

The French feminist philosopher Julia Kristeva has argued that the modernist poetry of Lautréamont, Mallarmé and others constitutes a 'revolutionary' form of writing. The modernist poem, with its abrupt shifts, ellipses, breaks and apparent lack of logical construction is a kind of writing in which the rhythms of the body and the unconscious have managed to break through the strict rational defences of conventional social meaning. Since Kristeva sees such conventional meaning as the structure that sustains the whole of the symbolic order – that is, all human social and cultural institutions – the fragmentation of symbolic language in modernist poetry comes for her to parallel and prefigure a total *social* revolution. For Kristeva, that is to say, there is a *specific practice of writing* that is itself 'revolutionary', analogous to sexual and political transformation, and that by its very existence testifies to the possibility of transforming the symbolic order of orthodox society from the inside.[5] One might argue in this light that Woolf's refusal to commit herself in her essays to a so-called rational or logical form of writing, free from fictional techniques, indicates a similar break with symbolic language, as of course do many of the techniques she deploys in her novels.

Kristeva also argues that many women will be able to let what she calls the 'spasmodic force' of the unconscious disrupt their language because of their strong links with the pre-Oedipal mother-figure. But if these unconscious pulsations were to take over the subject entirely, the subject would fall back into pre-Oedipal or imaginary chaos and develop some form of mental illness. The subject whose language lets such forces disrupt the symbolic order, in other words, is also the subject who runs the greater risk of lapsing into madness. Seen in this context, Woolf's own periodic attacks of mental illness can be linked both to her textual strategies and to her feminism. For the symbolic order is a patriarchal order, ruled by the Law of the Father, and any subject who tries to disrupt it, who lets unconscious forces slip through the symbolic repression, puts her or himself in a position of revolt against this regime. Woolf herself suffered acute patriarchal oppression at the hands of the psychiatric establishment, and *Mrs Dalloway* contains not only a splendidly satirical attack on that profession (as represented by Sir William Bradshaw), but also a superbly perspicacious representation of a mind that succumbs to 'imaginary' chaos in the character of Septimus Smith. Indeed Septimus can be seen as the negative parallel to Clarissa Dalloway, who herself steers clear of the threatening gulf of madness only at the price of repressing her passions and desires, becoming a cold but brilliant woman highly admired in patriarchal society. In this way Woolf discloses the dangers of the invasion of unconscious pulsions as well as the price paid by the subject who successfully preserves her sanity, thus maintaining a precarious balance between an overestimation of so-called 'feminine' madness and a too precipitate rejection of the values of the symbolic order.[6]

It is evident that for Julia Kristeva it is not the biological sex of a person, but the subject position she or he takes up, that determines their revolutionary potential. Her views of feminist politics reflect this refusal of biologism and essentialism. The feminist struggle, she argues, must be seen historically and politically as a three-tiered one, which can be schematically summarized as follows:

1. Women demand equal access to the symbolic order. Liberal feminism. Equality.

2. Women reject the male symbolic order in the name of difference. Radical feminism. Femininity extolled.

3. (This is Kristeva's own position.) Women reject the dichotomy between masculine and feminine as metaphysical.

The third position is one that has deconstructed the opposition between masculinity and femininity, and therefore necessarily challenges the very notion of identity. Kristeva writes:

> In the third attitude, which I strongly advocate – which I imagine?
> – the very dichotomy man/woman as an opposition between two
> rival entities may be understood as belonging to metaphysics.
> What can 'identity', even 'sexual identity', mean in a new theoret-
> ical and scientific space where the very notion of identity is
> challenged? ('Women's time', 33–4)

The relationship between the second and the third positions here
requires some comment. If the defence of the third position implies a
total rejection of stage two (which I do not think it does), this would
be a grievous political error. For it still remains *politically* essential for
feminists to defend women *as* women in order to counteract the patriarchal oppression that precisely despises women *as* women. But an
'undeconstructed' form of 'stage two' feminism, unaware of the metaphysical nature of gender identities, runs the risk of becoming an
inverted form of sexism. It does so by uncritically taking over the very
metaphysical categories set up by patriarchy in order to keep women
in their places, despite attempts to attach new feminist values to these
old categories. An adoption of Kristeva's 'deconstructed' form of feminism therefore in one sense leaves everything as it was – our positions
in the political struggle have not changed – but in another sense
radically transforms our awareness of the nature of that struggle.

Here, I feel, Kristeva's feminism echoes the position taken up by
Virginia Woolf some sixty years earlier. Read from this perspective, *To
the Lighthouse* illustrates the destructive nature of a metaphysical belief
in strong, immutably fixed gender identities – as represented by Mr
and Mrs Ramsay – whereas Lily Briscoe (an artist) represents the subject who deconstructs this opposition, perceives its pernicious
influence and tries as far as is possible in a still rigidly patriarchal
order to live as her own woman, without regard for the crippling
definitions of sexual identity to which society would have her con-
form. It is in this context that we must situate Woolf's crucial concept
of androgyny. This is not, as Showalter argues, a flight from fixed
gender identities, but a recognition of their falsifying metaphysical
nature. Far from fleeing such gender identities because she fears them,
Woolf rejects them because she has seen them for what they are. She
has understood that the goal of the feminist struggle must precisely be
to deconstruct the death-dealing binary oppositions of masculinity
and femininity. . . . The host of critics who . . . read Mrs Ramsay and
Mrs Dalloway as Woolf's ideal of femininity are thus either betraying
their vestigial sexism – the sexes are fundamentally different and
should stay that way – or their adherence to what Kristeva would call
a 'stage two' feminism: women are different from men and it is time
they began praising the superiority of their sex. These are both, I

believe, misreadings of Woolf's texts, as when Kate Millett writes that:

> Virginia Woolf glorified two housewives, Mrs. Dalloway and Mrs. Ramsay, recorded the suicidal misery of Rhoda in *The Waves* without ever explaining its causes, and was argumentative yet somehow unsuccessful, perhaps because unconvinced, in conveying the frustrations of the woman artist in Lily Briscoe. (139–40)

A combination of Derridean and Kristevan theory, then, would seem to hold considerable promise for future feminist readings of Woolf. But it is important to be aware of the political limitations of Kristeva's arguments. Though her views on the 'politics of the subject' constitute a significant contribution to revolutionary theory, her belief that the revolution within the subject somehow prefigures a later social revolution poses severe problems for any materialist analysis of society. The strength of Kristevan theory lies in its emphasis on the politics of language as a material and social structure, but it takes little or no account of other conflicting ideological and material structures that must be part of any radical social transformation. . . . It should nevertheless be emphasized that the 'solution' to Kristeva's problems lies not in a speedy return to Lukács, but in an integration and transvaluation of her ideas within a larger feminist theory of ideology.

A Marxist-feminist critic like Michèle Barrett has stressed the materialist aspect of Woolf's politics. In her introduction to *Virginia Woolf: Women and Writing*, she argues that:

> Virginia Woolf's critical essays offer us an unparalleled account of the development of women's writing, perceptive discussion of her predecessors and contemporaries, and a pertinent insistence on the material conditions which have structured women's consciousness. (36)

Barrett, however, considers Woolf only as essayist and critic, and seems to take the view that when it comes to her fiction, Woolf's aesthetic theory, particularly the concept of an androgynous art, 'continually resists the implications of the materialist position she advances in *A Room of One's Own*' (22). A Kristevan approach to Woolf, as I have argued, would refuse to accept this binary opposition of aesthetics on the one hand and politics on the other, locating the politics of Woolf's writing *precisely in her textual practice*. That practice is of course much more marked in the novels than in most of the essays.

Another group of feminist critics, centred around Jane Marcus, consistently argues for a radical reading of Woolf's work without recourse to either Marxist or post-structuralist theory. Jane Marcus claims Woolf as a 'guerrilla fighter in a Victorian skirt' (1), and sees in her a champion of both socialism and feminism. Marcus's article 'Thinking back through our mothers', however, makes it abundantly clear that it is exceptionally difficult to argue this case convincingly. Her article opens with this assertion:

> Writing, for Virginia Woolf, was a revolutionary act. Her alienation from British patriarchal culture and its capitalist and imperialist forms and values, was so intense that she was filled with terror and determination as she wrote. A guerrilla fighter in a Victorian skirt, she trembled with fear as she prepared her attacks, her raids on the enemy. (1)

Are we to believe that there is a causal link between the first and the following sentences – that writing was a revolutionary act for Woolf *because* she could be seen to tremble as she wrote? Or should the passage be read as an extended metaphor, as an image of the fears of any woman writing under patriarchy? In which case it no longer tells us anything specific about Woolf's particular writing practices. Or again, perhaps the first sentence is the claim that the following sentences are meant to corroborate? If this is the case, the argument also fails. For Marcus here unproblematically evokes biographical evidence to sustain her thesis about the nature of Woolf's writing: the reader is to be convinced by appeals to biographical circumstances rather than to the texts. But does it really matter whether or not Woolf was in the habit of trembling at her desk? Surely what matters is what she wrote? This kind of emotionalist argument surfaces again in Marcus's extensive discussion of the alleged parallels between Woolf and the German Marxist critic Walter Benjamin ('Both Woolf and Benjamin chose suicide rather than exile before the tyranny of fascism' (7)). But surely Benjamin's suicide at the Spanish frontier, where as an exiled German Jew fleeing the Nazi occupation of France he feared being handed over to the Gestapo, must be considered in a rather different light from Woolf's suicide in her own back garden in unoccupied England, however political we might wish her private life to be? Marcus's biographical analogies strive to establish Woolf as a remarkable individual, and so fall back into the old-style historical-biographical criticism much in vogue before the American New Critics entered the scene in the 1930s. How far a radical feminist approach can simply take over such traditional methods untransformed is surely debatable.

We have seen that current Anglo-American feminist criticism tends to read Woolf through traditional aesthetic categories, relying largely on a liberal-humanist version of the Lukácsian aesthetics, against which Brecht so effectively polemicized. The anti-humanist reading I have advocated as yielding a better understanding of the political nature of Woolf's aesthetics has yet to be written. The only study of Woolf to have integrated some of the theoretical advances of post-structuralist thought is written by a man, Perry Meisel, and though it is by no means an anti-feminist or even an unfeminist work, it is nevertheless primarily concerned with the influence on Woolf of Walter Pater. Meisel is the only critic of my acquaintance to have grasped the radically deconstructed character of Woolf's texts:

> With 'difference' the reigning principle in Woolf as well as Pater, there can be no natural or inherent characteristics of any kind, even between the sexes, because all character, all language, even the language of sexuality, emerges by means of a difference from itself. (234)

Meisel also shrewdly points out that this principle of difference makes it impossible to select any one of Woolf's works as more representative, more essentially 'Woolfian' than any other, since the notable divergence among her texts 'forbids us to believe any moment in Woolf's career to be more conclusive than another' (240). It is a mistake, Meisel concludes, to 'insist on the coherence of self and author in the face of a discourse that dislocates or decentres them both, that skews the very categories to which our remarks properly refer' (242).

The paradoxical conclusion of our investigations into the feminist reception of Woolf is therefore that she has yet to be adequately welcomed and acclaimed by her feminist daughters in England and America. To date she has either been rejected by them as insufficiently feminist, or praised on grounds that seem to exclude her fiction. By their more or less unwitting subscription to the humanist aesthetic categories of the traditional male academic hierarchy, feminist critics have seriously undermined the impact of their challenge to that very institution. The only difference between a feminist and a non-feminist critic in this tradition then becomes the formal political perspective of the critic. The feminist critic thus unwittingly puts herself in a position from which it becomes impossible to read Virginia Woolf as the progressive, feminist writer of genius she undoubtedly was. A feminist criticism that would do both justice and homage to its great mother and sister: this, surely, should be our goal.[7] □

Several critics have taken up Moi's gauntlet. Makiko Minow-Pinkney's *Virginia Woolf and the Problem of the Subject* (1987) was one of the first book-length studies of Woolf's work to make use of Kristevan theories, from which, for reasons of space, I can only briefly quote. This is Minow-Pinkney's reading of Lily Briscoe's final vision:

■ Lily's line represents an unsurpassable bar between lived experience and the symbolic order, which always objectively exists but comes to subjective consciousness as the result of a historical 'fall' from the plenitude of the Ramsays to the dearth suffered by the post-war generation. It is the necessary condition of the subject as such, and reacts back to interrogate the symbolic visions of the first half of the novel. The book's ambivalent attitude to this bar or gap is finally grounded in the daughter's fraught relation to the mother. Mrs Ramsay's death is the bleak loss of the possibility of total meaning, yet it also reveals an arbitrariness in the sign which reduces even her impressive symbols into fictional constructs with no compelling authority over the next generation.[8] □

This might almost serve as an allegory for the contribution of this new generation of Woolf criticism! No longer discerning unified meaning in closed totalising interpretations of Woolf's texts, critics now celebrate them for their endlessly transgressive free-playing signifiers, for their foregrounding of absences, gaps, and silences,[9] and for their presentation of radically deconstructed subjectivity. Woolf is no longer modernist, but postmodernist.[10] Although she approves Perry Meisel's prescient use of post-structuralist thought in his study of Woolf and Pater, and acknowledges in a footnote Gillian Beer's work as a precedent to her own,[11] Moi does not seem to have been aware of Gayatri Chakravorti Spivak's excellent essay, 'Unmaking and Making in *To the Lighthouse*' (1980), which puts forward a highly sophisticated, feminist, deconstructive reading. It is the source of the next extract.[12]

■ This essay is not necessarily an attempt to illuminate *To the Lighthouse* and lead us to a correct reading. It is rather an attempt to use the book by the deliberate superimposition of two allegories – grammatical and sexual – and by reading it, at moments, as autobiography. This modest attempt at understanding criticism not merely as a theoretical approach to the 'truth' of a text, but at the same time as a practical enterprise that produces a reading is part of a much larger polemic.[13] I introduce *To the Lighthouse* into this polemic by reading it as the story of Mr. Ramsay (philosopher-theorist) and Lily (artist-practitioner) around Mrs. Ramsay (text).

Virginia Woolf's *To the Lighthouse* can be read as a project to catch the essence of Mrs. Ramsay. A certain reading of the book would show how the project is undermined; another, how it is articulated. I will suggest that the undermining, although more philosophically adventurous, is set aside by Woolf's book; that the articulation is found to be a more absorbing pursuit.

On a certain level of generality the project to catch the essence of

Mrs. Ramsay is articulated in terms of finding an adequate language. The first part of the book ('The Window') looks at the language of marriage: is Mrs. Ramsay's 'reality' to be found there? The third part of the book ('The Lighthouse') uncovers the language of art: Lily catches Mrs. Ramsay in her painting. Or at least, a gesture on the canvas is implicitly given as a representation of a possible vision (implicitly of Mrs. Ramsay or the picture itself):

> With a sudden intensity, as if she saw it clear for a second, she drew a line there, in the centre. It was done; it was finished. Yes, she thought, laying down her brush in extreme fatigue, I have had my vision.[14]

The second part of the book couples or hinges I and III. In Part I, Mrs. Ramsay is, in the grammatical sense, the subject. In Part III, the painting predicates her.[15]

I could make a grammatical allegory of the structure of the book: Subject (Mrs. Ramsay) – copula – Predicate (painting). That would be the structure of the proposition, the irreducible form of the logic of non-contradiction, the simplest and most powerful sentence. Within this allegory, the second part of the book is the place of the copula. That too yields a suggestive metaphor. For the copula is not only the pivot of grammar and logic, the axle of ideal language, the third person singular indicative of 'to be'; it also carries a sexual charge. 'Copulation' happens not only in language and logic, but also between persons. The metaphor of the copula embraces Mr. Ramsay both ways. As the custodian of the logical proposition ('If Q is Q, then R . . .'), he traffics in the copula; and, as father and husband, he is the custodian of copulation. Lily seeks to catch Mrs. Ramsay with a different kind of copula, a different bridge to predication, a different language of 'Being', the language not of philosophy, but of art. Mr. Ramsay has seemingly caught her in the copula of marriage.

A certain rivalry and partnership develop between Lily and Mr. Ramsay in Part III. But this rivalry and partnership do not account for Part II, where the search for a language seems strangely unattached to a character or characters. One is tempted to say, this is the novel's voice, or, here is Woolf. I will suggest that, in this strange section, the customary division between work and life is itself vague, that the language sought here is the language of madness.

Within the grammatical allegory of the structure of the book, it would run thus: the strongest bond, the copula in the proposition, the bastion of language, the place of the 'is', is almost uncoupled in the coupling part of *To the Lighthouse*. How does that disarticulation and undermining take its place within the articulation of the project to catch the essence of Mrs. Ramsay in an adequate language?

The language of marriage seems a refusal of 'good' language, if a good language is that which brings about communication. When she speaks, Mrs. Ramsay speaks the 'fallen' language of a civility that covers over the harshness of interpersonal relations. (The most successful – silent – communication between herself and her husband is to deflect his fury at Mr. Carmichael's request for a second helping of soup!) When she and Mr. Ramsay speak to each other or read together, their paths do not cross. She knows marriage brings trouble, yet, when she speaks of marriage, it is with complete and prophetic optimism. Her own privileged moments are when words break down, when silence encroaches, or when the inanimate world reflects her. In the end she turns her refusal of discourse into an exclamation of triumph, the epitome, in this book, of a successful conjugal (copulative) relationship.

All of section twelve presents conjugal non-communication with a light touch. I quote two moments: 'All this phrase-making was a game, she thought, for if she had said half what he said, she would have blown her brains out by now' (106). 'And',

> looking up, she saw above the thin trees the first pulse of the full-throbbing star, and wanted to make her husband look at it; for the sight gave her such keen pleasure. But she stopped herself. He never looked at things. If he did, all he would say would be, Poor little world, with one of his sighs. At that moment, he said, 'Very fine,' to please her, and pretended to admire the flowers. But she knew quite well that he did not admire them, or even realize that they were there. (108)

If I were reading the relationship between her knowledge and her power, I would remark here on her matchmaking, or her manipulation of men through deliberate self-suppression. But I am interested only in establishing that she relies little on language, especially language in marriage. Her privileged moments (a privilege that is often nothing but terror), are when words disappear, or when the inanimate world reflects her. One such terrifying moment of privilege is when the men cease talking and the sea's soothing song stops:

> The gruff murmur, . . . which had kept on assuring her, though she could not hear what was said . . . that the men were happily talking; this sound, which had . . . taken its place soothingly in the scale of sounds pressing on top of her . . . had ceased; so that the monotonous fall of the waves on the beach, which for the most part . . . seemed consolingly to repeat over and over again as she sat with the children the words of some old cradle song . . . but at

other times . . . had no such kindly meaning, but like a ghostly roll
of drums remorselessly beat the measure of life . . . – this sound
which had been obscured and concealed under the other sounds
suddenly thundered hollow in her ears and made her look up with
an impulse of terror.

They had ceased to talk: that was the explanation. (27–8)

Why should language be an ally for her, or promise any adequation to
her selfhood? Her discourse with 'life', her 'old antagonist' – her
'parleying' (92) – though not shared with anyone, is 'for the most part'
a bitterly hostile exchange. Her sexuality, the stage for action between
son and husband, does not allow her more than the most marginal
instrument and energy of self-signification:

There was scarcely a shell of herself left for her to know herself by;
all was so lavished and spent; and James, as he stood stiff between
her knees, felt her rise in a rosy-flowered fruit tree laid with leaves
and dancing boughs into which the beak of brass, the arid scimitar
of his father, the egotistical man, plunged and smote, demanding
sympathy. (60)

It is not surprising that, when she feels free (both to 'go' and 'rest'),
'life sank down for a moment', and not only language, but personality
and selfhood were lost: 'This core of darkness could go anywhere. . . .
Not as oneself did one find rest ever . . . but as a wedge of darkness
losing personality . . .' (96). Any dream-dictionary would tell us that
knitting stands for masturbation. A text-dictionary would alert us that
one knits a web, which is a text. Woolf uses the image of Mrs.
Ramsay's knitting (an auto-erotic textuality) strategically. It may represent a reflexive act, a discursivity. It emphasises the second kind of
privileged moment that is Mrs. Ramsay's secret: when she leans
toward inanimate things, which reflect her. The structure of that
reflection is indeed that of sexual intercourse (copulation) and of self-
mirroring in the other. Within that structure, however, she is, in this
last move, the object not the subject, the other not the self. The
moment of self-privilege is now its own preservative yielding to the
world of things.

Imagining herself as a wedge of darkness, she 'looked out to meet
that stroke of the *Lighthouse,* the long steady stroke, the last of the
three, which was her stroke' (96). I must think of 'stroke' as the
predicate, the last stroke in the three-stroke sentence (S is P) of the
house of light, which, as any dictionary of symbols will tell us, is the
house of knowledge or philosophy. If Mrs. Ramsay recognizes her
own mark in being predicated rather than in subjectivity, she is still

caught within copulation. As Woolf knits into her text the image of a suspended knitting she moves us, through the near-identification ('like', 'in a sense') of mirroring, to deliver a satisfying image of the threshold of copulation ('a bride to meet her lover'):

> She looked up over her knitting and met the third stroke and it seemed to her like her own eyes meeting her own eyes. . . . It was odd, she thought, how if one was alone, one leant to inanimate things; trees, streams, flowers; felt they expressed one; felt they became one; felt they knew one, in a sense were one. . . . There rose, and she looked and looked with her needles suspended, there curled up off the floor of the mind, rose from the lake of one's being, a mist, a bride to meet her lover. (97–8)

'One' can be both 'identity' (the word for the unit), and 'difference' (an impersonal agent, not she herself); 'in a sense' might be understood both 'idiomatically' and 'literally' (meaning 'within a meaning').

But these are not the last words on Mrs. Ramsay in 'The Window'. Mostly she remains the protector (13), the manager (14), the imperialist governor of men's sterility (126). At the end of her section she mingles charmingly, as women will, the notions of love, beauty in the eye of the male beholder, and power. By refusing to say 'I love you', she has taken away his power to deny it; by saying 'you were right', she has triumphed:

> She never could say what she felt. . . . He was watching her. She knew what he was thinking. You are more beautiful than ever. And she felt herself very beautiful. . . . She began to smile, for though she had not said a word, he knew, of course he knew, that she loved him. . . .
>
> 'Yes, you were right.' . . . And she looked at him smiling. For she had triumphed again. She had not said it: Yet he knew. (186)

And what of the language of academic philosophy, Mr. Ramsay's tool for making a connection between subject and predicate? Words come easily to him. Woolf shows him to us as he plans a lecture (67). He assimilates the leaves of the trees into leaves of paper: 'Seeing again the . . . geraniums which had so often decorated processes of thought, and bore, written up among their leaves, as if they were scraps of paper on which one scribbles notes in the rush of reading . . .' (66). And he finds them dispensable: 'He picked a leaf sharply. . . . He threw away the leaf.' (67)

The most celebrated formulation of Mr. Ramsay is through the image of the keyboard-alphabet. Here is the traditional copular proposition in the service of the logic of identity and geometrical proof: If Q is Q, then R is . . .[16] . . . If Mrs. Ramsay repeatedly endorses the copulation of marriage – as in the case of the Rayleys – for the sake of a materialist genealogy, Mr. Ramsay would exploit the copulation of philosophy for the sake of paternalistic appropriation.[17] But the Rayleys' marriage comes to nothing, and Mr. Ramsay is convinced 'he would never reach R' (55). . . . A script, half design, half word, combining words and picturing, getting at the truth of things, expressing the body's feelings, this is Lily's desired 'discourse'. 'But what she wished to get hold of was that very jar on the nerves, the thing itself before it had been made anything' (287). Woolf's language, or Lily's, like all language, cannot keep these goals seamless and unified. It is the truth *of* things, the feelings *of* the body, and, as we can easily say since Derrida, 'any' is always already inscribed in 'the thing' for it to be open to being 'made anything'.[18] So she too, like the philosopher, must search for a copula, for her goal, however conceived, also splits into two. In a most enigmatic wish, perhaps she wishes beauty to be self-identical, as Q is Q: 'Beauty would *roll itself* up; the space would fill' (268; italics are mine). She wants to bridge a gap and make a sphere, not merely by a love of learning (philosophy) but a love of play, or a play of love: 'There might be lovers whose gift it was to choose out the elements of things and place them together and so, giving them a wholeness not theirs in life, make of some scene, or meeting of people (all now gone and separate), one of those lobed compacted things over which thought lingers, and love plays' (286). Perhaps she wants to erase 'perhaps' and make first and last coincide: 'Everything this morning was happening for the first time, perhaps for the last time' (288).

She grasps at two 'visions' that ostensibly provide a copula, a bridge between and beyond things. The first: 'One glided, one shook one's sails (there was a good deal of movement in the bay, boats were starting off) between things, beyond things. Empty it was not, but full to the brim. She seemed to be standing up to the lips in some substance, to move and float and sink in it, yes, for these waters were unfathomably deep' (285–6). Alas, since this is language, one can of course find traces of division here if one looks, if one wants to find them. But even beyond that, this sense of plenitude is betrayed by a broad stroke, the incursion of 'temporality', and the rhetoric of measure, of the 'almost'. For 'it was *some such* feeling of completeness *perhaps* which, *ten years ago*, standing *almost* where she stood now, had made her say that she must be in love with the place' (286; italics are mine).

The other vision is of Mrs. Ramsay. It is introduced gently, parenthetically, on page 290. 'A noise drew her attention to the drawing-room window – the squeak of a hinge. The light breeze [we are reminded of the empty house of 'Time Passes'] was toying with the window . . . (Yes; she realized that the drawing-room step was empty, but it had no effect on her whatever. She did not want Mrs. Ramsay now.)' By means of a delicate workwomanlike indirection, Lily makes the vision mature through eight-and-a-half pages. She is then rewarded:

> Suddenly the window at which she was looking was whitened by some light stuff behind it. At last then somebody had come into the drawing-room; somebody was sitting in the chair. For Heaven's sake, she prayed, let them sit still there and not come floundering out to talk to her. Mercifully, whoever it was stayed still inside; had settled by some stroke of luck so as to throw an odd-shaped triangular shadow over the step. It altered the composition of the picture a little. (299)

How is this indefiniteness ('somebody', 'whoever', 'by a stroke of luck') transformed into the certitude and properness of a vision? Through *declaring* this indefiniteness (a kind of absence) as a definiteness (a kind of presence), not through the fullness of presence itself. It is, in other words, turned into a sign of presence. The 'origin of the shadow' remains 'inside the room'. It is only the shadow that is on the steps. Lily *declares* that the origin of the shadow is not 'somebody' but Mrs. Ramsay. And, paradoxically, having forced the issue, she 'wants' *Mr.* Ramsay, now for he too reaches R only through a sign or symbol. He gets to the Lighthouse, although he 'would never reach R'. The 'metaphorical' language of art falls as short of the 'true' copula as the 'propositional' language of philosophy. . . . As Lily paints on the shore, Mr Ramsay must sail to the lighthouse. 'She felt curiously divided, as if one part of her were drawn out there – . . . the lighthouse looked this morning at an immense distance; the other had fixed itself doggedly, solidly, here on the lawn' (233–4). Mr. Ramsay on his boat is the tool for the actualization of her self-separation: a sort of shuttling instrumental copula. It is always a preserved division, never an androgynous synthesis. 'So much depends, Lily thought, upon distance' (284). With the same sort of modal uneasiness as in 'I have had my vision', she can only say 'he must have reached it' (308) rather than 'he has', when Mr. Ramsay springs upon the rock.

Let me say at once that I must read the alternating rhythm of Lighthouse-canvas in the last part of the book as a copulation. To sleep with father in order to make a baby (a painting, a book) is supposed to be woman's fondest wish. But, here as well, Woolf gives that brutal verdict a twist. For the baby *is* mother – it is a sublimated version of Mrs. Ramsay that Lily would produce – whereas Freud's point is that the emergence of this wish is to learn to hate the mother. Woolf's emphasis falls not on the phallus that reappears every other section, but on the workshop of the womb that delivers the work. In fact, in terms of the text, Mr. Ramsay's trip can begin because Lily 'decides' it must:

> She decided that there in that very distant and entirely silent little boat Mr. Ramsay was sitting with Cam and James. Now they had got the sail up; now after a little flagging and hesitation the sails filled and, shrouded in profound silence, she watched the boat take its way with deliberation past the other boats out to sea. (242)

[Postscript]

Knowledge as noncontradiction (identity) is put into question in 'The Window'; it is shown to be based on nothing more immutable than '*if* Q is then Q', and Mr. Ramsay's 'character' is shown to be weak and petulant. Marriage as copulation is also devalorized in 'The Window'; it is shown to be a debilitating and self-deceived combat, and Mrs. Ramsay's 'character' is shown to be at once manipulative and deceitful, and untrusting of language. 'Time Passes' allegorically narrates the terror of a (non-human or natural) operation without a copula. 'The Lighthouse' puts into question the possibility of knowledge (of Mrs. Ramsay) as trope; for a metaphor of art is also a copula (the copula is, after all, a metaphor) that joins two things.

Lily does not question this impasse, she merely fights it. She makes a copula by drawing a line in the center, which can be both an invitation to fill in a blank or a deliberate erasure. If the latter, then she erases (while keeping legible) that very part of the book that most energetically desires to recuperate the impasse, to achieve the undecidable, to write the narrative of madness – 'Time Passes' – for that section is 'in the centre'.

But Lily's 'line in the centre' is also part of a picture, the picture is part of a book, there is a product of some kind in the story as well as in our hands. I can read this more fully as an allegory of sexual rather than grammatical production: it is not only that Lily decides to copulate, she also shows us her wombing. A great deal of the most adventurous criticism in philosophy and literature for the last 15 years has been involved with putting the authority of the proposition (and, therefore, of the copula) into question.[19] This questioning has been often misunderstood as an invitation to play with the copula. I reserve the occasion for arguing that this 'new criticism' in fact asks for what might be called the 'feminine mode of critical production'.[20] Here I am reading *To the Lighthouse* as if it corrects that possible misunderstanding. As if it suggests that, for anyone (and the generic human exemplar is a woman) to play with the copula is to go toward the grim narrative of the discourse of madness and war. One must use the copula as a necessarily limited instrument and create as best one can.

(This is not as far-fetched as it might sound. In a recent essay in *Screen,* Stephen Heath collects once again the evidence to show how close the questioning of the copula comes to the psychoanalytic description of hysteria, 'the female ailment', where the patient is not sure if she has or has not a penis.[21] And Derrida, trying to catch Jean Genet's mother Mme. Genet in his book *Glas*, as Lily tries to 'catch' Mrs. Ramsay, stops at the fetish, of which no one may be sure if it signifies the possession or lack of a penis.[22] In this part of my essay I am suggesting that *To the Lighthouse*, in its emphasis not merely on copulation but on gestation, rewrites the argument from hysteria or fetishism.)

In her reading of Freud's late essay 'Femininity' the French feminist Luce Irigaray suggests that Freud gives the girl-child a growth (warped) by penis-envy (pre-Oedipally she is a boy!) because the Father (a certain Freud) needs to seduce through pronouncing the Law (42, 44), because once 'grown', she must console and hide man's anguish at the possibility of castration (6, 74) and because she is made to pay the price for keeping the Oedipus complex going (98). And then Irigaray asks, why did Freud not articulate vulvar, vaginal, uterine stages (29, 59), why did he ignore the work of the production of the child in the womb? (89)[23]

I am proposing, then, that it is possible to think that texts such as Woolf's can allow us to develop a thematics of womb-envy. I hasten to add that I do not advance womb-envy as a 'new' or 'original' idea. From Socrates through Nietzsche, philosophers have often wished to be midwives or mothers. I am only placing it beside the definition of the physical womb as a lack. I speculate that the womb has always been defined as a lack *by* man in order to cover over a lack *in* man, the lack, precisely, of a tangible place of production. Why does man say he 'gives' a child to a woman? Since we are in the realm of fanciful sex-vocabularies, it is not absurd to suggest that the question of 'giving' might be re-formulated if one thought of the large ovum 'selecting' among millions of microscopic spermatozoa, dependent for effectiveness upon the physiological cycles of the woman. Freud finds the ovum 'passive'.[24] It is just as appropriate to point out that, if one must allegorize, one must notice that the uterus 'releases', 'activates' the ovum. It is simply that the grave periodic rhythm of the womb is not the same as the ad hoc frenzy of the adjudicating phallus. And so forth. I hope the allegoric parallels with *To the Lighthouse* are clear. I am of course not discounting penis-envy, but simply matching it with a possible envy of the womb. As Michel Foucault has written, 'it's not a question of emancipating truth from every system of power . . . but of detaching the power of truth from the forms of hegemony (social, economic, and cultural) within which it operates at the present time.'[25] This might be the secret of 'the rivalry and partnership' between Lily Briscoe and Mr. Ramsay that I mention on the opening page of the essay.

To conclude, then, *To the Lighthouse* reminds me that the womb is not an emptiness or a mystery, it is a place of production. What the hysteron produces is not simply the contemptible text of hysteria, an experimental madness that deconstructs the copula. As a tangible place of production, it can try to construct the copula, however precarious, of art. I am not sure if this ennobling of art as an alternative is a view of things I can fully accept. I can at least honor it as an attempt to articulate, by using a man as an instrument, a woman's vision of a woman;[26] rather than to disarticulate because no human hand can catch a vision, because, perhaps, no vision obtains.[27] □

Spivak is not alone in putting the pleasures of punning to work in theoretically informed readings of Woolf. What follows is a virtuoso performance of such criticism by Garrett Stewart, who, in 'Catching the Stylistic D/rift: Sound Defects in Woolf's *The Waves*', playfully and productively draws on classical rhetoric, post-Saussurean linguistics, and Kristeva's theory of the semiotic. Rhoda, not Bernard, is now the focus of critical attention.

■ The eye of man hath not heard, the ear of man hath not seen . . .
— *A Midsummer Night's Dream*, 4.2.214–17

. . . the silver-grey flickering moth-wing quiver of words
— *The Waves*

I should like to begin by admitting that the verbal phenomenon this essay will be listening for in Virginia Woolf's *The Waves* is not really there. Or to be more exact, it is neither here nor there in any given unit of prose. It falls, or flashes, between words, as something they can be said to keep between themselves in enunciation, as for instance in the double glottal stop – become ligature – between 'wing' and 'quiver' in the epigraph. We may come to understand this aural, if not necessarily oral, phenomenon as a mode of ambiguity, but one whose doubleness is not primarily semantic. The ambivalence in question subtends not two senses of a word but two senses of the reading body. It divides between eye and ear, between script and a tacit voicing fractionally out of phase with it, overlapping the boundaries between written words. Such an ambiguity is a double take that becomes in the lexical sense dis-junctional. As a readable, though not directly legible, phenomenon, this drift of Woolf's later prose certainly does not appear on every page of *The Waves*, and it is rarely salient when it does show (or sound) itself. But neither can it be called an isolated phenomenon, for when it surfaces it tends to contaminate our ear for everything around it. Though disturbing the march of semantic notation with what could be compared to unwritten musical overtones, this effect has little to do with *The Waves* as a so-called 'lyric novel'. Rather, heard in this way, the prose of *The Waves* becomes an instance of a more generalized poetic function as recently defined by Julia Kristeva: a pulsional break with normal discourse, the breakthrough of phonic play into the chain of symbolic or discursive continuity.[28]

By playing specifically between the written and the read, between the lexeme and its phonic articulation, *The Waves* opens the contours of its prose to the counter-logical and subversive possibilities beneath and between the elements of syntactic accumulation. At such moments Woolf's prose is more permissive than expressive; it lets in as lingual disruption the stray reverberations ordinarily contained or suppressed by the marshalled effects of literary style. Woolf's phonic counterpoint to the rank and file of script, her syncopated collaboration between the written and the read, creates a poetic resonance that is at the same time a dissonance within the logic of inscription of textuality itself. In vibrating upon the ear, this conceptual discord between the graphic and the phonic matter of words appears to reroute the written text through the palpable, the palpitating upper body, its passively engaged organs of articulation. Not *back* through the body, as if voice were the privileged ground of all language. Rather, the body is not so much the recovered origin as the secondary medium of poetic utterance, sounding board rather than source.

This essay will return at the end to a further consideration of the body as the ultimate field for the poetic irregularities of Woolf's late style. In the meantime, we will need to examine the relation of Woolf's prose to the life and death of her suicidal heroine, Rhoda, the character who is quick to figure what is most unforgiving and disruptive in temporal consciousness as a precarious linguistic terrain and to find textual metaphors for the unyielding succession of her clocked, disjunctive moments. If Woolf's prose is in any functional sense to be read as an appeal to the articulating, tactile body – and thus perhaps as a concerted humanizing of script's regimentation – then we must note the manner in which such sensual apprehension fails at the same time, even by analogy, to anchor the novel's doomed female character in a meaningfully eased sense of temporal succession. In a diary entry dated January 7, 1931, while Woolf was at work on *The Waves*, she wrote, 'I want to make prose *move* – yes, I swear, move as never before.'[29] But movement, negotiated duration, is the very thing that terrifies and defeats her character Rhoda, who is tortured by script-like intervals that provide no respite, torn by the knowledge that getting on with it is always a getting-over of the dead spots. Rhoda's recurrent pre-psychotic lapses and eventual suicide may thus seem to embody in a single fictional character the notions of linguistically based subjectivity and its traumas prevalent both in post-structuralist theory at large and in the particular bearings of its feminist (or at least gender-oriented) investigations.

Even more than the deputized writer figures among Woolf's cast of characters in *The Waves*, Rhoda thereby offers the touchstone for the novel's underlying sense of language as not only a mode but a model of temporal duration. With Rhoda's crisis in view, I will begin by sketching out the rhythmic leniency of a prose in which the work of eye and ear are complicit with each other, though not always coincident. I will stress the radically poetic, rather than lyric or even stylistic, dimension of this prose – this language not entirely writing – precisely because such a manipulation of language reintroduces the articulating body into the circuit of textual production at the receiving end. The essay will then attempt to suggest what psycho-linguistic options for the maintenance of subjectivity such a feel for verbal duration as pulsional drive might seem to hold out, even as this one narrative withdraws its recurrent promise of rhythm and fluidity from the ruptured consciousness of a single female character.

[I]

Classical rhetoric calls the addition or subtraction of letters from a word a *metaplasm*. But the elusive phenomenon this essay will explore in Woolf's 'prose poetry', a phenomenon both inevitable to all speech and activated as discourse only by certain kinds of literary language, does not involve the inscription or removal of a letter. Rather, it negotiates the slippage of such a letter, or phonemic cluster, across the break between lexical segments, a phonic but not scriptive borrowing, less a strict metaplasm than an audible shift in the plastic stress of a line. In lieu of a received term, I will be calling this phenomenon, wherever detected, a trans-segmental (or, more illustratively, a *transegmental*) adhesion between units of discourse. I have so far been calling it a phenomenon, rather than a feature or stylistic effect, because it so often falls at the lowest limit of intentionality, a near accident of voicing implicated but not legible in script. Appearing momentarily, pivotally, as a phonic hinge between lexemes, it suggests something vaguely askew, indeed unhinged, in the discrete vocabulary of a given syntactic format – a sound effect as sound defect.

In Woolf's last novel, *Between the Acts* (1941), the heroine, Miss La Trobe retreats after the staging of her play into a crowded pub, where indirect discourse retreats further with her into a reverie on the nature of language. The printed version of the passage goes like this: 'Words of one syllable sank down into the mud. . . . The mud became fertile.'[30] But Woolf had originally thought to write: 'Words copulated; seethed, surged. Phrases began shouldering up from the mist,' with 'mist' at once changed, even at this stage of composition, to the more fecund 'mud'.[31] One is tempted to generalize from this passage, even though Woolf later euphemized it, to say that in Woolf's late style words shoulder each other as well as up, and in so doing, interlock, couple, give, and blend. Such an erotics of style is nowhere so directly referred to in Woolf's published prose. Yet what implications might it have for that implicit 'woman's sentence' she seems to call for in *A Room of One's Own*?[32] What kind of sensual charge, what yielding, what abandon, what giving way between the acts of wording, so to speak, would serve to feminize or diffuse the insistent syntactic drive of a male-preempted mother tongue? Or is this sexual differentiation, this gendering of utterance, a false lead even in Woolf's own dream of something beyond the 'man's sentence'? Might language perhaps lay claim instead to a sensual component apart from gender, where the rhythm of phrasing is itself sexualized without being co-opted by one sex or the other, where words 'copulate' with each other, fertilizing, generative, well before they can be commandeered by the forces of sexual politics? In some happy bafflement of eye and ear, might Shakespeare's sister, as imagined and mourned in *A Room of One's Own*, just possibly have survived after all, along with numerous experimental writers of both sexes, by speaking at times in the manner of Bottom's dream?

A certain conjunction of words across the border or blank of their normal scriptive segmentation proliferates with unusual frequency in *The Waves*. Examples may come baring their own characterization, as in that 'moth-wing quiver of words' (215), where the heard difference between g and q, even as read to oneself, depends on a mere quaver of voicing.[33] The sensuous or potentially erotic drift of such phonic undulation is even suggested by the fact that French names it with a term used for other couplings as well: the *liaison*. In phonetics, this is the rule that not only would dictate the pronunciation, for instance, of the otherwise silent *s* in the definite article of the French title, *Entre les actes*, but would also require its unbinding from that article and its enunciation as the virtual first letter of the adjacent morpheme '(*s*)*actes*'. This is rather the opposite effect from the double elision, say, in such a requisite French contraction as *l'entr'acte*. Far rarer in English, and thus more readily available for literary deployment, either instance – whether the dropping or the repositioning of a phoneme – falls within the general category I am terming the *transegmental drift*. To borrow again from the earlier draft version of *Between the Acts*, the seething of one word becomes a surging forward into the next, a penetration of the lexical boundary, a blending of phonemes that in effect, like the musical notation of ligature (*les actes*), glides over the hollows between the scriptive clusters known as words.

By the time of *The Waves*, Woolf had already developed and refined a style that could quietly (one resists saying silently) begin to bridge the interval between words, rendering the very seams of articulation polysemous. The structure of this late novel helps to thematize indirectly not only this verbal facility but its failures. According to Woolf's own provisional terms for the subdivisions of her eccentric text, *The Waves* is made up of italicized descriptive 'interludes' (concerned almost exclusively with describing the natural, the non-human world) alternating with 'episodes' that are merely a collection of separate monologues by the six main characters. They are noted as 'said' by the characters, but as Avrom Fleishman further notes, they rarely reach up from inner speech to voice, let alone to conversation.[34] They are, however, at their very origin thoughts *in* words, not just mental images translated *into* words. In what critics repeatedly call Woolf's most 'stylized' novel, language itself, inner articulation, thus becomes the only occupied zone of consciousness, as well as the sole domain of plot. At the same time, what is 'subjective' about such inner discourse can no longer be taken for granted. *The Waves* demonstrates more strenuously than any other novel by Woolf how the stream of consciousness, in its expressive projections, is licensed only by a simultaneous act of the unconscious which must attempt, often vainly, to posit, and position, a subject behind all its verbal *jection*. In this prose-poetic novel – whose chief characters are first a prose writer, a novelist in fact, second a poet, and third a woman consigned to and doomed by a nonaesthetic view of language – the drama of constituted subjectivity is played out within the soliloquies by the pressure of language exploiting its own clefts, ruptures, elisions, and deflections, its subjective continuity riven and recontrived, breached, appeased, or radically reconceived.

Among the characters of *The Waves*, this dispersal of self across the weft of language is most piercing a grief for Rhoda, an eventual suicide among those six friends whose collective evolution defines the novel, and most explicitly a metaphysical crisis for Bernard, the novelist of the group. This is because Bernard has all along had the greatest faith in the easing and healing power of language. For him 'words' are the potencies which, 'moving darkly, in the depths of your mind', will 'break up' the 'knot of hardness' (15) between separate selves. While other characters, for instance, 'cannot follow any word through its changes' (42), or 'sense themselves tied down with single words' (16), feel 'doomed', as one among them puts it, 'to be a clinger to the outside of words all my life', Bernard insists by contrast that 'we melt into each other with phrases' (16). As a novelist he is therefore 'dabbling always in warm soluble words' (68–9), shelling out 'the hot, molten effects', the 'lava flow of sentence into sentence' (79), by which language, dissolving under its own pressure, will burn away the borders of received distinctions.

Remembering that the working title of the narrative was originally *The Moths*, one understands better the sponsoring provenance of that self-exampling metaphor already quoted: 'the silver-grey flickering moth-win*g q*uiver of words' (215). Given the reduced junctural difference of *g* from *q*, the hyphen reads as a sub-phonemic filament binding the two sounds: an example of the transgressed segmentation to which this essay is directing attention. In addition to the incontestably, if barely, marked difference between the sound of *g* and the less guttural *q*, linguistics might resort also to the notion of 'suprasegmental phonemes', pitch, stress, and juncture, to enforce the lexical break between these magnetized, because nearly equivalent, letters.[35] Along similar lines, a greater problem yet for phonological 'disambiguation' arises with the attempt to distinguish aurally between such 'minimal pairs' as *an aim* and *a name*, *night rate* and *nitrate*, *light housekeeper* and *lighthouse keeper*.[36]

More likely in Woolf's (if not, say, in Joyce's) wordplay, however, is a differential alternative whose acoustic ambiguity depends on a blurring elision of two conflated letters rather than just on the quirky or defiant mobility of a single phoneme. We can see this, for instance, in the distinction between an idiomatic *eyes well* (with tears) and the actual phrasing Woolf has Susan utter at one point, which can be read simultaneously to contain that other expression of approximately the same thought: 'My eyes swell; my eyes prick with tears' (32–3). Anticipated by the narrowly achieved disjoining of internal rhyme in the doubled diphthong, which can be phonetically transcribed (M)/*ay*/ /*ay*/(s), the next requisite break at the doubled *s* is harder yet to ascertain and secure. Such a phonic crux has sometimes been addressed not only by the general notion of 'suprasegmentals' but by a sliding phoneme of 'zero' value, a so-called 'zero allophone of internal open juncture' that soundlessly inserts itself in one place or the other in order to assert the determining pause between morphemes.[37] For many linguists, however, this is a suspect account, a 'fiction' designed to rescue segmental autonomy.[38] As far as Woolf's adjusted and suspended junctures are concerned, one is advised to recall

Roman Jakobson's insistence on the inevitable dovetailing of phonemes: 'From a strictly articulatory point of view . . . there is no *succession* of sounds. Instead of following one another the sounds overlap.'[39] Woolf's style often seeks to maximize this fact. With 'eyes swell' it is also typical that her mitigation of the gap at the phonetic level, through a drifting sibilant, is matched at the semantic level by an ambivalence softened to the point of making no real substantive difference – except to the ear. We know that when Woolf was at work on the book still provisionally titled *The Moths*, she vowed explicitly to 'saturate every atom', and we can take this in part as a stylistic motto for the kind of effect I am here registering, as if she were out to make syllables themselves so replete that they spill over in that 'lava flow' of phrase sought by her novelist hero.[40]

Toward the end of the novel, however, Bernard has actually come to despair over the power of words to convey experience. Despite its plasticity, the opacity of language always sabotages its referential intent. 'There are no words' sufficient to his task, no words transparent enough. 'Blue, red – even they distract, even they hide with thickness instead of letting the light through' (287). Reality is masked rather than manifested by words. Unless of course, at the metalinguistic level, this phonic veiling, this lexical thickening and gathering, is precisely what such words are sometimes attempting to represent. A nexus like 'wi*th th*ickness' merely exaggerates the inevitable overlapping of phonemes either by an almost irresistible elision or by the laboured emphasis necessary to forestall it. Such phonemic clotting or 'thickening' at the edges can elsewhere suggest a merger or bleeding between semantic units, as when in an italicized interlude *'all the blades of the grass were run together in one fluent green blaze'* (149). Framing the whole clause is the phonemic matter of *'blades'* displaced to the undentalized, slightly compressed acoustic echo of *'blaze,'* not to mention the echo of *were run* in *one*. At the same time the entire verb phrase itself, *were run* (not just *re run*), slackened and rushed enough in enunciation, is pronounced as one swift blurred *run*. At most, however, this is only an acoustic collapse into a part term of the complete phrasal verb. The lexical segmentation succumbs at its border, but no new word emerges, no third term wrung from contiguity, or stretched between its scripted units. If this sentence had not been found in an italicized interlude, but in one of Rhoda's own paranoid speeches, we still would not have been disposed to hear in it, I think, either 'were untogether' or 'to get her,' because neither takes what we might call the path of least resistance in the complicity of eye and ear. These variant proposals flout respectively the norms of lexicon and vocal articulation, whereas a genuine transegmental effect slips in and out of audibility without doing comparable violence either to dictionary plausibility or to graphically signalled pronunciation.

Though 'were run' is thus likely to telescope only into an active (versus passive) version of itself, 'run', at other points in the novel a *liaison*, can – without fusing a usable new word – still seem to precipitate one at the close remove of internal rhymes. Jinny's fantasy of 'a thin dress shot wi*th red* threads' (34), for instance, involves a double stitch in the prose itself. Unamplified by such proximate repetition, there are also moments when the segmental border not only begins to give, but gives up a new verbal transform in the process: by an infinitesimal phonemic migration across the lexical gap. As usual, this occurs in the following example amid other, more salient manipulations of prose's acoustic wavelengths. After the syllabic but not orthographic play of the novel's opening italicized sentence, '*The SUN had not yet riSEN*' (matched at the start of the last interlude by '*Now the SUN had SUNk,*' 236), the second sentence of *The Waves* records how '*the SEA was slightly crEASed*' (7). To begin with, the chiastic gradation may suggest the chasm of the momentarily wave-opened valley it portrays. At the same time it frames a transegmental give in 'was slightly,' an easing of the shared sibilant. This drifting across the rift between words, what I am calling transegmental slippage, creates in this case only the virtually tautological ambiguity of 'lightly' versus 'slightly'. Nevertheless, it is in just such a slight wrinkle – or crease – that we glimpse most clearly the texturing momentum of Woolf's prose, a momentum that can elsewhere enact itself even more explicitly. In Bernard's last soliloquy, his flagging faith in language suddenly recovered, we hear that 'loveliness returns as one looks with all its *train* of phantom phrases' (287). Throughout the novel to this late point, a recurrent phantom in the successive train of Woolf's language has been the ghostly syllabic afterimage. In the present self-exampling case, the host word 'train' couples itself with the preceding sibilant to form upon its trace the new noun *strain*. To hear such a strain on the nexus of syntax in Woolf is to attune ourselves to a stylistics unpledged to the eye. This is what Joyce at the end of the decade, in a junctural pun that covertly labels the contradictory sensory allegiances of its own reading, calls in *Finnegans Wake*[41] 'an earsighted view'.[42] □

The final extract in this chapter is from Rachel Bowlby's influential study of Woolf, *Virginia Woolf: Feminist Destinations* (1988). In her chapter, 'Getting to Q: Sexual Lines in *To the Lighthouse*', she uses Freudian and Lacanian theories for a feminist interpretation of the novel.

■ A train arrives at a station. A little boy and a little girl, brother and sister, are seated in a compartment face to face next to the window through which the buildings along the station platform can be seen passing as the train pulls to a stop. 'Look', says the brother, 'we're at Ladies!'; 'Idiot!' replies his sister, 'Can't you see – we're at Gentlemen'.[43]

From this journey also dated the beginning of a 'phobia' of travelling by train, from which [Freud] suffered a good deal for about a dozen years (1887–99) before he was able to dispel it by analysis. It turned out to be connected with the fear of losing his home (and ultimately his mother's breast) – a panic of starvation which must have been in its turn a reaction to some infantile greed. Traces of it remained in later life in the form of slightly undue anxiety about catching trains.[44]

He was safe, he was restored to his privacy. He stopped to light his pipe, looked once at his wife and son in the window, and as one raises one's eyes from a page in an express train and sees a farm, a tree, a cluster of cottages as an illustration, a confirmation of something on the printed page to which one returns, fortified, and satisfied, so without his distinguishing either his son or his wife, the sight of them fortified him and satisfied him and consecrated his effort to arrive at a perfectly clear understanding of the problem which now engaged the energies of his splendid mind. (TL, 38–9)

This is Mr Ramsay securing sustenance from the image of his wife and son. The picture of familial harmony is analogous to the distant sight of the emblems of a pastoral idyll (farm, tree, 'cluster' of cottages), and the whole paragraph – a single sentence – is like an enactment in miniature of the structure of masculine subjectivity as Woolf analyses its impasses for both sexes in To the Lighthouse.

Mr Ramsay is (as if) on a train: he is moving at a fast rate along a line with a precise destination, and his 'effort' is 'to arrive' at a solution to his current 'problem'. In this endeavour, Mr Ramsay or the traveller is 'restored', 'fortified' and 'satisfied' – given strength, and given enough, like adequate nourishment – by seeing the image of rural completeness, and this is explicitly likened to the sight of the wife and child. In the same way, Mr Ramsay's 'problem' is validated in a quasi-religious sense – it is 'consecrated' – by the image of maternal wholeness. But the view from the train is also related to the text the passenger is reading. The far-off image gives 'confirmation' to what, it is implied, is the actual source of meaning on 'the printed page', but which is yet in some way lacking. It functions oddly both as secondary in relation to the meaning of the page, and as prior to the establishment of that meaning, 'to which one returns'.

This passage is immediately followed by another, much more

famous one, which by picking up on the 'splendid mind' might seem to act in turn as its 'confirmation':

> It was a splendid mind. For if thought is like the keyboard of a piano, divided into so many notes, or like the alphabet is ranged in twenty-six letters all in order, then his splendid mind had no sort of difficulty in running over those letters one by one, firmly and accurately, until it had reached, say, the letter Q. He reached Q. Very few people in the whole of England ever reach Q. . . . But after Q? What comes next? After Q there are a number of letters the last of which is scarcely visible to mortal eyes, but glimmers red in the distance. Z is only reached by one man in a generation. Still, if he could reach R it would be something. . . . Q he could demonstrate. If Q then is Q – R – (*TL*, 39)

We might liken this, first of all, to the simile of the previous paragraph. If Mr Ramsay is still in some way (like) a train passenger, the rails along which he travels have now become the letters of the alphabet, which also lead to a preordained destination that 'glimmers red in the distance' like the lights of a station. It is as if the letters on the printed page have been transposed so as to fuse with the stages of the journey: 'getting from A to B', in this account, would be equivalent to getting from A to Z. But the effect of this is to render them less, not more, meaningful. Whereas the page, by implication, could be understood to have a meaning of which the far-off picture was then a 'confirmation' – both the page and the image working as heterogeneous signs of the same meaning – the letters of the alphabet have no meaning at all but are simply listed, by convention, in one particular order, with each one being defined in terms of its adjacency to two others (or one other, in the case of the first and the last).

The 'splendid mind' makes of the moves from A to B to C a logical rather than simply a linear progression, and so lays claim to more significance than the alphabetically ordered lists of the British Museum reader in *A Room of One's Own* (*ROO*, 30–1). 'If Q then is Q – R –' takes up the notation of propositional logic, and suggests that each letter attained is an advance upon the previous one, not just a neutral point on a line made up of points of equal value. Woolf is able to get maximum comic mileage out of the fact that P and Q really are the letters conventionally used as signs in propositional logic, while Mr Ramsay's name begins with the 'next' letter, R. (There is extra mileage too, perhaps, for a certain V.W. from the fact that her own consecutive initials are further along; and in that R is indeed often wheeled on in formal logic examples where a third letter is required in addition to P and Q. . . .)

A further hint of an undermining of the main line of the simile occurs via the keyboard analogy, introduced at the beginning and then abandoned. For a keyboard's letters, though certainly sequential, go from A to G and then back to the beginning again: the bottom and top noted in terms of pitch may well have the 'same' name. And the move from the bottom to the top end of the keyboard – the piano being rather like the printed page with its implicit direction from left to right – involves repetitions rather than progression, when viewed in terms of letter names. The repercussions of this tacit conflation of the repetition and the sequence extend, as we shall see, to the differential and intersecting lines of each sex's 'normal' development.

In his *Three Essays on the Theory of Sexuality* (1905), Freud suggests a close connection between fantasies and trains: 'The shaking produced by driving in carriages and later by railway-travel exercises such a fascinating effect upon older children that every boy, at any rate, has at one time or other in his life wanted to be an engine driver or coachman.'[45] The fact that having first said that the fascination of trains affects 'older children' in general, Freud then signals this kind of dream as every boy's, is suggestive. Going back for a moment to Woolf's simile of the alphabet and piano ('If thought is like the keyboard . . .'), we might say: 'If masculine development is like a train journey . . .', and then see how far this takes us.

Woolf's explorations of what makes the difference of the sexes are uncannily close to Freud's in another key, and this may be related to the fact that his writings were much discussed in Woolf's social circle. The Hogarth Press, which she founded with her husband Leonard Woolf, published the first translations of Freud in Britain (and later in the 1950s and 1960s, the Standard Edition).[46] Woolf drew directly on psychoanalytic insights in her prose writings (especially *Three Guineas*), but she also made use of them in her fiction. *To the Lighthouse* is particularly interesting in this regard because Woolf said of its writing: 'I suppose I did for myself what psycho-analysts do for their patients. I expressed some very long felt and deeply felt emotion. And in expressing it I explained it and then laid it to rest' (*MB*, 94). This declaration gives one justification for the identification of Woolf with Lily Briscoe, the daughter figure and artist as outsider who then looks back at the relation between her 'parents' and hers to them.

In the psychoanalytic account of human development, there is no subjectivity without sexual difference, and there is no natural, programmed progression for those of either biological sex towards the achievement of the 'masculine' or 'feminine' identity socially ascribed. Because the dominant line is that of masculinity, the girl's understanding of the meaning of sexual difference implies coming to terms with her *de facto* eccentricity, forced to take up a position in relation to the norm from which she is by definition excluded: as the image of maternal fulfilment seen from the train window, as the 'woman' despised for her lack of the masculine attribute, or as an interloper into the compartment reserved for men.

One way of looking at masculine development would be to say, in the teleology of social purpose, that its object is to get the boy onto the train, headed for a respectable destination, but still fired at some level by the fantasy of being Casey Jones at the throttle. But this is to go too fast, or to look only from one direction: put the other way around, the same process appears also as an inevitable lack of fit between the situation of the social subject as passenger and his residual fantasy of being, in the end, a hero. The mother figures in both perspectives as the imagined plenitude of a childhood left behind, but still there as the source of meaning and authentication for the work or journey in progress. Freud says that a man seeks in adult life to find again, in the form of a wife, the figure of support to whom he 'returns' for reassurance of his powers and centrality. Yet this reassurance refers to what he nonetheless lacks, to the extent that the social train admits him only at the price of a ticket which makes him like every other conforming passenger who has accepted the conditions of travel.

Mr Ramsay's blundering towards a possible R which will never be the Z of 'one man in a generation' perfectly illustrates such a pattern. He is likened to the resigned leader of an unsuccessful expedition:

> . . . Who shall blame him? Who will not secretly rejoice when the hero puts his armour off, and halts by the window and gazes at his wife and son . . . and bending his magnificent head before her – who will blame him if he does homage to the beauty of the world? (*TL*, 40 2)

The 'expedition' – a journey with a goal, the attainment of which would ensure immortal fame to the leader – remains as the structuring fantasy for the philosopher resigned to getting no further than halfway, to being one of the 'plodding and persevering' rather than a man of 'genius': 'the gifted, the inspired who, miraculously, lump all the letters together in one flash' (40). And in the age of the train, the journey is figured in the more heroic imagery of the pioneering explorer.

Even Mr Ramsay's 'abstract' philosophical speculations seem to be related to the need to come to terms with a social hierarchy of men in which he does not necessarily occupy the place of 'genius':

> Does the progress of civilisation depend upon great men? Is the lot of the average human being better now than in the time of the Pharoahs? Is the lot of the average human being, however, he

asked himself, the criterion by which we judge the measure of civilisation? Possibly not. Possibly the greatest good requires the existence of a slave class. The liftman in the Tube is an eternal necessity. (*TL*, 67)

Here the path of the individual is transposed to the field of 'civilisation', which is also endowed with a hypothetical line of progression whose 'measure' can be decided. In this context of the great man *manqué*, it is the picture of maternal plenitude – his own wife and child, the reverenced 'beauty' of the woman – which provides, restores, a form of compensation. This is not incompatible with the fact that the acquisition of dependents in the form of wife and children – the settling down to the normality of the 'average' man – is also, in Mr Bankes's view, the reason for Mr Ramsay's failure to fulfil his early promise as a philosopher. The woman is placed in the contradictory position of being both source of meaning for the masculine project (that which 'fortifies' the traveller) and a constraint, the scapegoat for its necessary failure in the original heroic mode of its conception.

Mr Ramsay's relation to his wife suggests the man's wish to return to the position of the child in relation to a woman like his mother. According to Freud, it is insofar as she identifies with her mother that the woman

acquires her attractiveness to a man, whose Oedipus attachment to his mother it kindles into passion. How often it happens, however, that it is only his son who obtains what he himself aspired to! One gets an impression that a man's love and a woman's are a phase apart psychologically.[47]

The resentment of James – 'hating his father' (36) – for Mr Ramsay's prior claims to his mother parallels Freud's Oedipal scenario, where the boy wants nothing less than to put out of the way the father who asserts his rights to the mother. Looking at it from the husband's point of view, Mr Ramsay attempts to recover, with another woman, the relation of dependence and centrality in which he once stood, or imagines he once stood, to his own mother: after receiving the sympathy he claims from his wife, he is 'like a child who drops off satisfied' (44). Yet this harmony of oneness with the mother figure, which his wife is called upon to secure, can necessarily never be restored completely once it is posed in terms of a constitutive loss. Mr Ramsay's demands for reassurance of his uniqueness are doomed to be endlessly repeated: 'this was one of those moments when an enormous need urged him, without being conscious what it was, to approach any woman, to force them, he did not care how, his need was so great, to give him what he wanted: sympathy' (165). Only in fantasy can the exorbitant request be satisfactorily answered:

> Sitting in the boat, he bowed, he crouched himself, acting instantly his part – the part of a desolate man, widowed, bereft; and so called up before him in hosts people sympathising with him; staged for himself as he sat in the boat, a little drama; which required of him decrepitude and exhaustion and sorrow . . . and then there was given him in abundance women's sympathy, and he imagined how they would soothe him and sympathise with him. (*TL*, 181)

Other men in the novel are represented as threatened in similar ways in that identity, and seeking to have it given or restored to them through the intercession of an all-providing Mrs Ramsay. Charles Tansley, the young protégé of her husband, unburdens himself of his hard-luck story: 'He had wanted to tell her everything about himself' (18). She had first confided in him the story of Mr Carmichael's 'unfortunate marriage', with the comment that 'he should have been a great philosopher' (14). In reading this as a parable of proper relations between the sexes (and not, for example, noticing its ironic reference to Mrs Ramsay's own case, where the very dependence of Mr Ramsay, rather than the marriage's ending, is allegedly what has restrained his philosophising), Tansley is 'flattered':

> Charles Tansley revived. Insinuating, too, as she did the greatness of man's intellect, even in its decay, the subjection of all wives . . . to their husband's labours, she made him feel better pleased with himself than he had done yet, and he would have liked, had they taken a cab, for example, to have paid for it. As for her little bag, might he not carry that? . . . He would like her to see him, gowned and hooded, walking in a procession. (*TL*, 15)[48]

But the final result of 'that extraordinary emotion which had been growing all the walk' (18) is a revelation:

> In she came, stood for a moment silent . . . stood quite motionless for a moment against a picture of Queen Victoria wearing the blue ribbon of the Garter; and all at once he realised that it was this: it was this: – she was the most beautiful person he had ever seen.
>
> With stars in her eyes and veils in her hair, with cyclamen and wild violets – what nonsense was he thinking? She was fifty at least; she had eight children. (*TL*, 18)

Momentarily the virgin, the queen and the mother coalesce into a mute image which makes the man something more than what he took himself previously to be: 'for the first time in his life Charles Tansley felt an extraordinary pride' (18–19). The woman's perfection and summation of every part establishes the man's identity.

It is the asymmetry of Freud's 'phase apart' that now points the way towards a consideration of the difference in the developments of boys and girls. For if the metaphors of journey, destination, progression – indeed, of 'development' itself in so far as the word implies determinate stages towards an end already known – are useful in thinking of the case of the man, they are less obviously applied to that of the woman imagined as the sustaining object of the gaze from the window. It was the realisation of this asymmetry, prompted by the criticisms of other analysts including women, which led Freud, in what can appear retroactively as his own logical 'line' of intellectual development, to consider what was different in the girl's development to what is called femininity rather than to assume it as a progression along parallel lines to the boy's development to what is called masculinity.

It would seem that girls are placed in a structurally untenable position insofar as the main line of human development is concerned. For if subjectivity is figured by the place on the train, with the mother in the distance, left behind and idealised, but women in general devalued and despised for their lack of the attribute of masculinity, then women are effectively put in two places at once, both of which are undesirable. The third possibility is the place on the train, as part of the 'procession', but that is by definition deemed unwomanly as being reserved for men. The difficulty of reaching 'femininity' is emphasised by Freud when he speaks of no less than three possible 'lines of development' for girls after they have understood the meaning of sexual difference. Only one of these lines goes to 'normal' femininity (heterosexuality and motherhood); the other two, frigidity and homosexuality, each represent different versions of the refusal of the 'normal' feminine position.

'Anatomy is destiny', so often taken as the Freudian condemnation of women to a conventionally feminine fate, is rather the marking of the way that determinate social meanings are arbitrarily imposed upon subjects of either anatomical sex, and in far less tenable ways for the woman. Freud's account of the trials of the girl on her way to what is prescribed as normal femininity makes her development sound like a switchback railway journey thwarted by upheavals and potential reversals at every turn.[49] As has often been pointed out, these very difficulties can be taken as a kind of allegory of the impossibility for 'woman' of finding an approximate identity to match – to challenge and to fit in with – that of the masculine scenario which has already put her in certain contradictory positions. Masculine identity is permanently under threat, but 'femininity' never has the pretence to any positive content to begin with.

Mrs Ramsay seems to others the image of fulfilled womanhood, but does not sustain the equanimity she constantly proffers to assuage their doubts and floundering: 'for the most part, oddly enough, she must admit that she felt this thing that she called life terrible, hostile, and quick to pounce on you if you gave it a chance' (66). Her perpetual mothering represents for her the only way of holding at bay 'this thing' that is always ready to spring. 'She would have liked always to have had a baby' (65), and her demand upon others, 'that people must marry; people must have children' (67) is said to emanate not from assurance but from a negotiation of what would otherwise be despair. Mrs Ramsay's own capacity to ease the sufferings of those around her is exposed as resting on her acknowledgement that the alleviation is only a patching over of a fundamental discord:

> She had often the feeling, Why must they grow up and lose it all? And then she said to herself, brandishing her sword at life, nonsense. They will be perfectly happy. And here she was, she reflected, feeling life rather sinister again, making Minta marry Paul Rayley. (*TL*, 67)

The incompatibility of the marital relations upon which Mrs Ramsay nonetheless so vehemently insists is brought to the surface in the Grimm story she reads to James of the fisherman and his wife:

> Flounder, flounder, in the sea
> Come, I pray thee, here to me;
> For my wife, good Ilsabil,
> Wills not as I'd have her will. (*TL*, 63)

'"Well, what does she want then?" said the Flounder' (63), echoing – or anticipating – Freud's famous formulation. What he, Mr Ramsay, would have her will, she tries to will, and yet there remains a discrepancy after she has 'satisfied' him, after 'there throbbed through her . . . the rapture of successful creation' (61) which seems then to create or to comfort her too:

> Every throb of this pulse seemed, as he walked away, to enclose her and her husband, and to give to each that solace which two different notes, one high, one low, struck together, seem to give each other as they combine. Yet, as the resonance died, and she turned to the Fairy Tale again, Mrs Ramsay felt not only exhausted in body . . . but also there tinged her physical fatigue some faintly disagreeable sensation with another origin. (*TL*, 44)

Mrs Ramsay is 'discomposed' by the 'disagreeable sensation' which itself has more than one part: not liking the public aspect of 'his coming to her like that, openly' for reassurance; not liking 'to feel finer than her husband'; 'not being entirely sure' that he is as fine as she tells him he is to soothe him. Rather than 'the entire joy, the pure joy, of the two notes sounding together', the outcome of the exchange reminds her of a discordance, of what she calls (in the latest psychological language) 'the inadequacy of human relationships' (45). The image of perfect complementarity and reciprocity between the sexes shows itself to mask a basic disunity of parts that in fact do not fit, either within her or between the two of them.

If Mrs Ramsay endeavours to preserve the spectacle of the composure of feminine and masculine relationships, Lily Briscoe is placed outside this structure, fascinated by it but resisting incorporation into it as a woman who, in Mrs Ramsay's scheme, should marry Mr Bankes. Against Mrs Ramsay's urging that 'an unmarried woman has missed the best of life' (56), and Charles Tansley's running insistence that 'women can't paint, women can't write' (54), Lily 'would urge her own exemption from the universal law' (56); and this makes her, as when she is about to fail to give Mr Ramsay the solace he demands of her, 'not a woman' (165). 'That man, she thought, her anger rising in her, never gave; that man took. She, on the other hand, would be forced to give. Mrs Ramsay had given. Giving, giving, giving, she had died' (163).

In making of Lily a cultural and sexual rebel against 'the universal law', the novel seems to place her as the antithesis to Mrs Ramsay, whose energies are dedicated to the maintenance of all that Lily repudiates in her prescribed sexual destiny. Yet from another point of view, as has often been pointed out, their projects are analogous. The unification or bringing together of disparate things, of the 'discomposed', which Mrs Ramsay seeks to achieve by marryings and motherings, is also what Lily attempts in the field of art:

Mrs Ramsay making of the moment something permanent (as in another sphere Lily herself tried to make of the moment something permanent) – this was of the nature of a revelation. In the midst of chaos there was shape; this eternal passing and flowing . . . was struck into stability. (TL, 176)

This 'revelation' itself stands out in the narrative as a 'moment' to give coherence, a nodal point perhaps upon which to base a general interpretation of To the Lighthouse. Such a view lends itself readily to being brought into connection with Woolf's own interest in and endorsement of a particular modernist conception of the function of art: that the work of art makes in its own autonomous medium the unity which in the world itself is lacking. In the biographical reading of the Lily/Mrs Ramsay connection/opposition, Lily, like Virginia Stephen, represents the virginal artist daughter of the Victorian 'Angel in the House', moving tentatively away from the restrictions on female expectations to become what Mrs Ramsay thinks of as 'an independent little creature' (21). This parallel is borne out by the statements in Woolf's memoirs and her diary indicating that the writing of *To the Lighthouse* finally routed or put to rest the ghost of a too angelic mother who had haunted her since her death, when Virginia was only thirteen.

But it could be argued that the moment of unity, the apparently resolved triple sequence of times collected together in the completion of Lily Briscoe's picture, only emphasises all the more strongly the underlying lack of harmony in 'human relationships', as in the art or institutions which attempt to cover over their 'inadequacy'. This is the alternative I have stressed in examining what undermines the unity of the most apparently unifying or unified of characters and episodes in the novel. But this is not then to argue that it is more 'adequate' to posit a general flux and fragmentation than a final unification. Rather, *To the Lighthouse* explores both the insistence and the untenability of the prevailing constructions of masculine and feminine identities, showing how the two are neither complementary, making a whole, nor ever reached in their imaginary completion by individuals of either sex. In particular, the conquering hero and the angel in the house are (masculine) fantasies, and it is in relation to them that men and women have to take up their parts, more or less adequately.

The three sections of *To the Lighthouse* are distinguished by different forms of temporality. The first and third focus, as often in Woolf's novels, on a single day and the associative links which connect it, in the consciousnesses of the characters and along the narrative line, to other times and places. The 'present moment' is divided and encompasses more than one time, and this effect is multiplied by the number of characters in such a way that their coming together as a group – for instance, in the dinner party scene – constitutes only a tenuous and ephemeral connection of many heterogeneous parts. Woolf uses the classical structure of a tragedy, with the action taking place in the course of a single day, to unwind the schematic outlines according to which persons, lives and events appear as comprehensible and consistent. The multiple layers of the day and the question of the position from which the narrator sees what she sees detract from the plausibility of a straightforward narrative, which might be characterised as a confidence in asserting or retracing the single way in which 'one thing led to another' (*BA*, 47).[50]

The middle section, 'Time Passes', makes Mrs Ramsay's death

parenthetical, literally, to a general lack of differentiation from which identifiable human agency is absent, except for the ambivalent questioning of 'sea airs' (*TL*, 141), or the half-acknowledged place of the narrator:

> Night after night, summer and winter, the torment of storms, the arrow-like stillness of fine weather, held their court without interference. Listening (had there been anyone to listen) from the upper rooms of the empty house only gigantic chaos streaked with lightning could have been heard tumbling and tossing. (*TL*, 146–7)

In this part, 'time passing' is represented rather as cyclical repetition than as the multiple story lines or criss-cross networks – to the past, and to other places – of a day. Natural rhythms take precedence over the appeal to any kind of progression or linear development: there is no specificity of a differentiated past or elsewhere structuring the present. But the half-acknowledged narrator also identifies the abandoned house as a kind of aesthetic image of natural, self-contained peace.

> So loveliness reigned and stillness, and together made the shape of loveliness itself, a form from which life had parted; solitary like a pool at evening, far distant, seen from a train window, vanishing so quickly that the pool, pale in the evening, is scarcely robbed of its solitude, though once seen. (*TL*, 141)

Neither of these two forms of temporality, or atemporality – the changelessness of the 'form', 'the shape of loveliness', or the repeated movements of a chaotic nature – apparently bears any relation to the linearity identified as masculine: they are like obverse sides against which it appears as an arbitrary imposition.

The other kinds of time – that of night and day, of waves, of seasons and years, or that of still form, signify no progression but the bareness of natural cycles, permanent recurrence and alternation, or else static completeness. It is these times which are often associated with femininity as cyclical and 'reproductive', or as iconic and eternal, and which are differentiated in *To the Lighthouse* from the arbitrary sequences of masterful 'masculine' temporality.

Yet in terms of the sexual structuring of subjectivity, this difference is far from absolute: it is not a dualism of two unrelated types. As with the interconnection of repetition and linearity in the keyboard simile, the 'shape of loveliness itself', likened to a pool glimpsed from a train window, acquires its meaning in relation to the distance and direction of the place from which it is seen. What appears as the pure origin of life in Mrs Ramsay ('this delicious fecundity' (42–3)) is so only by virtue of its capacity to symbolise the antithesis of the end-directed cultural purposes of 'the fatal sterility of the male' (43). It is at once the basis of meaning to authenticate the otherwise indefinite and wavering series of A to Z, and a means of comfort, representing an attempted restoration of infantile dependence and centrality. It also represents freedom from the 'failure' (43) which threatens to engulf from the point at which a man joins the line of ambitious males headed and herded towards the letter R and beyond. The image of the succouring, nurturing woman serves to supply – and necessarily to fail to supply – the gap between R and Z, making up for his inevitable incapacity to get to the end of his line.

The absoluteness of the distinction between different times is also undermined in other ways. The repetitive work of the old women on the decaying house prevents rather than inducing a return to a natural state – 'the whole house would have plunged to the depths to lie upon the sands of oblivion' (151) – and is thus eminently a cultural enterprise. As if to underline this almost ironically, the restoration work is precipitated by the women's receipt of an imperious letter from the remnants of the Ramsay family: 'All of a sudden, would Mrs McNab see that the house was ready, one of the young ladies wrote' (209). This brings Mrs McNab closer to what Mr Ramsay abstracts into the 'possible eternal necessity' of 'the liftman in the Tube' (49) than to a figure for the eternal feminine. But Mrs McNab's work against the dereliction of the house is also similar in form to the time pattern of Mrs Ramsay's life of dailiness. For the latter, 'the monotonous fall of the waves on the beach' is either consoling or admonitory, warning 'her whose day had slipped past in one quick doing after another that it was all ephemeral as a rainbow' (20). So again, the clear division of different modes of temporality is made more complicated. The beat of the waves is not only a soothing return to cradle songs: it can also signify a forward march towards an end whose approach measures the dissipation of wasted days. The forms of feminine subjectivity cannot be separated from their position in relation to the governing order of masculine temporality.

If the 'Time Passes' section of *To the Lighthouse* figures as the antithesis against which the man's letters appear in sharpest outline and opposition, the first and third parts also – but differently – depart from that line, showing its multiple layers and complex crossings and intersections, like Mrs Ramsay's knitting. So different a view of the narrative line – without a place of mastery, and resembling a network or imbrication of many times, places, memories and fantasies – could be said to be feminine in that it looks beyond – just glimpses further than – the certainties of the recognisable, single line. If this is what constitutes the difference of modernist from realist narrative, it might also be what makes modernism in a certain sense 'feminine'.[51] For the time being, that 'feminine' is so by virtue of its pursuing different, less direct lines from those identified as masculine: by its moving away from what it regards, from another position, as the false neutrality and universality of the principal, masculine line.

To the Lighthouse makes evident the mapping of human subjectivity in terms of figurations inseparable from sexual difference, and it also shows the lack of fit, the 'phase apart', entailed by the discrepancy between the train of masculinity and the various outsider positions into which the woman is cast:

> ('Nature has but little clay,' said Mr Bankes once, hearing her voice on the telephone, and much moved by it though she was only telling him a fact about a train, 'like that of which she moulded you.' He saw her at the end of the line, Greek, blue-eyed, straight-nosed. How incongruous it seemed to be telephoning to a woman like that . . .) (*TL*, 46–7)

The woman moves the man to a poetic language quite different from the factual language of timetables. He imagines her as a Greek statue or goddess, returning backwards along a cultural line where artistic and feminine purity can be clearly seen, and which is marked by pathos through its necessary difference from the here and now associated with the mechanical lines of the railway and the phone. 'How incongruous it seemed to be telephoning to a woman like that' could be taken to condense all the features of the unparallel lines of masculine and feminine journeys. Just as the simile of the train passenger contrasted the straight progression along an arbitrary line with the image of the woman as restorer or giver of meaning, so Mr Bankes casts the lady in a mould of aesthetic perfection and endows her with the function of making up for the mechanical and routinised lines in the modern world.

The eventual arrival at the lighthouse, and the eventual completion or composition of Lily Briscoe's picture of James and Mrs Ramsay, are so belated in the novel as to put in question the very progression of which their achievement appears, at length, as a kind of formal culmination. This is no Z at the end of the alphabet, but rather the discovery of a different kind of line, contrary to the 'doomed expedition' (57) ordained for the forward march of masculine history. How to represent a more complex feminine or feminist temporality, against the simple lines of sequential progress, is one of the questions of *Mrs Dalloway*.[52] □

CHAPTER SIX

The 1990s: Historical, Materialist, Post-colonialist Readings

AT THE same time as sexual/textual deconstructive and psycho-analytical readings of *To the Lighthouse* and *The Waves* were developing, so too were contextual readings which examine Woolf's writing in relation to history, politics, culture, and 'the real world', as Alex Zwerdling puts it in his influential study (1986). This book did much to reassert Woolf's status as a politically engaged writer, but in comparison to recent developments in criticism, it remains limited by some of the preconceptions of earlier critics. Most notably, Zwerdling has little to say on *The Waves*, which he regards as the dead-end for Woolf's experimentalist prose.[1] It is this very novel, however, that in the 1990s has become the focus of renewed historico-political readings in Woolf. Whereas book titles such as Moi's encapsulate the concerns of the last chapter, the concerns of this one are expressed by titles such as that of Zwerdling's monograph or of Mark Hussey's collection, *Virginia Woolf and War: Fiction, Reality, and Myth* (1991).[2] Another influential work from the 1980s is Kate Flint's essay, 'Virginia Woolf and the General Strike' (1986),[3] which reads the central section of *To the Lighthouse* with reference to the political upheavals that formed the context to its composition.[4] 'Time Passes', for so long considered a flight of experimental lyric prose or philosophical reverie, is thus opened up to historical materialist analysis. Woolf and her husband gave considerable support to the strikers, but Flint's reading draws on Woolf's diary entries during the strike which show her ambivalent feelings toward the crisis, her desire for reconciliation, and some contradictory attitudes toward the working class. This is a more empirically-based than theoretically-engaged study, but it stands nevertheless as an influential and informative contribution to criticism of *To the Lighthouse*.

The two extracts for this chapter are from the 1990s. The first is from Jane Marcus's ground-breaking essay on *The Waves* as anti-imperialist text; and the second is from Janet Winston's recent analysis of imperial discourses in *To the Lighthouse*. Just as some of the psychoanalytical and deconstructive criticism we looked at in the last chapter is not without awareness of political, cultural and historical implications, so the criticism represented here may be seen to engage with elements of 'sexual/textual' criticism. And just as Flint causes us to rethink our understanding of the high modernist aesthetics of Woolf's prose, so Marcus, in abandoning her earlier view of its interrelated feminism and mysticism, has confronted us with new ways of reading that Ur-modernist text, *The Waves*.

■ What has made it impossible for us to live in time like fish in water, like birds in air, like children? It is the fault of Empire! Empire has created the time of history. Empire has located its existence not in the smooth recurrent spinning time of the cycle of the seasons but in the jagged time of rise and fall, of beginning and end, of catastrophe. Empire dooms itself to live in history and plot against history. One thought alone preoccupies the submerged mind of Empire: how not to end, how not to die, how to prolong its era. By day it pursues its enemies. . . . By night it feeds on images of disaster.

– J.M. Coetzee, *Waiting for the Barbarians*

The waves drummed on the shore, like turbaned warriors, like turbaned men with poisoned assegais who, whirling their arms on high, advance upon the feeding flocks, the white sheep.

– Virginia Woolf, *The Waves*

[*Rise and Fall*]

Canon building is Empire building. Canon defense is national defense. Canon debate, whatever the terrain, nature and range (of criticism, of history, of the history of knowledge, of the definition of language, the universality of aesthetic principles, the sociology of art, the humanist imagination), is the clash of cultures. And *all* of the interests are vested.

– Toni Morrison, 'Unspeakable Things Unspoken'

Virginia Woolf's novel *The Waves* (1931) has consistently been read critically as a work of High Modernism, a novel of the thirties that is not a thirties novel. Its canonical status has been based on a series of misreadings of this poetic text and of Woolf herself as synonymous with and celebratory of upper-class genteel British culture. My reading claims that *The Waves* is the story of 'the submerged mind of empire'. Woolf has, to use Coetzee's terms (133), set her experimental antinovel in 'the jagged time of rise and fall', explicitly repeating the words 'rise and fall and rise again' throughout the text. But this text (roman typeface as opposed to the italics recording the rise and setting of the sun) of humans making their life history (plotting against history?) is surrounded by an italicized text of 'spinning time' in the cycle of the seasons. These italicized interludes take the form of a set of Hindu prayers to the sun, called Gayatri, marking its course during a single day. These (Eastern) episodes surround a (Western) narrative of the fall of British imperialism. Imperialist history is divided into chapters called 'the rise of . . .' or 'the fall of . . .'. *The Waves* explores the way in which the cultural narrative 'England' is created by an Eton/ Cambridge elite who (re)produce the national epic (the rise of . . .) and elegy (the fall of . . .) in praise of the hero. The poetic language and experimental structure of this modernist classic are vehicles for a radical politics that is both anti-imperialist and anticanonical.[5]

Woolf dramatizes the death of the white male Western author, Bernard, his fixation with 'how not to die,' while exposing the writer's collusion in keeping alive the myth of individualism and self-hood that fuels English patriotism and nationalism. This violent homosocial narrative of English national identity, in its simple-minded racism (and sexism) and nostalgia for class bias, which Woolf merci-lessly parodies in an infantilized fictional focalization of 'he said' and 'she said', is nevertheless so powerful in its intertextuality with hundreds of lines from familiar Romantic poems that readers for five decades have been taught to read Percival and Bernard as Hero and Poet, without recognizing Woolf's fictional prophecy of fascist charac-ters. *The Waves* quotes (and misquotes) Shelley, not to praise him but to bury him. Woolf is infusing her discourse about Orientalism in England at the beginning of the post-colonial period with Shelley's Orientalism, exposing the implications of race and gender in the still-living English Romantic quest for a self and definition of the (white male) self against the racial or sexual Other. There has been so much critical resistance to Woolf's politics that her anti-imperialist effort of enclosing a Western narrative in an Eastern narrative in order to critique Western philosophy and politics in *The Waves* may have seemed too radical for a descendant of Anglo-Indian policymakers. But as a socialist, feminist, and pacifist, Woolf had far more reason to explore Indian history and religion than T.S. Eliot did, for example, whose references to the great Indian texts are taken seriously. It is my contention that Woolf uses Shelley's poems, specifically 'The Indian Girl's Song,' to create a discourse for an alienated Western woman like Rhoda to have a 'heroic death', like Indian widows in sati.

In creating Rhoda's internal speech out of the texts of Shelley's poems, Woolf participates in and exposes at least two historical Orientalisms that force us to look at race and gender in relation to colonialism. Shelley's visions of Indian love/death come from his readings of Sydney Owenson's (Lady Morgan's) novel *The Missionary* (1811), as hers came from reading Sir William Jones, an early English 'Orientalist'. The abjection of Rhoda's suicide is politicized by mirroring the acts of Shelley's Indian maidens, though her Western sati is death by water, not by fire. Rhoda's silence invokes the silence of the Indian woman (Gramsci and Spivak's 'subaltern'?), so verbal and intellectual a figure in Owenson but transformed in Shelley into a Romantic suicide, thereafter speechless, absent, or dead in Western texts. Shelley's Romanticization of sati recalls British colonial chivalry, arguing that colonialism would free Indian women from such 'barbaric' practices, as one patriarchy invokes its superiority to another patriarchy, in the same way that the overturned bullock cart, righted by Percival, recalls the throngs of worshipers run over and killed by Krishna's cart at religious celebrations, another excuse for English intervention.

The history of the reception of the text, particularly its rejection by those leftist critics whose ideology it presumably shares, exposes an awkward gender and class bias, a certain paternalism in British Left criticism from Leavis to Williams, which cannot come to terms with a Marxist novel that is not realist, an anti-imperialist novel that is not (I am sorry to say) written by a man.[6] The failure of the text to reach its contemporary intended audience, and its subsequent status as 'difficult' or only available to an elite, have ensured its relegation to the unread, except in formalist or philosophical terms, and have operated as a cultural imperative that continues to deprive Virginia Woolf of readers of color or of the working class. Left-wing guardians of English culture steered such readers to Lawrence and Orwell for their moral and political heritage, rather than to the radicalism of Woolf. What a different narrative of modernism might have emerged if Jameson had read *The Waves* with Conrad's *Lord Jim* as exposing the ideology of the British ruling class. Perhaps he would have been forced to question his privileging of *Lord Jim*.

Said's praise of *Kim* and Jameson's exploration of fascist modernism are moves that seem deliberately to avoid reading or acknowledgement of the profound critique of imperialism and the class system in Virginia Woolf's work. Some very astute critics are unable to accept Woolf's irony about an author figure so like herself in the portrait of Bernard; they ignore the antipatriotic and anti-imperialist outbursts in the text because they are inconsistent with these critics' notion of the author's politics, based on her gender and class. The interpretative history of *The Waves* for a socialist feminist critic, then, is largely a negative burden, for *The Waves* simply does not exist as a cultural icon of the 1930s, as part of the discourse about (the rise of . . .) fascism, war, and imperialism in which it participated. The critical act of replacing it in this discourse is an aggressive cultural move made possible now, I would argue, by the legitimation of cultural studies and the combined methodologies of feminism, Marxism, revisionist Orientalism, and the recognition of certain postmodern characteristics in some modernist texts.

The rescue of the text, which I here attempt, is addressed to those deeply indoctrinated by the Leavisite legacy of a mythical 'Virginia Woolf', created to stand for that elite, effete English culture against which the democratic Great Tradition strenuously struggled. Adena Rosmarin has theorized the cultural process of recuperative reading: 'the argument that best accounts for the work is coincident with the argument that best accounts for the manifold histories of its reworkings' (21), an idea that moves me to say it is the project of cultural studies that now allows one to read *The Waves* as a narrative about culture making. Exploring the relations between race, class, and gender in the text and in the history of its production allows us to see those forces at work in criticism as well. Bernard in *The Waves* authorizes his role as inheritor of civilization by summoning a recurring vision of a 'lady at a table writing, the gardeners with their great brooms sweeping' (192). This is a vision in which English culture is represented as an aristocratic female figure in a grand country house called Elvedon, leisure for creativity provided by the security of the fixed class position of servants. Bernard insists that the two figures are inseparable, that you cannot have one without the other. As inheritor of culture, he will always have a Mrs. Moffat to 'sweep it all up'. The figure of the lady represents the gentleman artist; once the reader pries apart Bernard's pairing of the writing classes and the sweeping classes and questions the inevitability of Elvedon as a figure for art, it is possible to read the novel as a critique of the culture-making process, and especially as Woolf's feminist exploration of the patriarchal representation of Woman as Culture, a representation that nevertheless silences and intimidates women like Rhoda. Bernard's fetishized Portrait of the Artist as a Lady has more to do with his own image as a ruling-class writer than the possibility of women's producing culture. (Desmond MacCarthy, the model for Bernard, would never concede that there were any great women writers.)

Marina Warner, in *Monuments and Maidens: The Allegory of the Female Form*, discusses the allegorical use of female figures for national and imperial projects. She wittily points out the irony in the history of the symbolism of Britannia, in recent years portentously figuring official state power in cartoons of Mrs. Thatcher as the armed warrior woman when, in fact, Britannia was originally a figure on coins struck by the Roman emperors Hadrian and Antoninus Pius to celebrate the colonisation of Britain. In the seventeenth century Britannia was mythologised as the British constitution and the triumphant naval nation, and engraved with Neptune yielding his sceptre to her. In 1740 James Thomson's poem 'Rule, Britannia!' with music by Thomas Arne, was sung as the finale of his masque *Alfred*; it did not become a popular unofficial national anthem until the next century. Thomson's text reflects the tension between free democracy and the dread ruler of subject nations: Britannia is commanded to rule as if in fearful memory of Roman subjection; other nations are joyfully given over to tyrants while Britons shout their determination never, never to be slaves. This is a fitting anthem for imperialists.

As nineteenth-century figures of Britannia began to impersonate Athena, the democratic persona gave way to the figure of might and power. Warner writes: 'It is noteworthy that Britannia appears more frequently on the stamps of subject nations than on the stamps of Great Britain herself, revealing her shift from personification of a free people to symbol of the authority which endorses it' (49). My calling upon the figure of Britannia in the title of this essay is meant to convey the national anxiety of the former colony about the colonizing process itself, as if there were no other role but colonizer or colonized. The Lady at a Table Writing serves as a 'Britannia' figure and an allegory for Bernard. But in order to read it this way, one has to be open to irony in Woolf's voice, particularly toward Bernard, the writer figure, and be aware of and open to Woolf's critique of class and empire. Bernard is a parody of authorship; his words are a postmodern pastiche of quotation from the master texts of English literature.

Woolf's 'biographeme', her model for the character of Bernard, is Desmond MacCarthy, the man of letters, editor of *Life and Letters*, prominent reviewer and arbiter of taste, writing as 'Affable Hawk' a series of judgements of literary value in which he claims that there is no such thing as a 'great' woman artist (Woolf argued the point with him in 'The Intellectual Status of Women', but he never wavered). This process by which the actual Desmond and the fictional Bernard figure Woman as Culture while denying either women or the working class the possibility of creating culture, to follow Rosmarin again, can be plotted both in formalist and materialist readings of *The Waves* and in the problematic scapegoating of Virginia Woolf herself. She may represent culture, but she may not create it. Insofar as Elvedon *is* Bloomsbury in the novel and Bloomsbury/Virginia Woolf is an enormous inflated straw woman against whom both the Left and Right may fulminate (and did; and still do?) from the 1930s to the present, we notice that the figure of Woman as Culture in *The Waves* is constructed as demanding the continued oppression of the working class, a move that allows certain Marxists to continue their misreading. Such interpretations of the author's class and gender as 'lady' denied feminism a founding place in modernism or in English Left criticism by insisting on its inability to ally itself with the working class. This deprived socialist women of a model critic and founding mother and foreclosed the possibility of inserting, at an earlier historical date, gender (and race) into a predominantly class-centered oppositional narrative.

Other cultural narratives about Virginia Woolf were invented and circulated around this master narrative of the lady: Quentin Bell's biography was constructed backward from the suicide and produced versions of madwoman and victim; feminist narratives of the survivor of child abuse were fashioned; American feminists revived *A Room of One's Own* as a founding text for women's studies as a field, a practice that sometimes ignored the class narrative in the text. Also problematic was the explicit rejection of Woolf as the origin of modern socialist feminist critical practice by American empiricist feminists, responding, it appears, to the demand of English Left cultural authority. Woolf alienated a contemporary leftist audience in 'The Leaning Tower' by exposing the way leftist intellectuals romanticised the working class and neglected the political education of their own class. (Their heroizing of Lawrence is as problematic as the demonizing of Woolf.) Her fiction relentlessly connects imperialism to patriarchy; *Three Guineas*, for example, insists that the origin of fascism is in the patriarchal family, not in Italian or German nationalism, a politics recuperated by certain 1970s feminisms but certainly not by the British Left.

It is not my purpose to claim subaltern status for Woolf or for *The Waves*, or even to claim that my reading of its politics is a restoration of a lost original text. But what becomes apparent in reading *The Waves* with the benefit of recent cultural methodologies is that the text itself provides strategies for readers excluded from the cultural inheritance it represents. Woolf provides such strategies through Bernard's demand as an artist for an audience of 'other people's eyes' (I's, ayes). Bernard's is an act of literary hegemony; he absorbs the voices of his marginalized peers into his own voice – he needs 'other people's eyes' to read him and other people's I's, their lives and selves, to make his stories. As Bernard's audience, however, we are made to see this act of appropriation. The text as a whole thus invokes a reader who can read as a barbarian or outsider, not just as a Greek or inheritor of the tradition. As readers, prying open the difference between the two positions allows us to enter into the racial/colonial narrative in the way that opening the lady/sweeper pairing assists in the interrogation of class.

I argue here that *The Waves* is a thirties novel and that it is concerned with race, class, colonialism, and the cultural politics of canonicity itself. In *The Waves* Woolf interrogates the color problem, setting a metropolitan 'whiteness' against the colored colonial world as a vast desert against which an intellectual elite like the Bloomsbury Group creates itself as culture. *The Waves* might have been called *Waiting for the Barbarians* because of its emotional evocation of white fear and guilt for colonial and class oppression, the national dream of being assailed by the assegais of the savage enemy as 'white sheep'. But fifty years of readings are difficult to displace – just as readers of Edith Sitwell's *Façade* have been prevented from hearing its profound critique of British naval power because of a narrow notion that the political is foreign to a performative aesthetic emphasising sound, dance, and nonsense children's rhymes. Postmodern performance art may allow us to recuperate Sitwell's text, music, and megaphone, as well as the mockery of English maritime power she shared with Woolf. We might think of Woolf's rehearsal for *The Waves* in her youthful participation in the 'Dreadnought Hoax' in 1910, a prank in which she and her friends, posing as the emperor of Abyssinia and his court, successfully boarded a formidable secret man-of-war of which her cousin, William Fisher, was flag commander.

Consistent with the socialist politics and antifascist ethics of *The Years* and *Three Guineas*, which explore the relation of the patriarchal family and state institutions to fascism, *The Waves* investigates the origin of cultural power in the generation or group formed by the British public school and in its values. Woolf mocks snobbish, eternally adolescent male bonding around the ethos of 'the playing fields of Eton' and she exposes the cult of the hero and the complicity of the poet in the making of culture as he exudes cultural glue (in the form of an elegy for the dead hero) as a source of social cohesion, the grounding for nationalism, war, and eventually fascism. I claim here that in 1931, despite her personal privilege in class terms, Woolf prophesized the doom of the insular civilisation that produced her by specifically problematizing whiteness as an issue. If, as I have argued, *A Room of One's Own* is an elegy for all the lives of women left out of history, then *The Waves* deconstructs the politics of the elegy as an instrument of social control. In the process of inventing a new name for her fictions, Woolf thought 'elegy' might do. But in exploring its function, she revealed the ethical problems to be faced in using this patriarchal genre. Bernard's production of culture is authorised by the politics of the elegy in the history of poetry; his writing mourns the death of Percival in India:

He was thrown, riding in a race, and when I came along Shaftesbury Avenue tonight, those insignificant and scarcely formulated faces that bubble up out of the doors of the Tube, and many obscure Indians, and people dying of famine and disease, and women who have been cheated, and whipped dogs and crying children – all these seemed to me bereft. He would have done justice. He would have protected. . . . No lullaby has ever occurred to me capable of singing him to rest. (243)

The Waves insists that the modernist epic-elegy *is* a melodrama for beset imperialists. (*The Waste Land, Ulysses*, etc., might be read in the same way.) It marks the end of empire, but to read it this way, as part of what I call the 'postcolonial carnivalesque,' one must be willing to read the comic and ironic and perhaps even regard with relief the death of the author which it enacts.

The study of the silenced colonial other and the search for the subaltern voice, while not articulated in Woolf's text, do lead us to recognize the power of the white woman's critique of herself and her social system, and of the complicity of English literature with imperialism and class oppression, especially when such a critique is not to be found in the writing of modernist men. The gardeners and the natives do not speak in *The Waves*; they are pictures taken under Bernard's imaginary Western eyes. But their presence, and that of Mrs. Moffat, the charwoman, and Bernard's nanny-muse, suggests that we ask whose interest was served by marking this text apolitical for five decades.

Virginia Woolf self-consciously creates here a literature of color, and that color is white, a literature written under the protection of the 'white arm' of imperialism and defining itself by the brown and black of colonized peoples, ideologically asserting itself even in the unconscious of oppressed and silenced women in Rhoda's fantasy of her white flower fleet. The Haule-Smith concordance reports 117 instances of 'white' or 'whiteness' in this very short text, evidence of Woolf's effort to interrogate the color problem of whiteness as ideology. A barbarian reading notices *The Waves* as a white book, as Toni Morrison's provocative reading of Melville recalls the moment in American history

when whiteness became ideology. . . . And if the white whale is the ideology of race, what Ahab has lost to it is personal dismemberment and family and society and his own place as a human in the world. The trauma of racism is, for the racist and the victim, the severe fragmentation of self. (15–16)

Bernard's 'world without a self' is the white postcolonial world. The fragmented selves of the 'civilized' characters in *The Waves* are directly related to the politics of British imperialism. If Bernard is an Ahab figure, then the vision of a 'fin in a waste of waters' may belong to his own white whale, his obsession with Percival and India. (We know that Woolf read *Moby Dick* on February 14, 1922, and again on September 10, 1928; her centenary article on Melville, for which she read all his works, appeared in *TLS* on August 7, 1919. Her diary mentions *Moby Dick* in connection with Desmond MacCarthy [*Diary* III, 195], and she also jokes about Moby Dick's whiteness.)

This Occidental tribe of alienated characters, so often read as figures in a roman à clef of Bloomsbury intellectuals, collectively inscribe their class and race superiority only by imagining a world of the Savage Other in India and Africa, where their representative, Percival (a Siegfried, a Superman, the strong silent bully who will by the end of the decade be a fascist idol), secures their privilege by violent exertions of brute force. As *Orlando* writes the history of English literature based on a founding gesture of violence and conquest, Orlando slicing at the shrunken head of a Moor, the trophy of a violent British adventure against African blacks, *The Waves* reveals that the primal narrative of British culture is the (imperialist) quest. Bernard and his friends idolize Percival, the violent last of the British imperialists, as his (imagined) life and death in India become the story of their generation. Percival embodies their history, and Bernard, the man of letters, ensures by his elegies to Percival that this tale, the romance of the dead brother/lover in India, is inscribed as the story of modern Britain. My reading of the novel goes against the grain of its reception as ahistorical and abstract by insisting that it records a precise historical moment – the postcolonial carnivalesque – in Percival's quixotic ride on a flea-bitten mare and his fall from a donkey, of England's fall from imperial glory and the upper-class angst of the intellectuals, their primal terror in imagining the assegais of subject peoples turned against them, their agony at contact with the masses and the classes at home, who threaten the order of their whiteness with blood and dirt. The success of Woolf's postmodern practice is evident in her ambivalence about the 'fall,' unless she was joking when she wrote to Quentin Bell in 1935 that she shed a tear at the film *Bengal Lancers* ('that's what comes of being one generation nearer to Uncle Fitzy' [*Letters* V, 383]).

The Waves is about the ideology of white British colonialism and the Romantic literature that sustains it. Its parody and irony mock the complicity of the hero and the poet in the creation of a collective national subject through an elegy for imperialism. In its loving misquotation and textual appropriation of Romantic poetry, *The Waves* may participate more fully in postmodernism as Linda Hutcheon defines it than it does in that modernism where its tenuous canonical place is earned by praise for technical difficulty and apparent antirealism as a representation of consciousness. *The Waves* undermines humanistic faith in the individual coherent subject while exposing the role writing plays in shoring up national subjectivity; it challenges the idea of the artist's integrity. In its allusion to Romantic poetry, and, specifically, to Shelley's earlier Orientalism, Woolf's text recalls another historical moment of English fetishization of selfhood and individualism as the struggle against death. It questions the white man's anxiety about identity as universal. Woolf mocks the Western valorization of individual selfhood in her exhaustion of the form of soliloquy, and she disposes of the notion of individual literary genius by an overdetermined intertextuality with Romantic poetry, which simultaneously pokes fun at Romantic diction and ideology and demonstrates how powerful certain phrases and images are in the invocation of patriotism and nationalist claims for English genius. Harold Bloom completely misses this aspect of Woolf's cultural critique when he interprets *The Waves* as belated Romanticism and calls Bernard's last speech a 'feminization of the Paterian aesthetic stance' (5). This canonical move denies the politics of Woolf's parody of the English culture-making machinery in which one genius succeeds another. *The Waves* is the swan song of the white Western male author with his Romantic notions of individual genius, and his Cartesian confidence in the unitary self. Byronic man, the Romantic artist-hero, sings his last aria against death.[7]

The waves that interest me in this essay are the waves called up in the English national anthem, 'Britannia Rules the . . .', waves that surround an island imperialist culture defining itself as civilisation against the perceived savagery of those whom it has conquered across the seas, specifically, in this text, India. The children of empire, the British ruling class of the 1930s, six characters lacking patronymics and fixed forever in their first names by an absent authority, fixate on the seventh, Percival, the hero, the man of action, the figure whose body they all identify with England. (Since they address only themselves and not each other, and the women don't even call themselves by name, Woolf enacts a discursive infantilization that she emphasises by the use of the pure present – 'I come; I go.') Her authorial hand had torn these characters from the bosoms of their families as if to isolate for scientific study the peer group as carrier of ideology. While *To the Lighthouse* and *The Years* provide acute social critiques of marriage and the family, *The Waves* examines the role of childhood friendships and schooling in the formation of individual, group, and national identity, and the group's production of the figures of hero and poet in the consolidation of cultural hegemony. The school scenes are in fact an indictment of the British public school systems, exposing the barbarism and cruelty by which upper-class boys learn to be 'Greeks', inheritors of culture, what Woolf's cousin J.K. Stephen first called 'the intellectual aristocracy.'

Woolf exposes as well the way that white women are implicated in, rather than exempt from, this imperialistic project. Correctly, I think, she reveals the way each of the white women in their Foucauldian roles as sexualized social beings – Rhoda the hysteric, Ginny the prostitute, and Susan the mother – collaborates in Bernard's plot to canonize the physical and verbal brutality, class arrogance,and racial intolerance of Percival. Feminist readings often argue that Bernard's fluency depends upon the suppression of Rhoda, that her silence is necessary for his speech. But in their roles as victims, silenced subjects, the women still participate in imperialist practice.[8] □

Patrick McGee is one of the first critics to respond to Marcus' essay, which he acknowledges for having

■ articulated a new space for reading *The Waves* – a space that should become the enabling ground for future readings of the novel. By articulating this space in the form of a political interpretation, she also makes visible the internal boundary or blank space that any interpretation hollows out for itself. □

He proceeds to offer a corrective account of the political discourses of *The Waves* by returning to a more textually based methodology:

■ By subordinating the novel's form to its context without paying sufficient attention to the process of mediation, Marcus tends to overlook the politics of literary form at the heart of *The Waves* and possibly of the modernist project itself.[9] □

McGee's is a fascinating essay, but I have chosen for the last critical word of this guide an extract from an essay on *To the Lighthouse* which has also put Marcus' innovations to good use. Janet Winston, in '"Something Out of Harmony": *To the Lighthouse* and the Subject(s) of Empire' (1996), turns our attention once again to the portrait(s) of Mrs Ramsay in that novel, and offers a stimulating reading which addresses, in the best Woolfian tradition, both aesthetic form and political context. What follows is the first part of Winston's article which concludes by considering the 'meta-textual' question of the representation of imperialism in the light of an analysis of the political implications of Lily Briscoe's painting:

■ The novel ends with an abstract description of an abstract painting; the reader is not made to 'see' the finished abstraction on Lily's canvas but must instead configure it herself. In this way, the reader becomes the viewer of non-representational art, who must develop new ways of seeing.[10] □

Like so many commentators on *To the Lighthouse* before her, Winston reads this final vision of Mrs Ramsay with an alertness to Tansley's earlier vision, and yet still finds in this most scrutinised of literary images 'new ways of seeing'.

■ On the occasion of her Diamond Jubilee in 1897, Queen Victoria rode through the streets of London behind marching battalions from every colony of the British Empire in what has been described as imperial Britain's 'last confident celebration of unchallenged power' (Chapman and Raben). An allegorical illustration of her Golden Jubilee (1887) representing *The Jubilee in the East* shows turbaned subjects – some on horseback, others genuflecting – parading through a colonial city while exaltedly carrying the Queen above their heads. The specific image of Victoria represented here is a common one, found in many paintings and sketches of the period: the Queen stares impassively; on her head sits the Imperial Crown, signifying her status as the Empress of India, while the official blue ribbon of the Garter emblazons her bodice. As in the many statues of her erected throughout the colonies, she is depicted, in imperialist fashion, as 'the Great White Queen' who, in Victoria's words, would 'protect the poor natives and advance civilisation', an allegory for Empire itself.[11] Yet, this is no ordinary pictorial rendering. For the Empress appears in the scene not as an 'actual' presence, but as a mimesis – a two-dimensional framed portrait hoisted up by ropes and poles, adorned with a crown of flags. The effect of this portrait within a picture is to draw attention to both the Queen's and the picture's status as representations, and specifically to their representational function as imperial allegories.

Given the allegorical signification of mimetic images of the Queen such as this one, one wonders about the significance of another picture of Victoria, one also foregrounded as representation, yet found not in an engraving whose occasion is the celebration of Empire but in a novel whose subject is not ostensibly British imperialism: Virginia Woolf's *To the Lighthouse*. Early in the novel, Charles Tansley accompanies Mrs. Ramsay on her errands in town, all the while thinking 'she was the most beautiful person he had ever seen' and desiring to serve her by carrying her handbag (14). During this scene in which (Tansley imagines) Mrs. Ramsay finally 'let herself be', Tansley's gaze is directed at her as she 'stood quite motionless for a moment against a picture of Queen Victoria wearing the blue ribbon of the Garter . . .' (14). At this moment, the text positions Mrs. Ramsay spatially in the place of Queen Victoria by superimposing the linguistic description of her upon the ekphrastic image of the Queen.[12] In effect the text displaces the Queen's image with that of Mrs. Ramsay. Through this process of representational displacement, Mrs. Ramsay metonymically assumes the role of Queen Victoria, emblem of Empire, to be figured allegorically as the subject of art.[13] Tansley's ontological musing on Mrs. Ramsay – her status of 'be[ing]' versus 'pretending' – only reinforces this idea (14). The notion that Mrs. Ramsay is most genuinely *being* herself while standing in front of the Queen's portrait (as compared to 'pretending up there' as she ministers to an ill woman) suggests that the portrait somehow represents her – or, put otherwise, she is the subject of the portrait. Thus, in the act of letting herself *be* as she stands in front of the portrait, Mrs. Ramsay becomes Queen Victoria.

This moment in the novel at which the portrait of Victoria and the character of Mrs. Ramsay converge offers a glimpse of what Jenny Sharpe, in her reading of another text of Victorian ekphrasis, identifies as an 'anterior sign' system at work in the novel. In her discussion of allegory and Paul Scott's *The Jewel in the Crown*, Sharpe explains that

[u]nlike metaphor, which signifies a synchronic relationship between two signs, allegory (from *allos* and *agoreuein* meaning 'to speak otherwise') relies on complexes of codes for its meaning. It proceeds not only by metaphor (superimposed levels of meaning) but also by metonymy (a sequential relation of signs to anterior signs). Since each sign always refers to an anterior sign, allegory draws attention to the pre-existing codes on which an interpretation relies. (*Allegories* 140)

By yoking together the character of Mrs. Ramsay and an official portrait of the Imperial Queen, Woolf's text invites us to read not only with attention to codes of imperialist representation but to Mrs. Ramsay's role as Queen in a text of imperial allegory.

This method of reading Woolf's fiction for its underlying engagement with the subject of British imperialism finds support in Fredric Jameson's conception of the modernist text's 'political unconscious'. Specifically, in his essay 'Modernism and Its Repressed', Jameson argues that

modernist works are not, as the older Marxism would have it, simply ways of distracting us from reality, and of substituting trivial concerns and encouraging 'decadent' values and activities. . . . [T]hey do not speak about something essentially different from the content and raw material of revolutionary art; rather, the same fears and concerns, the same historical perceptions and political anxieties pass through them also, only what they attempt to do is

> not to express, but rather to *manage* those fears, to disguise them, and drive them underground. (179)

Countering the notion that modernist writing is concerned solely with aesthetics, Jameson suggests a method of reading modernist texts which uncovers their repressed political content. In his essay 'Modernism and Imperialism', Jameson argues specifically that in high modernist texts it is the system of British imperialism that is repressed yet erupts from the text in the form of the modernist style (50, 55).

That the high modernist Virginia Woolf was concerned with the system of British imperialism is borne out in her essays. In 'Mr. Kipling's Notebook', for example, her 1920 review of Rudyard Kipling's *Letters of Travel*, Woolf criticises Kipling for jingoistically glorifying British imperialism in stilted prose (*BP* 65). She concludes, 'Whether grown-up people really play this game, or whether, as we suspect, Mr. Kipling makes up the whole British Empire to amuse the solitude of his nursery, the result is curiously sterile and depressing' *(BP* 66). More substantially, in her anti-war treatise *Three Guineas* she excoriates British patriarchal society for its imperialist exploits abroad, comparing such actions to German fascism and the subjection of women domestically. In contrast to these essays, Woolf usually approaches the subject of British imperialism in her fiction more obliquely. As several critics have shown in recent years, Woolf's novels, while manifestly focusing on other subjects, are rife with allusions to imperial figures, places, and objects of expropriation.[14] Notable among these critics is Jane Marcus, whose essay 'Britannia Rules *The Waves*' examines Woolf's critique in *The Waves* of 'the ideology of white British colonialism and the Romantic literature that sustains it' (235). Indeed with 'Britannia', Marcus paves the way for a new approach in Woolf criticism: one informed by colonial historiography and postcolonial theory.

To the Lighthouse – itself a voyage narrative in the tradition of Conrad's *Heart of Darkness* and Woolf's own *The Voyage Out* – has received considerably less attention in this area.[15] In what follows, I offer a reading of the novel as an imperial allegory, foregrounding the many tropes of imperialism embedded in the text and the conflicting ideologies these tropes suggest. My approach to the novel as allegorical, and hence my method of reading through juxtaposition and analogy, draws from current critical discussions of the significance of allegory to postcolonial studies.[16] Much has been written on Jameson's provocative yet problematic essay 'Third-World Literature in the Era of Multinational Capitalism' in which he argues that so-called Third World texts are necessarily national allegories.[17] More relevant to this essay is the claim, which underlies his thesis, that:

one of the determinants of capitalist culture, that is, the culture of the western realist and modernist novel, is a radical split between the private and the public, between the poetic and the political. . . We have been trained in a deep cultural conviction that the lived experience of our private existences is somehow incommensurable with the abstractions of economic science and political dynamics. Politics in our novels, therefore is, according to Stendhal's canonical formulation, a 'pistol shot in the middle of a concert'. (69)

According to Jameson, this split manifests itself in 'allegorical structures' that are 'unconscious' in 'first-world cultural texts' (79).

Revisiting and in some important ways revising Jameson by writing on the use of allegory in several postcolonial texts as a specific cultural practice of 'anti-colonialist critique', Stephen Slemon notes that

within the discourse of colonialism allegory has always functioned as an especially visible technology of appropriation; and if allegory literally means 'other speaking', it has historically meant a way of speaking for the subjugated Others of the European colonial enterprise – a way of subordinating the colonised, that is, through the politics of representation. ('Monuments' 10, 8)

In his examination of postcolonial literature, Slemon suggests, however, 'that allegory can itself be used to dismantle the system of allegorical thinking that underwrites the act of colonisation' ('Post-Colonial Allegory' 163). He explains:

[P]ost-colonial allegorical writing builds the provisional, discursive nature of history into the structure and narrative mode of the text so that it becomes approachable only in an act of reading that foregrounds its secondary or conditional nature, its link to fictionality. . . . [T]he binocular lens of allegory refocuses our concept of history as fixed monument into a concept of history as the creation of a discursive practice, and in doing so it opens history, fiction's 'other', to the possibility of transformation. ('Post-Colonial Allegory' 160–1)

Thus, by strategically deploying allegory to demonstrate the constructedness of imperial history and by 'historicis[ing] the conditions of their own possibility', '[t]hese texts,' Slemon argues, 'establish an oppositional, disidentificatory voice within the sovereign domain of the discourse of colonialism . . .' ('Monuments' 13). While *To the Lighthouse* neither engages in a wholesale 'technology of appropriation', as Slemon describes, nor enacts a dismantling of allegory itself, it does concern itself with the 'politics of representation', including those dictated by structures of imperialist ideology. Indeed, Woolf's experimentation with narrative and notions of time in the 'Time Passes' section of the novel, in particular the relegation of private and public (World War I) deaths to mere parenthetical phrases, suggests that, like the allegorical postcolonial texts that Slemon discusses, *To the Lighthouse* challenges the notion of history, both personal and national, as 'fixed monument.'[18] In its specific use of imperial allegory, however, Woolf's text is somewhat ambivalent: it is invested in 'establishing oppositional voices' which question the legitimacy of imperialist ideologies at the same time that it is implicated in these ideologies' discursive repetition.

Such ideological ambivalence in the novel, I will argue, is linked to Woolf's own ambivalence about the artist's role as an agent for progressive social reform at a time of great social and economic upheaval in Britain following the First World War. In a diary entry, Woolf broaches this subject as it specifically relates to opposition to British imperialism. Having attended a lecture in 1919 by Annie Besant, the Irish-English social reformer who agitated for India's home rule (Strobel 64), Woolf writes in her diary:

> She . . . began by comparing London . . . with Lahore. And then she pitched into us for our maltreatment of India, she, apparently, being 'them' & not 'us'. But I don't think she made her case very solid, though superficially it was all believable. . . . It seems to me more & more clear that the only honest people are the artists, & that these social reformers & philanthropists get so out of hand, & harbour so many discreditable desires under the guise of loving their kind, that in the end there's more to find fault with in them than in us. But if I were one of them? (*D1* 293)

Woolf's pique at Besant calling herself one of 'them' (the Indians) and not one of 'us' (the English imperialists) betrays her skepticism about the possibility of disinterested philanthropic or political action. Her assertion of the artist's ethically superior position by virtue of her commitment to 'honesty' gives way, however, to a sense of doubt represented by the final question. Here, Woolf wonders what her perspective on the matter would be 'if she were one of them', i.e. the Indians, while at the same time acknowledging, with some regret, her distance from being 'one of them', i.e. the social reformers.

Woolf's ambivalence about the role of the artist, and indeed of art, in a world of social and political crises comes from questioning the notion of a 'radical split' between the political and the poetic, which Jameson describes as being ingrained in capitalist culture. Such questioning finds its way into *To the Lighthouse*. Take for example the following passage in 'Time Passes':

> [T]hose who had gone down to pace the beach and ask of the sea and sky what message they reported or what vision they affirmed had to consider among the usual tokens of divine bounty . . . something out of harmony. . . . There was the silent apparition of an ashen-coloured ship for instance, come, gone; there was a purplish stain upon the bland surface of the sea as if something had boiled and bled, invisibly, beneath. This intrusion into a scene calculated to stir the most sublime reflections and lead to the most comfortable conclusions stayed their pacing. It was difficult blandly to overlook them; to abolish their significance in the landscape. . . . (133–4)

Juxtaposed as it is in the novel with a bracketed parenthetical phrase about Andrew Ramsay's death by shelling, this passage can be read as an example of those repressed political anxieties, in this case about World War I,[19] latent in the modernist novel: the 'purplish stain' – suggestive of the commingling of the red blood of soldiers and the blue waters of the sea – is a blight on the beautiful British landscape. Woolf's vision-seekers – 'the hopeful', who search the landscape for truth and beauty (131–2) – are the artists, whose pursuit of pure aesthetic inspiration in nature is untenable in an age of world war. Those called to reflect on the sublimity of nature must instead contend with that which intrudes on nature, so-called civilisation. Specifically, political and material realities – in this case a ship and a stain – inevitably impinge upon the artists' vision and necessarily 'bleed into' their finished work.

Metaphorically describing how political realities may 'haunt' a work of art, the above passage from *To the Lighthouse* suggests a method of reading that foregrounds political allegory. For this passage may be read meta-textually, signalling the reader to look within the landscape of the text itself for 'stains' beneath its beautiful seamless surface. In this sense those who 'pace the beach', 'the hopeful', who 'dream . . . of finding in solitude . . . an answer' to the point of their existence (134) are the novel's readers. The 'ship' and the 'stain' signal the reader to uncover what is submerged in Woolf's text: not just the events of World War I but rather the entire institution of British imperialism, which made World War I inevitable.

The image of the ship foregrounded in this meta-textual moment underscores this idea of the submerged imperial subtext: A 'ship . . . come, gone' has sunk or at least passed out of sight; in its place a 'stain' has risen to the surface and a 'silent apparition' of the ship haunts the scene. This image of a sunken ship – evocative of the shipwreck in that ur-text of imperialism, *The Tempest* – resonates with 'the quest-voyage motif' characteristic of European explorer narratives (Said, *Culture* 210–11). Thus, it is not surprising that the image of the sunken ship functions in *To The Lighthouse* as a trope through which the subject of imperialism gets expressed. For just as the sunken ship haunts this scene, so too the process of sinking pervades the novel. In 'Time Passes', for example, both the passing away of the protagonist, Mrs. Ramsay, and the gradual decay and sinking of the Ramsay house dominate this section of the novel, the former for its shocking, because off-handed, presentation in a double parenthetical phrase (128);[20] the latter for its anthropomorphic status as protagonist in this section of the novel:

> The house was left; the house was deserted. It was left like a shell on a sandhill to fill with dry salt grains now that life had left it. The long night seemed to have set in; the trifling airs, nibbling, the clammy breaths, fumbling, seemed to have triumphed. . . . One feather, and the house, sinking, falling, would have turned and pitched downwards to the depths of darkness. (137–8)

Fighting the antagonist 'Time', the Ramsays' summer home – both its inhabitants and its architecture – gives way to the forces of nature, biological and tectonic.[21]

This sinking, this gradual deterioration, also characterises the Hebrides island on which the home stands. In 'The Window' section of the novel during a moment of existential musing, Mr. Ramsay contemplates 'his fate . . . to come out thus on a spit of land which the sea is slowly eating away' (43–4). During the expedition to the lighthouse, Cam thinks that '[t]he island had grown so small that it scarcely looked like a leaf any longer' (204). Finally, at the end of the novel, the island seems to disappear completely as Cam watches Mr. Ramsay 'staring at the frail blue shape which seemed like the vapour of something that had burnt itself away' (207).

The image of the sinking ship – like 'the silent apparition' of the sunken vessel in 'Time Passes' – also haunts the text in this final section. Macalister's story of the 'great storm last winter' during which '[t]hree [ships] had sunk' (163–4) merges with the fragments of the William Cowper poem (D3 19n), which Mr. Ramsay and Cam recite incantationally: '[Cam] was murmuring to herself, "We perished, each alone", for her father's words broke and broke again in her mind. . . . And she went on telling herself a story about escaping from a sinking ship. . .' (167, 190).

Taking seriously Edward Said's remarks that 'empire is everywhere a crucial setting' in the British novel and that '[i]mperialism and the culture associated with it affirm both the primacy of geography and an ideology about control of territory' (*Culture* 63, 78), I read these multiple images of sinking in Woolf's text – home(lands), islands, ships – as representing a pervasive anxiety[22] about the sinking British Empire, whose political and economic hegemony in the world was rapidly declining in the first half of the twentieth century.[23] □

BIBLIOGRAPHY

Elizabeth Abel, *Virginia Woolf and the Fictions of Psychoanalysis* (Chicago: University of Chicago Press, 1989)

Erich Auerbach, 'The Brown Stocking', *Mimesis: The Representation of Reality in Western Literature* (1946), trans. Willard R. Trask (Princeton: Princeton University Press, 1953)

John Batchelor, *Virginia Woolf: The Major Novels* (Cambridge: Cambridge University Press, 1991)

Nancy Topping Bazin, *Virginia Woolf and the Androgynous Vision* (New Brunswick: Rutgers University Press, 1973)

Morris Beja (ed.), *Critical Essays on Virginia Woolf* (Boston: G. K. Hall, 1985)

Quentin Bell, *Virginia Woolf: A Biography*, 2 vols. (London: The Hogarth Press, 1972)

Gillian Beer, 'Hume, Stephen, and Elegy in *To the Lighthouse*', *Essays in Criticism* 34 (1984) 33–55

— *Arguing with the Past: Essays in Narrative from Woolf to Sydney* (London: Routledge, 1989)

— *Virginia Woolf: The Common Ground. Essays by Gillian Beer*, Edinburgh: University of Edinburgh Press, 1997)

Joseph L. Blotner, 'Mythic Patterns in *To the Lighthouse*', *PMLA* 71 (1956) 547–62

Rachel Bowlby, *Virginia Woolf: Feminist Destinations* (Oxford: Blackwell, 1988)

— (ed.), *Virginia Woolf* (London and New York: Longman, 1992)

— *Feminist Destinations and Further Essays on Virginia Woolf* (Edinburgh University Press, 1997)

Pamela L. Caughie, *Virginia Woolf and Postmodernism: Literature in Quest and Question of Itself* (Urbana and Chicago: University of Illinois Press, 1991)

Mary Ann Caws, *Women of Bloomsbury: Virginia, Vanessa and Carrington* (London: Routledge, 1990)

David Daiches, *Virginia Woolf* (London: Poetry London, 1942)

Floris Delattre, *Le roman psychologique de Virginia Woolf* (Paris, 1932)

Maria DiBattista, *Virginia Woolf's Major Novels: The Fables of Anon* (New Haven: Yale University Press, 1980)

David Dowling, *Bloomsbury Aesthetics and the Novels of Forster and Woolf* (London: Macmillan, 1985)

Rachel Blau DuPlessis, 'Woolfenstein', *Breaking the Sequence: Women's Experimental Fiction*, ed. Ellen G. Friedman and Miriam Fuchs (Princeton: Princeton University Press, 1989)

Bridget Elliott and Jo-Ann Wallace, *Women Artists and Writers: Modernist (im)positionings* (London: Routledge, 1994)

Daniel Ferrer, *Virginia Woolf and the Madness of Language*, trans. Geoff Bennington and Rachel Bowlby (London: Routledge, 1990)

Kate Flint, 'Virginia Woolf and the General Strike', *Essays in Criticism* 36 (1986) 319–34

Diane Filby Gillespie, *The Sisters' Arts. The Writing and Painting of Virginia Woolf and Vanessa Bell* (Syracuse, NY: Syracuse University Press, 1988)

Ralph Freedman (ed.) *Virginia Woolf: Revaluation and Continuity* (Berkeley: University of California Press, 1980)

Jane Goldman, *The Feminist Aesthetics of Virginia Woolf: Modernism, Post-Impressionism and the Politics of the Visual* (Cambridge: Cambridge University Press, forthcoming)

J. W. Graham, 'Point of View in *The Waves*: Some Services of the Style', *University of Toronto Quarterly* XXXIX (1969–70) 193–211

Jean Guiguet, *Virginia Woolf et Son Oeuvre: L'Art et l Quête du Réel* (Paris: Didier, 1962); *Virginia Woolf and Her Works*, trans. Jean Stewart (London: The Hogarth Press, 1965)

James Hafley, *The Glass Roof: Virginia Woolf as Novelist* (Berkeley: University of California Press, 1954)

Geoffrey H. Hartman, 'Virginia's Web', *Beyond Formalism: Literary Essays 1958–1970* (New Haven: Yale University Press, 1970)

Carolyn Heilbrun, *Towards Androgyny: Aspects of Male and Female in Literature* (1963; reprinted London: Victor Gollancz, 1973)

Winifred Holtby, *Virginia Woolf: A Critical Memoir* (London: Wishart, 1932)

Margaret Homans (ed.), *Virginia Woolf: A Collection of Critical Essays* (Englewood Cliffs, New Jersey: Prentice Hall, 1993)

Mark Hussey, *The Singing of the Real World. The Philosophy of Virginia Woolf's Fiction* (Columbus, 1986)

— (ed.), *Virginia Woolf and War: Fiction, Reality, and Myth* (Syracuse: Syracuse University Press, 1991)

— *Virginia Woolf A–Z: A Comprehensive Reference for Students, Teachers and Common Readers to Her Life, Works and Critical Reception* (USA: Oxford University Press, 1996)

Alice Van Buren Kelley, *The Novels of Virginia Woolf: Fact and Vision* (Chicago: University of Chicago Press, 1973)

Shiv K. Kumar, *Bergson and the Stream of Consciousness Novel* (London and Glasgow: Blackie, 1962)

Patricia Ondek Laurence, *The Reading of Silence: Virginia Woolf in the English Tradition* (Stanford: Stanford University Press, 1991)

Mitchell A. Leaska, *Virginia Woolf's Lighthouse: A Study in Critical Method* (London: The Hogarth Press, 1970)

Hermione Lee, *The Novels of Virginia Woolf* (London: Methuen, 1977)

— *Virginia Woolf* (London: Chatto & Windus, 1996)

Jane Lilienfeld, '"The Deceptiveness of Beauty": Mother Love and Mother Hate in *To the Lighthouse*', *Twentieth-Century Literature* 23 (1977) 345–76

Jean O. Love, *Worlds in Consciousness: Mythopoetic Thought in the Novels of Virginia Woolf* (Berkeley, Los Angeles and London, 1970)

Frank D. McConnell, '"Death Among the Apple Trees": *The Waves* and the World of Things', *Bucknell Review* 16 (1968) 23–29

Patrick McGee, 'The Politics of Modernist Form: Or, Who Rules *The Waves*?'. *Modern Fiction Studies* 38 3 (Autumn 1992) 631–650

Allen McLaurin, *Virginia Woolf: The Echoes Enslaved* (Cambridge: Cambridge University Press, 1973)

Robin Majumdar and Allen McLaurin (eds.), *Virginia Woolf: The Critical Heritage* (London: Routledge & Kegan Paul, 1975)

Jane Marcus (ed.), *New Feminist Essays on Virginia Woolf,* (London: Macmillan, 1981)

— (ed.), *Virginia Woolf: A Feminist Slant* (Lincoln: University of Nebraska Press, 1983)

— (ed.), *Virginia Woolf and Bloomsbury: A Centenary Celebration* (Basingstoke: Macmillan, 1987)

— *Art and Anger: Reading Like a Woman* (Ohio: Ohio State University Press for Miami University, 1988)

— *Virginia Woolf and the Languages of Patriarchy* (Indiana University Press, 1988)

— 'Britannia Rules *The Waves*', *Decolonizing Tradition: New Views of Twentieth-Century 'British' Literary Canons*, ed. Karen Lawrence (Urbana: University of Illinois Press, 1992) [136–162]

Herbert Marder, *Feminism and Art: A Study of Virginia Woolf* (Chicago: University of Chicago Press, 1968)

Perry Meisel, *The Absent Father: Virginia Woolf and Walter Pater* (New Haven: Yale University Press, 1980)

John Mepham, 'Figures of Desire: Narration and Fiction in *To the Lighthouse*', *The Modern English Novel* (London: Open Books, 1976)

— *Criticism in Focus: Virginia Woolf* (London: Bristol Classical Press, 1992)

Makiko Minow-Pinkney, *Virginia Woolf and the Problem of the Subject* (Brighton: Harvester, 1987)

Ruth C. Miller, *Virginia Woolf: The Frames of Art and Life* (New York: St Martin's Press, 1989)

Toril Moi, *Sexual/Textual Politics: Feminist Literary Theory* (London: Methuen, 1985)

Madeline Moore, *The Short Season Between Two Silences: The Mystical and the Political in the Novels of Virginia Woolf* (London: Allen & Unwin, 1984)

James Naremore, *The World Without a Self: Virginia Woolf and the Novel* (New Haven: Yale, 1973)

Kathy J. Phillips, *Virginia Woolf Against Empire* (Knoxville: University of Tennessee Press, 1994)

Suzanne Raitt, *Virginia Woolf's* To the Lighthouse (Hemel Hempstead: Harvester, 1990)

— *Vita and Virginia: The Work and Friendship of Vita Sackville-West and Virginia Woolf* (Oxford: Clarendon Press, 1993)

Su Reid (ed.), *New Casebooks:* Mrs Dalloway *and* To the Lighthouse. *Critical Essays* (Basingstoke: Macmillan, 1993)

Harvena Richter, *Virginia Woolf: The Inward Voyage* (Princeton: Princeton University Press, 1970)

John H. Roberts, '"Vision and Design" in Virginia Woolf', *PMLA*, LXI (1946), 835–47

Sue Roe, *Writing and Gender: Virginia Woolf's Writing Practice* (Hemel Hempstead: Harvester, 1990)

Phyllis Rose, *Virginia Woolf: Woman of Letters* (London: Routledge & Kegan Paul, 1978)

Lucio P. Ruotolo, *The Interrupted Moment: A View of Virginia Woolf's Novels* (Stanford: Stanford University Press, 1986)

Bonnie Kime Scott (ed.), T*he Gender of Modernism: A Critical Anthology* (Bloomington and Indianapolis: Indiana UP, 1990)

Elaine Showalter, 'Virginia Woolf and the Flight into Androgyny', *A Literature of Their Own: British Women Novelists from Brontë to Lessing* (Princeton: Princeton University Press, 1977)

Gayatri Chakravorti Spivak, 'Unmaking and Making in *To the Lighthouse*', *Women and Language in Literature and Society*, ed. Sally McConnell-Ginet, Ruth Barker and Nelly Furman (New York: Praeger 1980); *In Other Worlds: Essays in Cultural Politics* (London: Methuen, 1987)

Claire Sprague (ed.), *Virginia Woolf: A Collection of Critical Essays* (Englewood Cliffs, New Jersey: Prentice Hall, 1971)

Garrett Stewart, 'Catching the Stylistic D/rift: Sound Defects in Woolf's *The Waves*'. *English Literary History* 54 (1987) 421–61

Jack F. Stewart, 'Existence and Symbol in *The Waves*', *Modern Fiction Studies* 18, 3 (Autumn 1972) 433–47

— 'Light in *To the Lighthouse, Twentieth Century Literature* 23 (1977) 377–389

— 'Spatial Form and Color in *The Waves*', *Twentieth Century Literature* 28 (1982) 86–101

— 'Color in *To the Lighthouse*', *Twentieth Century Literature* 31 (1985) 438–458

Eric Warner, *Virginia Woolf. The Waves* (Cambridge: Cambridge University Press, 1987)

Patricia Waugh, *Feminine Fictions: Revisiting the Postmodern* (London: Routledge, 1989)

J. H. Willis Jr., *Leonard and Virginia Woolf as Publishers; The Hogarth Press, 1917–41* (Charlottesville and London: University Press of Virginia, 1992)

Janet Winston, '"Something Out of Harmony": *To the Lighthouse* and the Subject(s) of Empire', *Woolf Studies Annual* 2 (1996) 39–70

Alex Zwerdling, *Virginia Woolf and the Real World* (Berkeley: University of California Press, 1986)

Virginia Woolf

— *A Room of One's Own* (London: The Hogarth Press, 1929)

— *Between the Acts* (London: The Hogarth Press, 1941)

— *Jacob's Room* (London: The Hogarth Press, 1922)

— *Kew Gardens* (London: The Hogarth Press, 1919)

— *Mr Bennett and Mrs Brown* (London: The Hogarth Press, 1924)

— *Mrs Dalloway* (London: The Hogarth Press, 1925)

— *Night and Day* (London: Duckworth, 1919)

— *Orlando. A Biography* (London: The Hogarth Press, 1928)

— *Roger Fry: A Biography* (London: The Hogarth Press, 1940)

— *The Voyage Out* (London: Duckworth, 1915)

— *The Waves* (London: The Hogarth Press, 1931)

— *'The Waves': The Two Holograph Drafts*, ed. J. W. Graham (London: The Hogarth Press, 1976)

— *The Waves*, ed. Gillian Beer (Oxford: Oxford University Press, 1992)

— *The Waves*, ed. Kate Flint (Harmondsworth: Penguin, 1992)

— *To the Lighthouse* (London: The Hogarth Press, 1927)

— *'To the Lighthouse': The Original Holograph Draft*, ed. Susan Dick (London: The Hogarth Press, 1983)

— *To the Lighthouse*, ed. Margaret Drabble (Oxford: Oxford University Press, 1992)

— *To the Lighthouse*, ed. Stella McNichol (Harmondsworth: Penguin, 1992)

— *Walter Sickert. A Conversation* (London: The Hogarth Press, 1934)

— *A Passionate Apprentice. The Early Journals 1897–1909*, ed. Mitchell A. Leaska (London: The Hogarth Press, 1990)

— *A Writer's Diary*, ed. Leonard Woolf (London: The Hogarth Press, 1953)

— *Collected Essays*, 4 vols. ed. Leonard Woolf (London: Chatto & Windus, 1966)

— *Granite and Rainbow: Essays* (London: The Hogarth Press, 1958)

— 'Introductory Letter to Margaret Llewelyn Davies', *Life As We Have Known It*, by Co-operative Working Women, ed. Margaret Llewelyn Davies (London: The Hogarth Press, 1931)

— *Moments of Being: Unpublished Autobiographical Writings*, ed. Jeanne Schulkind, Second Edition (London: The Hogarth Press, 1985)

— *The Captain's Death Bed and Other Essays* (London: The Hogarth Press, 1950)

— *The Common Reader* (London: The Hogarth Press, 1925)

— *The Common Reader: Second Series* (London: The Hogarth Press, 1932)

— *The Complete Shorter Fiction of Virginia Woolf*, New Edition, ed. Susan Dick (London: The Hogarth Press, 1989)

— *The Death of the Moth and Other Essays* (London: The Hogarth Press, 1942)

— *The Diary of Virginia Woolf*, 5 vols., ed. Anne Olivier Bell and Andrew McNeillie (London: The Hogarth Press, 1977–1984)

— *The Essays of Virginia Woolf*, 4 vols [more to come], ed. Andrew McNeillie (London: The Hogarth Press, 1986–1992)

— *The Letters of Virginia Woolf*, 6 vols., ed. Nigel Nicolson and Joanne Trautmann (London: The Hogarth Press, 1975–1980)

— *The Moment and Other Essays* (London: The Hogarth Press, 1947)

— *The Virginia Woolf Manuscripts: from the Henry W. and Albert A. Berg Collection at the New York Public Library* (Woodbridge, Conn., 1993)

— *Virginia Woolf: A Woman's Essays*, ed. Rachel Bowlby (Harmondsworth: Penguin, 1992)

— *Women and Writing*, ed. Michèle Barrett (London: The Women's Press, 1979)

NOTES

INTRODUCTION

1 Woolf, *The Letters of Virginia Woolf*, 6 vols, ed. Nigel Nicolson and Joanne Trautmann (London: The Hogarth Press, 1975–80), IV, p. 402.

2 The footnote to Woolf's letter tells us (ibid.): 'On 29 September 1931, in the first of ten BBC talks on "The New Spirit in Modern Literature", Harold Nicolson labelled as "modernist" VW, T.S. Eliot, D.H. Lawrence, James Joyce and Evelyn Waugh. He excluded J. Galsworthy, James Barrie, J.B. Priestley and Hugh Walpole on the grounds that "from the scientific standpoint, they are old-fashioned."' (*The Listener*, 30 September 1931).

3 The 'preliminary searches' of Laura Sue Fuderer, for example, in preparing a check-list of Woolf criticism to December 1990, 'produced 1,171 citations . . . not including dissertations'. See Laura Sue Fuderer, 'Criticism of Virginia Woolf from 1972 to December 1990: A Selected Checklist', *Modern Fiction Studies* 38 1 (Spring 1992) 303–42. This supplements Barbara Weiser, 'Criticism of Virginia Woolf from 1956 to the Present: A Selected Checklist with an Index to Separate Works', *Modern Fiction Studies* 18 3 (Autumn 1972) 447–86, which supplements Maurice Beebe, 'Criticism of Virginia Woolf: A Selected Checklist with an Index to Studies of Separate Works', *Modern Fiction Studies* (Spring 1956) 36–45.

4 *Jacob's Room* is the third of Woolf's novels after the more conventional *The Voyage Out* (1915) and *Night and Day* (1919).

5 *The Diary of Virginia Woolf*, ed. Anne Olivier Bell and Andrew McNeillie (London: The Hogarth Press, 1977–84), III, p. 34.

6 Woolf, *Orlando. A Biography* (London: The Hogarth Press, 1928).

7 *Diary*, III, p. 131.

8 *Ibid.*, III, p. 113.

9 *Ibid.*, IV, p. 10.

10 *Letters*, IV, p. 204.

11 *Diary*, IV, p. 53.

12 See Woolf, 'Character in Fiction' ['Mr Bennett and Mrs Brown'] (1924), *The Essays of Virginia Woolf*, ed. Andrew McNeillie (London: The Hogarth Press, 1986–92), III, p. 421. In a review of Hugh Walpole's novel, *The Green Mirror* (1918), Woolf says of his characters: 'they must belong to that composite group of English families created by Mr Galsworthy, Mr Arnold Bennett and Mr E.M. Forster.' *The Essays*, II p. 215. See also Hugh Walpole, 'Virginia Woolf', *New Statesman and Nation* XXI (14 June 1941), pp. 602–3.

13 Robert Graves and Alan Hodge, *The Long Week-End: A Social History of Great Britain 1918–1939* (London: Faber & Faber, 1940), p. 198.

14 'Simon Pure' [Frank Swinnerton], review [of Woolf's essay 'Character in Fiction', later published as 'Mr Bennett and Mrs Brown'], *Bookman* (New York), October 1924, pp. 193–5.

15 May Sinclair, 'The Novels of Dorothy Richardson' (1918), *The Gender of Modernism: A Critical Anthology*, ed. Bonnie Kime Scott (Bloomington and Indianapolis: Indiana UP, 1990), p. 444.

16 J.H. Willis Jr., *Leonard and Virginia Woolf as Publishers: The Hogarth Press, 1917–41* (Charlottesville and London: University Press of Virginia, 1992).

17 Alex Zwerdling, *Virginia Woolf and the Real World* (Berkeley, London: University of California Press, 1986).

18 Jane Marcus, 'Thinking back through our mothers', *New Feminist Essays on Virginia Woolf*, ed. Jane Marcus (London: Macmillan, 1981).

19 Louise DeSalvo, *Virginia Woolf: The Impact of Childhood Sexual Abuse on her Life and Work* (London: The Women's Press, 1989).

20 Quentin Bell, *Virginia Woolf: A Biography*, 2 vols (London: The Hogarth Press, 1972).

21 Hermione Lee, *Virginia Woolf* (London: Chatto & Windus, 1996). There are a number of other good biographies, of which I particularly recommend Phyllis Rose, *Virginia Woolf: Woman of Letters* (London: Routledge & Kegan Paul, 1978).

22 Woolf, *Moments of Being: Unpublished Autobiographical Writings*, ed. Jeanne Schulkind (first published, Sussex University Press, 1978; second edition, London: The Hogarth Press, 1985).

23 'To the Lighthouse': The Original Holograph Draft, ed. Susan Dick (London: The Hogarth Press, 1983); 'The Waves': The Two Holograph Drafts, ed. J.W. Graham (London: The Hogarth Press, 1976). See also the manuscript material available on microfilm and CD-ROM: The Virginia Woolf Manuscripts: from the Henry W. and Albert A. Berg Collection at the New York Public Library (Woodbridge, Conn., 1993).

24 Woolf, The Common Reader (London: The Hogarth Press, 1925). The Common Reader: Second Series (London: The Hogarth Press, 1932).

25 There are a number of critical studies of Woolf's essays. See Leila Brosnan, Virginia Woolf: Essays and Journalism (Edinburgh: Edinburgh University Press, 1997); Juliet Dusinberre, Virginia Woolf's Renaissance: Woman Reader or Common Reader? (Basingstoke: Macmillan, 1997).

26 See Collected Essays, vols 1–4, ed. Leonard Woolf (London: Chatto & Windus, 1966); The Essays of Virginia Woolf, vols 1–4 (and more to come), ed. Andrew McNeillie (London: The Hogarth Press, 1986–92).

27 William Empson, 'Virginia Woolf', Scrutinies II, ed. Edgell Rickword (London: Wishart, 1931), p. 211.

28 'Modern Fiction' and 'Mr Bennett and Mrs Brown' are frequently anthologised. See, for example, Peter Faulkner (ed.), A Modernist Reader: Modernism in England 1910–1930 (London: Batsford, 1986); David Lodge (ed.), Twentieth Century Literary Criticism: A Reader (London: Longman, 1972).

29 Woolf, 'Introductory Letter to Margaret Llewelyn Davies', Life As We Have Known It, by Co-Operative Working Women, ed. Margaret Llewelyn Davies (London, 1931), pp. xv–xxxix (reprinted elsewhere as 'Memories of a Working Women's Guild'). Woolf's article was first published in the Yale Review (September, 1930) with a number of differences also kept in reprints by Leonard Woolf.

30 Bonnie Kime Scott (ed.), The Gender of Modernism; Gillian Hanscombe and Virginia L. Smyers, Writing for Their Lives: The Modernist Women, 1910–1940 (London: The Women's Press, 1987); Shari Benstock,

Women of the Left Bank: Paris, 1900–1940 (London: Virago, 1987); Sandra M. Gilbert and Susan Gubar, No Man's Land: The Place of the Woman Writer in the Twentieth Century, vols 1–3 (New Haven, London: Yale University Press, 1988–94).

31 See, for example, Hugh Kenner's (nevertheless excellent) The Pound Era: The Age of Ezra Pound, T.S. Eliot, James Joyce and Wyndham Lewis (London: Faber, 1972).

32 Woolf, 'Character in Fiction' ['Mr Bennett and Mrs Brown'] (1924), The Essays, III, p. 421.

33 Woolf, 'Modern Fiction', The Common Reader (London, 1925), p.189.

34 William Troy, 'Virginia Woolf: The Novel of Sensibility', Literary Opinion in America, ed. Morton Dauwen Zabel (New York: Harper & Row, 1937), pp. 324–37.

35 Randall Stevenson, Modernist Fiction: An Introduction (Hemel Hempstead: Harvester, 1992), p. 59. See also Malcolm Bradbury and James McFarlane, 'The Name and Nature of Modernism', Modernism 1890–1930, ed. Malcolm Bradbury and James McFarlane (Harmondsworth: Penguin, 1976), p. 25.

36 M.H. Levenson, A Genealogy of Modernism: A Study of English Literary Doctrine, 1908–1922 (Cambridge: Cambridge University Press, pp. 154–5.

37 Ezra Pound, 'The Hard and the Soft in French Poetry', Poetry XI 5 (Feb. 1918); Literary Essays of Ezra Pound, ed. T.S. Eliot (London: Faber, 1954).

38 T.E. Hulme, 'Romanticism and Classicism' (1914), Speculations. Essays on Humanism and the Philosophy of Art, ed. Herbert Read (1924).

39 See Frances Spalding, Roger Fry: Art and Life (London: Granada, 1980), pp. 185–88. Wyndham Lewis savaged Woolf in his satires The Apes of God (London: Grayson & Grayson, 1930), and Men Without Art (London: Cassell, 1934), pp. 158–71.

40 G.E. Moore, Principia Ethica (Cambridge: Cambridge University Press, 1903).

41 General studies of the Bloomsbury Group include: Quentin Bell, Bloomsbury (London: Weidenfeld & Nicolson, 1968); Leon Edel, Bloomsbury: A House of Lions (Harmondsworth: Penguin, 1979); J.K.

Johnstone, *The Bloomsbury Group: A Study of E.M. Forster, Lytton Strachey, Virginia Woolf, and Their Circle* (London: Secker & Warburg, 1954); S.P. Rosenbaum (ed.), *The Bloomsbury Group: A Collection of Memoirs, Commentary and Criticism* (London: Croom Helm, 1975); and Raymond Williams, 'The Bloomsbury Fraction', *Problems in Materialism and Culture* (London: Verso, 1980). On Woolf and the aesthetics of Fry and Bell see: Allen McLaurin, *Virginia Woolf: The Echoes Enslaved* (Cambridge: Cambridge University Press, 1973); David Dowling, *Bloomsbury Aesthetics and the Novels of Forster and Woolf* (London: Macmillan, 1985).

42 See: Jane Marcus (ed.), *Virginia Woolf and Bloomsbury: A Centenary Celebration* (Basingstoke, Macmillan, 1987); Diane Filby Gillespie, *The Sisters' Arts. The Writing and Painting of Virginia Woolf and Vanessa Bell* (Syracuse, NY: Syracuse UP, 1988).

43 Su Reid, 'Introduction', *New Casebooks: Mrs Dalloway and* To the Lighthouse. *Critical Essays*, ed. Su Reid (Basingstoke, Macmillan, 1993), p. 1.

44 *Diary*, IV, p. 45.

CHAPTER ONE

1 See *Diary*, III, p. 232: 'And I made £2,000 out of Orlando & can bring Leonard here & buy a house if I want.'

2 Quentin Bell, *Virginia Woolf*, II, p. 129.

3 Robin Majumdar and Allen McLaurin (eds), *Virginia Woolf: The Critical Heritage* (London: Routledge, 1975).

4 Ms Appendix A, *'To the Lighthouse': The Original Holograph Draft*, ed. Susan Dick (London: The Hogarth Press, 1983), pp. 44–5.

5 See Jacqueline V. Falkenheim, *Roger Fry and the Beginnings of Formalist Art Criticism* (Ann Arbor: UMI Research Press, 1980).

6 Woolf, Letter to Roger Fry, 27 May 1927, *Letters*, III, p. 385.

7 For an introduction to their ideas, see Roger Fry, *Vision and Design* (London: Chatto & Windus, 1920); Clive Bell, *Art* (London: Chatto & Windus, 1914); and the introductions to the catalogues of the 1910 and 1912 post-impressionist exhibitions in J.B. Bullen (ed.), *Post-Impressionists in England* (London: Routledge, 1988).

8 *Diary*, III, pp. 18–19.

9 See *Diary*, III, p. 208: 'I used to think of him & mother daily; but writing The Lighthouse laid them in my mind.' And *MB*, p. 90: 'When [*To the Lighthouse*] was written, I ceased to be obsessed by my mother. I no longer hear her voice; I do not see her.'

10 Vanessa Bell, Letter to Virginia Woolf, 11 May 1927, Bell, *Selected Letters of Vanessa Bell*, ed. Regina Marler (London: Bloomsbury, 1993), p. 317.

11 Jean O. Love, *Worlds in Consciousness: Mythopoetic Thought in the Novels of Virginia Woolf* (Berkeley, Los Angeles and London, 1970) p. 70.

12 Louis Kronenberger, review, *New York Times*, 8 May 1927, p. 2; *Virginia Woolf: The Critical Heritage*, p. 197.

13 *Diary*, III, p. 61: 'all these people will read it & recognise poor Leslie Stephen & beautiful Mrs Stephen in it'.

14 F.R. Leavis, 'After *To the Lighthouse*', *Scrutiny* 10 (January 1942) 295–8.

15 Unsigned review, *Times Literary Supplement*, 5 May 1927, p. 315; *Virginia Woolf: The Critical Heritage*, pp. 193–5.

16 Louis Kronenberger, review, *New York Times*, 8 May 1927, p. 2; *Virginia Woolf: The Critical Heritage*, pp. 195–8. He quotes the passage from *To the Lighthouse* (London: The Hogarth Press, 1927), p. 198: 'But what after all is one night' to 'plates of brightness'.

17 Arnold Bennett, review, *Evening Standard*, 23 June 1927, p. 5; *Virginia Woolf: The Critical Heritage*, pp. 200–201.

18 Edwin Muir, review, *Nation and Athenaeum*, 2 July 1927, p. 450; *Virginia Woolf: The Critical Heritage*, pp. 209–10.

19 Arnold Bennett, review, *Evening Standard*, 23 June 1927, p. 5; *Virginia Woolf: The Critical Heritage*, pp. 200–201.

20 Conrad Aitken, 'The Novel as Work of Art', *Dial* (Chicago), July 1927, vol. 83, pp. 41–4; *Virginia Woolf: The Critical Heritage*, pp. 205–8.

21 *Letters*, III, p. 374. See also Jane Goldman, 'Metaphor and Place in *To the Lighthouse*: Some Hebridean Connections', *Tea and Leg-Irons: New Feminist Readings from Scotland*, ed. Caroline Gonda (London: Open Letters, 1992).

22 *Letters*, III, p. 379.

23 Unsigned review, *Times Literary*

Supplement, 30 October 1919, p. 607; *Virginia Woolf: The Critical Heritage*, p. 78.

24 Joan Bennett, *Virginia Woolf: Her Art as a Novelist* (Cambridge, Cambridge University Press, 1945), p. 79.

25 For helpful discussion of mysticism in *The Waves* see Eric Warner, *Virginia Woolf. The Waves* (Cambridge: Cambridge University Press, 1987), pp. 26–33.

26 *Diary*, IV, pp. 10–11.

27 Woolf, Letter to Ethel Smythe, 1 January 1933, *Letters*, V, p. 144.

28 Harold Nicolson, review, *Action*, 8 October 1931, p. 8; *Virginia Woolf: The Critical Heritage*, p. 266.

29 *Letters*, IV, p. 401.

30 *Diary*, IV, p. 10.

31 Vanessa Bell, Letter to Virginia Woolf, 15 October 1931, *Selected Letters of Vanessa Bell*, p. 367.

32 *Letters*, IV, p. 397.

33 Vanessa Bell, Letter to Virginia Woolf, 15 October 1931, *Selected Letters of Vanessa Bell*, p. 361.

34 Gerald Bullett, review ['Virginia Woolf Soliloquises'], *New Statesman and Nation*, 10 October 1931, Literary Supplement, p. x; *Virginia Woolf: The Critical Heritage*, pp. 268–9.

35 L.P. Hartley, review, *Week-end Review*, 24 October 1931, p. 518; *Virginia Woolf: The Critical Heritage*, p. 272.

36 Louis Kronenberger, *New York Times Book Review*, 25 October 1931, p. 5; *Virginia Woolf: The Critical Heritage*, pp. 273–5.

37 Storm Jameson, review, *Fortnightly Review*, November 1931, pp. 677–8; *Virginia Woolf: The Critical Heritage*, pp. 276–8.

38 Robert Herrick, review ['The Works of Mrs Woolf'], *Saturday Review of Literature* (New York), 5 December 1931, p. 246; *Virginia Woolf: The Critical Heritage*, pp. 278–81.

39 Earl Daniels, letter to the editor, *Saturday Review of Literature* (New York), 5 December 1931, p. 352; *Virginia Woolf: The Critical Heritage*, pp. 281–3.

40 Unsigned review, *Times Literary Supplement*, 8 October 1931, p. 733; *Virginia Woolf: The Critical Heritage*, pp. 263–5.

41 See 'Simon Pure' [Frank Swinnerton], review [of Woolf's essay 'Character in

Fiction', later published as 'Mr Bennett and Mrs Brown'], *Bookman* (New York), October 1924, pp. 193–5; *Virginia Woolf: The Critical Heritage*, pp. 130–2.

42 Frank Swinnerton, review, *Evening News*, 9 October 1931, p. 8; *Virginia Woolf: The Critical Heritage*, pp. 267–8.

43 See T.S. Eliot, 'The Metaphysical Poets', *Times Literary Supplement* 1031 (20 October, 1921), 669–70.

44 David Daiches, *Virginia Woolf* (London: Poetry London, 1942), p. 105.

45 Gerald Bullett, review ['Virginia Woolf Soliloquises'], *New Statesman and Nation*, 10 October 1931, Literary Supplement, p. x; *Virginia Woolf: The Critical Heritage*, pp. 268–70.

46 Gerald Sykes, review, *Nation* (New York), 16 December 1931, pp. 674–5; *Virginia Woolf: The Critical Heritage*, pp. 284–6.

47 Edwin Muir, review, *Bookman* (New York), December 1931, pp. 362–7; *Virginia Woolf: The Critical Heritage*, pp. 286–94.

CHAPTER TWO

1 For example, Deborah Newton, *Virginia Woolf* (Melbourne: Melbourne UP, 1946), and David Daiches, *Virginia Woolf* (London: Poetry London, 1942).

2 Floris Delattre, *Le Roman psychologique de Virginia Woolf* (Paris: Libraire Philosophique J. Vrin, 1932).

3 Floris Delattre, 'La Durée Bergsonienne dans le roman de Virginia Woolf', *Revue Anglo-Americaine* (December 1931), pp. 97–108; *Virginia Woolf: The Critical Heritage*, pp. 299–300. This article was incorporated in *Le Roman psychologique de Virginia Woolf*.

4 William Empson, 'Virginia Woolf', *Scrutinies* II, ed. Edgell Rickword (London: Wishart, 1931), p. 211; *Virginia Woolf: The Critical Heritage*, pp. 301–7.

5 M.C. Bradbrook, 'Notes on the Style of Mrs Woolf', *Scrutiny* (May 1932); *Virginia Woolf: The Critical Heritage*, p. 309. Bradbrook later revised her views and refused Morris Beja permission to reprint her article. See Suzanne Raitt, *Virginia Woolf's* To the Lighthouse (Hemel Hempstead: Harvester, 1990), p. 11; Morris Beja, 'Introduction', *'To the Lighthouse': A*

Casebook (London: Macmillan, 1970), p. 20.

6 F.R. Leavis, 'After *To the Lighthouse*', *Scrutiny* 10 (January 1942) 295–8.

7 Tom Paulin, 'J'Accuse', *Without Walls*, Channel 4, 29 January 1991.

8 See, for example, Hermione Lee, 'Introduction', *To the Lighthouse*, ed. Stella McNichol (Harmondsworth: Penguin, 1992), p. xxv: 'It's unfortunate that Virginia Woolf is so distant from her working class characters that she describes them as half-witted troglodytes.' For discussion of the cleaning woman, Mrs McNab, in particular, see Madeline Moore, *The Short Season Between Two Silences: The Mystical and the Political in the Novels of Virginia Woolf* (London: Allen & Unwin, 1984), pp. 78–81; Makiko Minow-Pinkney, *Virginia Woolf and the Problem of the Subject* (Brighton: Harvester, 1987), p. 101; and Rachel Bowlby, *Virginia Woolf: Feminist Destinations* (Oxford: Blackwell, 1988), p. 77. For interesting discussion of class in *The Waves*, see Gillian Beer, 'Introduction', *The Waves*, ed. Gillian Beer, p. xxxvi: 'Woolf . . . recognized her own limits. . . . She drew back from her first intention to include working-class speech.'

9 Margaret Homans, 'Introduction', *Virginia Woolf: A Collection of Critical Essays*, ed. Margaret Homans (Englewood Cliffs, New Jersey: Prentice Hall, 1993), p. 7.

10 Quentin Bell, *Guardian*, 21 March 1982, quoted Jane Marcus, 'Quentin's Bogey', *Critical Inquiry* 11 (1985), p. 492. See also Quentin Bell, 'A "Radiant" Friendship', *Critical Inquiry* 10 (1984) 557–66. All cited by Homans, 'Introduction', p. 7.

11 Winifred Holtby, *Virginia Woolf: A Critical Memoir* (London: Wishart, 1932). See also Ruth Gruber, *Virginia Woolf: A Study* (Leipzig: Tauchniz, 1935).

12 Holtby, *Virginia Woolf: A Critical Memoir*, pp. 147, 159–60.

13 Woolf, 'Introductory Letter to Margaret Llewelyn Davies', *Life As We Have Known It*, by Co-Operative Working Women, ed. Margaret Llewelyn Davies (London, 1931), pp. xv–xxxix (reprinted elsewhere as 'Memories of a Working Women's Guild'). Woolf's article was first published in the *Yale Review* (September, 1930) with a number of differences also kept in reprints by Leonard Woolf.

14 Holtby, *Virginia Woolf: A Critical Memoir*, p. 186.

15 See Marion Shaw, '"Alien Experiences": Virginia Woolf, Winifred Holtby and Vera Brittain in the Thirties' in *Rewriting the Thirties: Modernism and After*, ed. Keith Williams and Steven Matthews (London and New York, 1997).

16 *Letters*, V, p. 97

17 *Diary*, IV, p. 125.

18 *Letters*, V, p. 108.

19 *Ibid.*, p. 114.

20 Claire Sprague, 'Introduction', *Virginia Woolf: A Collection of Critical Essays*, ed. Claire Sprague (Englewood Cliffs, New Jersey: Prentice Hall, 1971), p. 3.

21 E.M. Forster, 'Virginia Woolf' (the Rede Lecture, Cambridge 1941).

22 John Mepham, *Criticism in Focus: Virginia Woolf* (London: Bristol Classical Press, 1992), p. 23.

23 David Daiches, *Virginia Woolf* (London: Poetry London, 1942), p. 99.

24 Joan Bennett, *Virginia Woolf: Her Art as a Novelist* (New York: Harcourt Brace, 1945), pp. 13, 106–7. See also R.L. Chambers, *The Novels of Virginia Woolf* (Edinburgh and London: Oliver & Boyd, 1947).

25 Bernard Blackstone, *Virginia Woolf: A Commentary* (London: The Hogarth Press, 1949), p. 109.

26 Rachel Bowlby, *Virginia Woolf*, ed. Rachel Bowlby (London and New York: Longman, 1992), p. 20.

27 *To the Lighthouse* (London: The Hogarth Press, 1927), pp. 45–51: 'And even if it isn't fine . . .' to '"Let's find another picture to cut out," she said.'

28 Erich Auerbach, 'The Brown Stocking', *Mimesis: The Representation of Reality in Western Literature* (1946), trans. Willard R. Trask (Princeton: Princeton University Press, 1953), pp. 525–41.

CHAPTER THREE

1 Woolf, *A Writer's Diary*, ed. Leonard Woolf (London: The Hogarth Press, 1953).

2 Noel Annan, *Leslie Stephen: His Thought and Character in Relation to his Time* (London: MacGibbon & Kee, 1951).

3 J.K. Johnstone, *The Bloomsbury Group: A Study of E.M. Forster, Lytton Strachey, Virginia Woolf, and Their Circle* (London: Secker & Warburg, 1954). For comments on *To the Lighthouse* see pp. 346–56, and *The Waves*, pp. 357–68.

4 James Hafley, *The Glass Roof: Virginia Woolf as Novelist* (Berkeley: University of California Press, 1954), p. 80. He quotes John Graham, 'Time in the Novels of Virginia Woolf', *University of Toronto Quarterly* (January 1949), p. 151.

5 James Hafley, *The Glass Roof*, p. 124. See pp. 78–92 for discussion of *To the Lighthouse*, and pp. 106–27 for *The Waves*.

6 See Josephine Schaefer, *The Three-Fold Nature of Reality in the Novels of Virginia Woolf* (The Hague: Mouton, 1965); N.C. Thakur, *The Symbolism of Virginia Woolf* (1965).

7 Su Reid, 'Introduction', *New Casebooks: Mrs Dalloway and* To the Lighthouse. *Critical Essays*, ed. Su Reid (Basingstoke, Macmillan, 1993), pp. 1–2.

8 Suzanne Raitt, *Virginia Woolf's* To the Lighthouse (Hemel Hempstead: Harvester, 1990), pp. 12–13.

9 D.S. Savage, *The Withered Branch: Six Studies in the Modern Novel* (London: Eyre & Spottiswood, 1950), p. 95; quoted Arnold Kettle, *An Introduction to the English Novel* (London: Hutchinson, 1953), vol. II, p. 105.

10 Kettle, *An Introduction to the English Novel*, vol. II, p. 110.

11 Walter Allen, *The English Novel: A Short Critical History* (London: Phoenix House, 1954), pp. 327, 330.

12 *Ibid.*, p. 333.

13 *Ibid.*, p. 335.

14 'Romance and the Heart', *Nation & Athenaeum*, 19 May 1923; *The Essays*, p. 367.

15 Walter Allen, *The English Novel*, p. 337.

16 Raitt, p. 13. See Glenn Pederson, 'Vision in *To the Lighthouse*', *PMLA* 73 (1958) 585–600.

17 T.S. Eliot, '*Ulysses*, Order and Myth', *The Dial* LXXV 5 (November 1923), p. 483.

18 C.G. Jung and C. Kerényi, *Essays on a Science of Mythology*, trans. R.F.C. Hull (New York, 1949) pp. 25, 152.

19 For a statement of this position see Bernard Blackstone, *Virginia Woolf* (London and New York, 1949) p. 99; Edwin B. Burgum, 'Virginia Woolf and the Empty Room', in *Antioch Review*, III (Dec. 1943) 596–611; and John H. Roberts, 'Toward Virginia Woolf', in *Virginia Quarterly Review*, X (Oct 1934), 587–602.

20 Virginia Woolf, 'The Novels of E.M. Forster', in *Atlantic Monthly*, CXL (Nov 1927) 642–8.

21 There is another factor which confirms Lily's role as a Persephone figure in this interpretation. Mrs Ramsay's characterisation of her as prim and old maidish is nothing more than emphasis and re-emphasis of a characteristic of Persephone, 'whose salient feature was an *elemental virginity*' (Jung and Kerényi, p. 207).

22 *The Basic Writings of Sigmund Freud*, ed. and trans. A.A. Brill (New York, 1938) p. 308.

23 Joseph L. Blotner, 'Mythic Patterns in *To the Lighthouse*', *PMLA* 71 (1956) 547–62. See also Edward A. Hungerford, 'Mrs Woolf, Freud, and J.D. Beresford', *Literature and Psychology* V (August 1955) 49–51.

24 Leon Edel, *The Psychological Novel, 1900–1950* (New York: Lippincott, 1955); Melvin Friedman, *Stream of Consciousness: A Study in Literary Method* (New Haven: Yale University Press, 1955); Robert Humphrey, *Stream of Consciousness in the Modern Novel* (Berkeley: University of California Press, 1954).

25 An interesting later account of stream of consciousness is to be found in James Naremore, *The World Without a Self: Virginia Woolf and the Novel* (New Haven: Yale, 1973).

26 Shiv K. Kumar, *Bergson and the Stream of Consciousness Novel* (London and Glasgow: Blackie, 1962), p.69. See Paul Douglass, 'The Gold Coin: Bergsonian Intuition and Modernist Aesthetics', *Thought: A Review of Culture and Idea*, 58 (June 1983), 234–50; Josalba Ramalho Vieira, 'Henri Bergson's Idea of Duration and Virginia Woolf's Novels', *Ilha do Desterro: A Journal of Language and Literature*, 24 No.2 (1990), 9–20; Suzanne Raitt, *Vita and Virginia: The Work and Friendship of Vita Sackville-West and Virginia Woolf* (Oxford: Clarendon Press,

1993), p.140.

27 Henri Bergson, *Time and Free Will: An Essay on the Immediate Data of Consciousness* (1889), trans. F.L. Pogson (London: Macmillan, 1910), p. 108.

28 Bergson, *Time and Free Will*, p. 116.

29 *Ibid.*, pp. 231–2.

30 Randall Stevenson, *Modernist Fiction: An Introduction* (Hemel Hempstead: Harvester, 1992), pp. 104–5.

31 Tony Inglis, 'Virginia Woolf and English Culture', first published in French in *Virginia Woolf et le groupe de Bloomsbury*, ed. Jean Guiguet (Paris, 1977); first English version in *Virginia Woolf*, ed. Rachel Bowlby (London: Longman, 1992), p. 48.

32 Marcel Proust, *Time Regained* (trans. Stephen Hudson), London, 1951, p. 433.

33 Henry James, 'London Notes' in *Notes on Novelists*, London, 1914, p. 349.

34 Virginia Woolf, *The Common Reader* (Second Series), London, 1932, pp. 79–80. (Italics mine.)

35 Laurence Sterne, *Tristram Shandy*, London, 1948, p. 151. (Italics mine.)

36 Cf. William James' statement: 'Such words as 'chain' or 'train' do not describe consciousness . . . . It is nothing jointed; it flows', *The Principles of Psychology*, Vol. I, p. 239.

37 Bergson, *Time and Free Will*, London, 1950, p. 100.

38 V. Woolf, *To the Lighthouse*, London, 1949, p. 76.

39 *Ibid.*, p. 229.

40 Proust, *The Captive* (translated by Scott-Moncrieff), Pt 2, London, 1929, p. 249.

41 *To the Lighthouse*, pp. 318–20. (Italics mine.)

42 *Ibid.*, p. 229.

43 Unlike Dorothy Richardson, her interests in interweaving 'vision and design' are paramount. 'The problem is how to bring Lily and Mr. R. together', she observes in her diary, 'and make a combination of interest at the end'. *A Writer's Diary*, p. 99. *La durée* is the principle which enables her to achieve this effect.

44 V. Woolf, *The Waves*, London, 1950, p. 169.

45 *Ibid.*, p. 178.

46 William James, *The Principles of Psychology*, Vol. I, p. 243.

47 *The Waves*, pp. 210–11.

48 *Ibid.*, p. 194. (Italics mine.)

49 V. Woolf, *The Common Reader* (First Series), London, 1925, p. 90.

50 Bergson, *Mind-Energy*, p. 45.

51 *The Waves*, p. 183.

52 If a metaphysician were to realise personality in its ceaseless becoming, he would have to invent 'fluid concepts' – 'I mean supple, mobile and almost fluid representations always ready to mould themselves on the fleeting forms of intuition', Bergson, *An Introduction to Metaphysics*, p. 18.

53 *The Waves*, pp. 67–8. As originally conceived under the title *The Moths*, this novel was supposed to present 'the idea of some continuous stream. . . .', *A Writer's Diary*, p. 108.

54 *The Waves*, p. 81.

55 *Ibid.*, p. 177. (Italics mine.)

56 *Ibid.*, p. 181. (Italics mine.)

57 *To the Lighthouse*, p. 241.

58 *The Waves*, p. 187.

59 *Ibid.*, p. 93.

60 *To the Lighthouse*, p. 246.

61 *Ibid.*, p. 308.

62 *An Introduction to Metaphysics*, p. 9.

63 Bergson, *La Perception du Changement*, Oxford, 1911, p. 26.

64 V. Woolf, *The Common Reader* (First Series), London, 1925, p. 189.

65 Kumar, *Bergson and the Stream of Consciousness Novel* (London and Glasgow: Blackie, 1962), pp. 68–102.

66 Jean Guiguet, *Virginia Woolf et Son Oeuvre: L'Art et la Quête du Réel* (Paris: Didier, 1962); *Virginia Woolf and Her Works*, trans. Jean Stewart (London: The Hogarth Press, 1965), p. 51.

67 John Mepham, *Criticism in Focus: Virginia Woolf* (London: Bristol Classical Press, 1992) p. 88.

68 Guiguet, *Virginia Woolf and Her Works*, pp. 461, 460.

69 Harvena Richter, *Virginia Woolf: The Inward Voyage* (Princeton: Princeton University Press, 1970).

70 Cf. D.H. Lawrence, Letter to Edward Garnett, 5 June, 1914. Quoted by A. Huxley in *Stories, Essays and Poems* (London:

Dent, 1938), p. 342: '. . . You must not look in my novel for the old stable ego of the character. There is another ego, according to whose action the individual is unrecognisable, and passes through, as it were, allotropic states which it needs a deeper sense than any we've been used to exercise, to discover are states of the same single radically unchanged element (Like as diamond and coal are the same pure single element of carbon).'

71 Cf. A. Bennett in the *Evening Standard*, 23 June, 1927. '. . . The middle part does not succeed. It is a short cut that does not get you anywhere. . . .'

72 Cf. Ch. III, pp. 75–95.

73 *A Writer's Diary*, p. 108.

74 *Ibid.*, p. 105.

75 *Ibid.*, p. 137.

76 Published for the first time in *The Moment and Other Essays*. It is interesting to note that Leonard Woolf's preface tells us that this was the first draft, a typescript copiously corrected by hand. Although no precise data entitle one to make the assumption, considering the affinities between this sketch and *The Waves* it is tempting to suppose that they date from the same period, and even that this is one of those little 'sketches' that she wrote every morning 'to amuse' herself while brooding over her novel (cf. *A Writer's Diary*, p. 142).

77 *The Moment and Other Essays*, p. 9.

78 *Ibid.*

79 *The Common Reader* I, p. 189.

80 *Ibid.*

81 *The Moment and Other Essays*, p. 9.

82 *Ibid.*, p. 10.

83 Cf. *The Waves* p. 158: '. . . I perceived, from your coats and umbrellas, even at a distance, how you stand embedded in a substance made of repeated moments run together . . .'.

84 ' . . . the thing that we have made, that globes itself here. . . . Let us hold it for one moment . . . this globe whose walls are made of Percival, of youth and beauty, and something so deep sunk within us that we shall perhaps never make this moment out of one man again', *The Waves*, p. 104.

85 *The Waves*, p. 197. Cf. *A Writer's Diary*,

p. 139: '. . . to give the moment whole; whatever it includes. . . .'

86 *The Waves*, p. 153.

87 Cf. particularly *Ibid.* p. 159.

88 *Ibid.*, p. 211. The last sentence in the book. Cf. p. 166, where in the acceptance of life we feel a tragic tension that shows how far the two attitudes are complementary.

89 *Ibid.*, p. 83. Cf. p. 135.

90 Cf. Joan Bennett, *Virginia Woolf*, p. 98; Gerald Bullitt, 'Virginia Woolf Soliloquizes: *The Waves* by V.W.' in *New Statesman & Nation*, 10 Oct., 1931; David Daiches, *Virginia Woolf*, New Directions, p. 111; Irène Simon, *Formes du Roman Anglais de Dickens à Joyce*, p. 385.

91 In 'O'Neill's Own Story of *Electra* in the Making' (reproduced in Barrett H. Clark, *European Theories of the Drama*, p. 534) we read: '. . . have strong feeling there should be much more definite interrelationship between characters' masks and soliloquies, *that soliloquies should be arbitrarily set in a stylised form that will be the exact expression of stylised mask symbol*'. The passage in italics justifies Daiches' comparison; this sentence might in fact serve as text for my own analysis of the monologues in *The Waves*, so much so that source-hunters would doubtless have found this a vein worth exploiting, did not the dates forbid it categorically: on 19 July, 1930, where O'Neill wrote the words, Virginia Woolf was working on the second version of *The Waves*; and when they were printed in the *New York Herald Tribune* of 8 Nov., 1931, *The Waves* had been published for over a month (8 Oct., 1931).

92 D. Daiches, *Virginia Woolf*, New Directions, p. 111.

93 Guiguet, *Virginia Woolf and Her Works*, trans. Jean Stewart (London: The Hogarth Press, 1965), pp. 252–302.

94 *The Romantic Ventriloquists* (Seattle, Wash., 1963), pp. 3–7.

95 *The Death of the Moth* (New York, 1942), p. 125. Later citations refer to this edition.

96 New York, 1925, p. 122.

97 New York, 1962.

98 London, 1965, p. 105.

99 *A Writer's Diary* (London, 1965), p. 137.

100 *Ibid.*, p. 108.

101 *Ibid.*, pp. 1–4.

102 *Jacob's Room and The Waves* (New York, 1959), p. 307. This edition is cited throughout.

103 This is remarkably like W.K. Wimsatt's famous definition of romantic metaphor as the 'tenor' generating its own 'vehicle', in *The Verbal Icon* (New York, 1963).

104 Sartre, in speaking of the incompatibility of conscious and 'phenomenal' being, makes the following point: 'If we suppose an affirmative in which the affirmed comes to fulfil the affirming and is confused with it, this affirmation cannot be affirmed – owing to too much of plenitude and the immediate inherence of the noema in the noesis. It is there that we find being … in connection with consciousness. It is the noema in the noesis; that is, the inherence in itself without the least distance.' (*Being and Nothingness*, trans. Hazel Barnes [New York, 1966], p. lxv.) It can be readily seen how Percival in *The Waves*, as both 'hero' of consciousness and full objective corporeality, is precisely this self-creating and therefore 'silent' affirmation.

105 *Virginia Woolf et son oeuvre* (Paris, n.d.), p. 281.

106 Interestingly, one anticipation of this oceanic world-without-human-consciousness may well be the last vision of the Time Traveller, of the final disappearance of man aeons in the future, in H.G. Wells' *The Time Machine*.

107 One of the earliest essays on *The Waves* is that of Floris Delattre, *Le roman psychologique de Virginia Woolf* (Paris, 1932), containing the following comment: 'The successive monologues are long asides which the actors pronounce before the stage-set, without distinguishing themselves from each other, and in which we see only far-off reflections of the drama playing itself out (p. 199, my translation).' It is interesting to compare this with Robbe-Grillet's ideas of eliminating 'the illusion of depth' from the novel in *For a New Novel* (New York, 1965).

108 This is much like the purely 'phenomenal' and hence terrifying vision of the Marabar Caves in *A Passage to India*.

109 Alain Robbe-Grillet, *The Erasers*, trans. Richard Howard (New York, 1964), p. 7.

110 See R.M. Adams, 'Down Among the Phenomena', *Hudson Review*, XX (1967), 255–67.

111 See Arthur Koestler, 'The Novelist's Temptations', in *The Yogi and the Commissar* (London, 1965); and John Edward Hardy, *Man in the Modern Novel* (New York, 1966).

112 Frank D. McConnell, '"Death Among the Apple Trees": *The Waves* and the World of Things' in *Bucknell Review* 16 (1968) 23–9.

CHAPTER FOUR

1 *To the Lighthouse* (London: The Hogarth Press, 1927), p. 286.

2 See 'The New Biography' (1927), *The Essays*, IV, p. 476: 'And if we think of truth as something of granite-like solidity and of personality as something of rainbow-like intangibility and reflect that the aim of biography is to weld these two into one seamless whole, we shall admit that the problem is a stiff one and that we need not wonder if biographers have for the most part failed to solve it.'

3 *A Room Of One's Own* (London: The Hogarth Press, 1929), pp. 66–7.

4 *A Room of One's Own*, p. 148.

5 See Jane Lilienfeld, '"The Deceptiveness of Beauty": Mother Love and Mother Hate in *To the Lighthouse*', *Twentieth-Century Literature* 23 (1977) pp. 345–76.

6 Geoffrey H. Hartman, 'Virginia's Web', *Beyond Formalism: Literary Essays 1958–1970* (New Haven: Yale University Press, 1970).

7 J.W. Graham, 'Point of View in *The Waves*: Some Services of the Style', *University of Toronto Quarterly* XXXIX (1969–70) 193–211.

8 Graham, 'Point of View in *The Waves*', pp. 193, 201.

9 *Ibid.*, pp. 210, 211.

10 Raitt, *Virginia Woolf's* To the Lighthouse, p. 14.

11 Mitchell A. Leaska, *Virginia Woolf's Lighthouse: A Study in Critical Method* (London: The Hogarth Press, 1970), p. 140. See also Herbert Marder, *Feminism and art: A Study of Virginia Woolf* (Chicago: University of Chicago Press, 1968).

12 Hermione Lee, *The Novels of Virginia*

Woolf (London: Methuen, 1977).

13 Carolyn Heilbrun, *Towards Androgyny: Aspects of Male and Female in Literature* (1963; reprinted London: Victor Gollancz, 1973).

14 Alice Van Buren Kelley, *The Novels of Virginia Woolf: Fact and Vision* (Chicago: University of Chicago Press, 1973).

15 Elaine Showalter, 'Virginia Woolf and the Flight into Androgyny', *A Literature of Their Own: British Women Novelists from Brontë to Lessing* (Princeton: Princeton University Press, 1977).

16 Nancy Topping Bazin, *Virginia Woolf and the Androgynous Vision* (New Brunswick: Rutgers University Press, 1973) p. 124.

17 Madeline Moore, *The Short Season Between Two Silences: The Mystical and the Political in the Novels of Virginia Woolf* (London: Allen & Unwin, 1984), p. 91.

18 Virginia Woolf, *Women and Writing*, ed. Michèle Barrett (London: The Women's Press, 1979).

19 *A Room of One's Own*, pp. 62–3.

20 Jane Marcus (ed.), *New Feminist Essays on Virginia Woolf* (London: Macmillan, 1981); ed., *Virginia Woolf: A Feminist Slant* (Lincoln: University of Nebraska Press, 1983); ed., *Virginia Woolf and Bloomsbury: A Centenary Celebration* (London: Macmillan, 1987); *Art and Anger: Reading Like a Woman* (Ohio: Ohio State University Press for Miami University, 1988); *Virginia Woolf and the Languages of Patriarchy* (Indiana University Press, 1988).

21 Jane Marcus, 'The Niece of a Nun: Virginia Woolf, Caroline Stephen, and the Cloistered Imagination', *Virginia Woolf: A Feminist Slant*, ed. Jane Marcus (Lincoln: University of Nebraska Press, 1983), p. 27.

22 Marcus, *Ibid*. See, Catherine Smith, 'Jane Lead: Mysticism and the Woman Cloathed with the Sun', in *Shakespeare's Sisters: Feminist Essays on Women Poets*, (Bloomington, 1979). Madeline Moore is also converted to similar views about Woolf after reading Smith's essay.

23 Allen McLaurin, *Virginia Woolf: The Echoes Enslaved* (Cambridge, Cambridge University Press, 1973), p. 191.

24 John H. Roberts, '"Vision and Design" in Virginia Woolf', *PMLA*, LXI (1946), 835–47.

25 See, for example, David Seed, 'The Vision of the Artist: Painting and Experimentation in the Fiction of Virginia Woolf' in *Proceedings of the English Association North 5*, (1990); Jonathan R. Quick, 'Virginia Woolf, Roger Fry and Post-Impressionism', *The Massachusetts Review*, 547–70; Frank Gloversmith, 'Autonomy Theory: Ortega, Roger Fry, Virginia Woolf', *The Theory of Reading*, ed. Frank Gloversmith (Brighton: Harvester, 1984); David Dowling, *Bloomsbury Aesthetics and the Novels of Forster and Woolf* (London: Macmillan, 1985).

26 Jack F. Stewart, 'Existence and Symbol in *The Waves*', *Modern Fiction Studies*, 18, 3 (Autumn 1972) 433–47; 'Light in *To the Lighthouse*, *Twentieth Century Literature*, 23 (1977) 377–89; 'Spatial Form and Color in *The Waves*', *Twentieth Century Literature*, 28 (1982) 86–101; 'Color in *To the Lighthouse*', *Twentieth Century Literature*, 31 (1985) 438–58.

27 Diane Filby Gillespie, *The Sisters' Arts. The Writing and Painting of Virginia Woolf and Vanessa Bell* (Syracuse, NY: Syracuse UP, 1988), p. 220. See also: Marianna Torgovnick, *The Visual Arts, Pictorialism and the Novel: James, Lawrence and Woolf*, (Princeton: Princeton University Press, 1985); Mary Ann Caws, *Women of Bloomsbury: Virginia, Vanessa and Carrington* (London: Routledge, 1990); Jane Dunn, *Virginia Woolf and Vanessa Bell: A Very Close Conspiracy* (London: Cape, 1990; 1996); Bridget Elliott and Jo-Ann Wallace, *Women Artists and Writers: Modernist (im)positionings* (London: Routledge, 1994).

28 *To the Lighthouse*, pp. 296–7.

29 *Ibid.*, pp. 43–4.

30 *Ibid.*, p. 44.

31 *Ibid.*, pp. 241–2.

32 *Ibid.*, p. 26.

33 *Ibid.*, p. 83.

34 *Vision and Design*, p. 52.

35 *To the Lighthouse*, pp. 84–5.

36 *Ibid.*, p. 85.

37 *Ibid.*

38 *Ibid.*, pp. 85–6.

39 *Ibid.*, p. 77.

40 *Ibid.*, p. 42.

41 *Ibid.*, pp. 40–1.

42 *Virginia Woolf*, pp. 87–8.

43 *To the Lighthouse*, p. 12.

44 *Ibid.*, p. 207.

45 *Ibid.*, p. 210.

46 *Ibid.*, p. 52.

47 G.E. Moore, *Principia Ethica* (1903; Cambridge University Press, 1959), p. 10.

48 *To the Lighthouse*, p. 51.

49 *Ibid.*, p. 275.

50 *Ibid.*, p. 207.

51 *Ibid.*, pp. 199–200. (Virginia Woolf gives the sense of yearning by denying the satisfaction of the 'accustomed curve' of the sentence. After 'but, . . . he stretched his arms out' we might have expected something like 'in vain', but the sentence halts abruptly and we are left with emptiness.)

52 *Ibid.*, p. 198.

53 *Ibid.*, pp. 63, 126.

54 *Ibid.*, p. 267.

55 Allen McLaurin, *Virginia Woolf: The Echoes Enslaved* (Cambridge: Cambridge University Press, 1973), pp. 189–95, 198–9.

56 Perry Meisel, *The Absent Father: Virginia Woolf and Walter Pater* (New Haven: Yale University Press, 1980), pp. 199–205.

57 See Elissa Greenwald, 'Casting Off From "The Castaway": *To the Lighthouse* as Prose Elegy', *Genre* (Spring 1986) 37–57; John Mepham, 'Mourning and Modernism', *Virginia Woolf: New Critical Essays*, ed. Patricia Clements and Isobel Grundy (London: Vision Press, 1983), pp. 137–56; Peter Knox-Shaw, '*To the Lighthouse*: The Novel as Elegy', *English Studies in Africa*, 29, 1 (1986) 3152; Stevie Davies, 'Elegy', *Virginia Woolf: To the Lighthouse* (Harmondsworth: Penguin, 1989), pp. 100–39.

58 Raitt, *Virginia Woolf's* To the Lighthouse, p. 123.

59 David Hume, *A Treatise on Human Nature* (1736), ed. T.H. Green and T.H. Grose (London, 1874), Vol. I, p. 534. All further references are to this edition and appear in the text in parentheses.

60 *The Diary of Virginia Woolf*, ed. Anne Olivier Bell (London, 1980), Vol. III, p. 208. Further page references appear in the text in parentheses.

61 Leslie Stephen, *English Thought in the Eighteenth Century*, two vols (London, 1876). Page references appear in the text in parentheses.

62 Virginia Woolf, *To the Lighthouse* (London, 1927). All page references are to this first edition and appear in the text in parentheses.

63 For discussion of this topic, see Allen McLaurin, *Virginia Woolf: The Echoes Enslaved* (Cambridge, 1973).

64 Gillian Beer, 'Hume, Stephen, and Elegy in *To the Lighthouse*', *Essays in Criticism* 34 (1984) pp. 33–43.

CHAPTER FIVE

1 See *New French Feminisms: An Anthology*, ed. Elaine Marks and Isabelle de Courtivron (Hemel Hempstead: Harvester, 1980); *French Feminist Thought: A Reader*, ed. Toril Moi (Oxford: Blackwell, 1987).

2 Michèle Barrett (ed.), *Virginia Woolf: Women and Writing* (London: The Women's Press, 1979); Jane Marcus, 'Thinking back through our mothers' in *New Feminist Essays on Virginia Woolf*, ed. Jane Marcus (London: Macmillan, 1981), pp. 1–30; Kate Millett, *Sexual Politics* (1969; London: Virago, 1977).

3 For further discussion of this point, see [Moi's] section on Gilbert and Gubar pp. 37–69.

4 For an introduction to Derrida's thought and to other forms of deconstruction see [Christopher Norris, *Deconstruction. Theory and Practice* (London: Methuen, 1982)].

5 My presentation of Kristeva's position here is based on her *La Révolution du langage poétique* [(Paris: Seuil, 1974)].

6 One feminist critic, Barbara Hill Rigney [*Madness and Sexual Politics in the Feminist Novel* (Madison: The University of Wisconsin Press, 1978)], has tried to show that in *Mrs Dalloway* 'madness becomes a kind of refuge for the self rather than its loss' (52). This argument in my view finds little support in the text and seems to depend more on the critic's desire to preserve her Laingian categories than on a responsive reading of Woolf's text.

7 Toril Moi, *Sexual/Textual Politics: Feminist Literary Theory* (London: Methuen, 1985), pp. 7–18.

8 Makiko Minow-Pinkney, *Virginia Woolf and the Problem of the Subject* (Brighton: Harvester, 1987), p. 116.

9 See Patricia Ondek Laurence's (excellent) *The Reading of Silence: Virginia Woolf in the English Tradition* (Stanford: Stanford University Press, 1991).

10 For further, helpful, discussion of this, see Pamela L. Caughie, *Virginia Woolf and Postmodernism: Literature in Quest and Question of Itself* (Urbana and Chicago: University of Illinois Press, 1991).

11 Moi, *Sexual/Textual Politics*, p. 175: 'Beer, in her essay "Beyond determinism: George Eliot and Virginia Woolf" [*Women Writing and Writing About Women*, ed. Mary Jacobus (London: Croom Helm, 1979) 80–99] raises the same kind of objections to Showalter's reading of Woolf as I have done in this paper. In her 1984 essay, "Subject and object and the nature of reality: Hume and elegy in *To the Lighthouse*" [sic], Beer develops this approach in a more philosophical context.'

12 Spivak's essay has both (italicised) foot-notes and endnotes, all of which are reproduced here as endnotes. I have left what originally were footnotes in italics.

13 *The simplest articulation of the polemic, which 'starts' with Martin Heidegger's approach to the tradition of philosophy, is still Jacques Derrida's* Of Grammatology *(Baltimore: Johns Hopkins University Press, 1976), pp. 157–64. I have tried to follow Derrida's sugges-tion regarding productive or 'forced' readings in my piece (in preparation) 'Marx after Derrida'.*

14 Virginia Woolf, *To the Lighthouse* (New York: Harcourt, Brace & Company, 1927), p. 310. Subsequent page references are included in my text.

15 *This sort of allegorical fancy should of course not be confused with the 'narrative typology' outlined in Tzvetan Todorov, 'Narrative Transformations,'* The Poetics of Prose, *trans. Richard Howard (Ithaca: Cornell University Press, 1977), pp. 218–33. Todorov indicates in that essay the precursors of his own approach.*

16 *It is not insignificant that he draws strength for his splendid burst of thinking from a glance at that safe symbol, his wife-and-child as a func-tioning unit: 'Without his distinguishing either his son or his wife, the sight of them fortified him and satisfied him and consecrated his effort to arrive at a perfectly clear understanding of the problem which now engaged the energies of his*

splendid mind' (53).

17 *Here are bits of Mrs. Ramsay's maternalist endorsement of marriage. 'Divining, through her own past, some deep, some buried, some quite speechless feeling that one had for one's mother at Rose's age' (123). 'All this would be revived again in the lives of Paul and Minta; "the Rayleys" – she tried the new name over. . . . It was all one stream. . . . Paul and Minta would carry it on when she was dead' (170–1). As for Mr. Ramsay's enterprise, the irony is sharpened if we remind ourselves that Virginia Stephen's father was engaged in compiling* The Dictionary of National Biography.

18 *I am referring to the idea of supplementarity. Derrida has suggested that, if a hierarchical opposition is set up between two concepts, the less favored or logically posterior concept can be shown to be implicit in the other, supply a lack in the other that was always already there. See 'The Supplement of the Copula', trans. James Creech and Josué Harari, Georgia Review 30 (Fall 1976), 527–64.*

19 *Once again I am thinking of the deconstruc-tive criticism of Jacques Derrida. The proposition is dismantled most clearly in* Speech and Phenomena and Other Essays on Husserl's Theory of Signs, *trans. David Allison (Evanston: Northwestern University Press, 1973). Among other texts in the field are Jacques Lacan, 'La Science et la vérité,'* Ecrits *(Paris: Seuil, 1966), pp. 855–77 and Gilles Deleuze,* Logique du sens *(Paris: Minuit, 1969).*

20 *It is from this point of view that the many helpful readers' reports on this study troubled me as well. They reflected the desire for theoreti-cal and propositional explicitness that, via Woolf and the 'new criticism', I am combating here: 'There is something coy about this paper and all its "copulas", but at the same time, the reading of Wolf [sic] is genuinely suggestive and I found myself ever convinced by the power of what seemed a pun [it is in response to this that I wrote my first paragraph]. It is difficult to understand just what the author's interest in language (as a formal system, with copulae, etc.) is concerned with, where it comes from and why she thinks it should lead to the sorts of insights she discovers. Some sort of theoretical explicitness would help here!'*

21 Stephen Heath, 'Difference', *Screen* 19.3. (Autumn 1978), pp. 56–7.

22 Jacques Derrida, *Glas* (Paris: Galilée, 1974), p. 290b.

23 Luce Irigaray, 'La tâche aveugle d'un vieux rêve de symétrie', *Speculum: de l'autre femme* (Seuil, Paris, 1974). Subsequent references to this essay are included in my text. For a critique of Irigaray's position, read Monique Plaza, '"Phallomorphic Power" and the Psychology of "Woman": a Patriarchal Chain', *Ideology and Consciousness* 4 (1978), 5–36.

24 Sigmund Freud, 'Femininity', *The Complete Psychological Works of Sigmund Freud*, ed. James Strachey (London: The Hogarth Press, 1961), XXII, p. 114.

25 Interview with Michel Foucault, *Politique-Hébdo*, no. 247 (29 Nov. to 6 Dec., 1976), p. 33. Trans. Colin Gordon, 'The Political Function of the Intellectual', *Radical Philosophy*, no. 17 (Summer 1977).

26 This aspect of the book allows me to justify our use of theories generated, surely in part by historical accident, by men.

27 Gayatri Chakravorti Spivak, 'Unmaking and Making in *To the Lighthouse*' (1980), *In Other Worlds: Essays in Cultural Politics* (London: Methuen, 1987), pp. 30–45.

28 See Julia Kristeva, *Revolution in Poetic Language*, trans. Margaret Waller (New York: Columbia Univ. Press, 1984), esp. the section on 'The Semiotic and the Symbolic', pp. 19–90. In a book published after my writing of this essay (*Sexual/Textual Politics: Feminist Literary Theory* (London and New York: Methuen, 1985)), Toril Moi urges a 'combination of Derridean and Kristevan theory . . . for future feminist readings of Woolf'. See her 'Introduction: Who's Afraid of Virginia Woolf?', p. 15.

29 *The Diary of Virginia Woolf*, ed. Anne Olivier Bell (London: Hogarth Press, 1982), 4:4, where she is speaking in particular of the attempt in Bernard's soliloquy to 'break up, dig deep'.

30 Virginia Woolf, *Between the Acts* (New York: Harcourt Brace, 1941), p. 212.

31 'Longer version' of *Between the Acts*, p. 230, continued from 'Typescript with author's ms. corrections, unsigned, dated throughout from April 27, 1938–July 30, 1939, 186 pp.,' the Berg Collection, New York Public Library.

32 Virginia Woolf, *A Room of One's Own* (New York, Harcourt Brace, 1929), p. 79, where the aspiring female writer is said to find no 'common sentence ready for her use', only 'a man's sentence'.

33 Virginia Woolf, *The Waves* (New York, Harcourt, 1931), p. 15. Subsequent parenthetical references are to this edition in its separate paperback issue (1978).

34 Avrom Fleishman, *Virginia Woolf: A Critical Reading* (Baltimore: The Johns Hopkins University Press, 1975); concerning 'he said' or 'she said', Fleishman comments that 'even this locution is equivocal since the speeches are thought, not spoken', p. 152.

35 Jan G. Kooij, *Ambiguity in Natural Language: An Investigation of Certain Problems in Linguistic Description* (Amsterdam: North-Holland Publishing Co., 1971), p. 19.

36 *Ibid.*, p. 15.

37 *Ibid.*, p. 19.

38 *Ibid.*, p. 18.

39 Roman Jakobson, *Six Lectures on Sound and Meaning*, trans. John Mapham (Cambridge: MIT Press, 1978), p. 11.

40 *Diary*, 3:209, 28 November, 1928, where she is still referring to her novel-in-progress as *The Moths*.

41 James Joyce, *Finnegans Wake* (New York: Viking, 1938), p. 143, 1.9.

42 Garrett Stewart, 'Catching the Stylistic D/rift: Sound Defects in Woolf's *The Waves*', *English Literary History* 54 (1987) [421–61], pp. 421–9. See also Rachel Blau DuPlessis' narratological exploration of *The Waves*: 'Woolfenstein', *Breaking the Sequence: Women's Experimental Fiction*, ed. Ellen G. Friedman and Miriam Fuchs (Princeton: Princeton University Press, 1989).

43 Jacques Lacan, 'The agency of the letter in the unconscious' (1957), in *Ecrits*, trans. Alan Sheridan (London: Tavistock, 1977), p. 152.

44 Ernest Jones, *Sigmund Freud: Life and Work*, vol. I (London: Hogarth Press, 1956), p. 14.

45 Freud, *Three Essays on the Theory of Sexuality* (1905), Pelican Freud Library, vol. 7, p. 121.

46 Details of the Hogarth Press publications of translations of Freud in the seventies

and of the later negotiations to publish the Standard Edition chiefly translated by James Strachey, are to be found in Leonard Woolf's autobiography, particularly the fourth volume: *Downhill All the Way: An Autobiography of the Years 1919–1939* (London: Hogarth Press, 1962), pp. 163–8, and the fifth, *The Journey Not the Arrival Matters: An Autobiography of the Years 1939–1969* (New York: Harcourt Brace & World, 1970), pp. 117–18.

47 Freud, 'Femininity' (1933), Pelican Freud Library, vol. 2, p. 168.

48 This, incidentally, would show up another side to the harmonious view of the couple getting into the taxi in *A Room of One's Own*.

49 In two ways in particular the girl has to accomplish a more difficult journey: by changing the sex of the object of love (from female to male: the boy has only to substitute another woman for the mother) and by changing the chief site of erotic arousal (from clitoris to vagina). Initially, there is no difference in the sexuality of boys and girls; it is only after the girl has understood the meaning of sexual difference – an understanding which Freud mythically attaches to sightings of the genitals of the other sex – that (in the 'normal' course of development) she regards herself as lacking and gives up the forms of sexuality that are now, retroactively, identified as masculine. In addition to the texts cited above see further on this 'Some Psychical Consequences of the Anatomical Distinction Between the Sexes' (1925) and 'Female Sexuality' (1931), both in Pelican Freud Library, vol. 7. Two recent studies of *To the Lighthouse* look at Woolf's undermining of the Freudian scenario of feminine development. See Margaret Homans, 'Mothers and Daughters in Virginia Woolf's Victorian Novel' in *Bearing the Word: Language and Female Experience in Nineteenth-Century Women's Writing* (Chicago: University of Chicago Press, 1986), pp. 277–88, and Gayatri C. Spivak, 'Unmaking and Making in *To the Lighthouse*', in Sally McConnell-Ginet, Ruth Barker and Nelly Furman (eds), *Women and Language in Literature and Society* (New York: Praeger 1980), pp. 310–27. Other sugges-

tive work includes Anne Juranville, 'La Figure de la mère chez Virginia Woolf', *Psychanalyse à l'université*, 7, 26 (Mars 1982), pp. 219–49; and Françoise Defromont, *Virginia Woolf*, especially pp. 100–27. Both these studies are written from a Lacanian point of view, part of Defromont's is translated as 'Mirrors and Fragments' in Rachel Bowlby, ed., *Virginia Woolf*, Longman Critical Readers (Harrow: Longman, 1992), pp. 62–76.

50 On the temporality of *To the Lighthouse*, see the classic final chapter, 'The Brown Stocking', of Erich Auerbach's *Mimesis: The Representation of Reality in Western Literature* (1946), trans. Willard R. Trask (Princeton: Princeton University Press, 1953) [. . .] On narrative and temporality in Woolf's novels generally, see the two final chapters of J. Hillis Miller, *Fiction and Repetition: Seven English Novels* (Cambridge: Harvard University Press, 1982), on *Mrs Dalloway* and *Between the Acts;* and Paul Ricoeur, *Temps et récit* (Paris: Seuil), vol. II (1984), pp. 152–67, and vol. III (1985), pp. 184–202, also on *Mrs Dalloway*.

51 For two perspectives on the idea of a 'feminine' quality of texts which subvert the realist norm, see Julia Kristeva, 'From One Identity to an Other' (1975), in her *Desire in Language: A Semiotic Approach to Literature and Art* (Oxford: Blackwell, 1980), ed. Leon S. Roudiez, pp. 124–47, and Hélène Cixous, *The Newly Born Woman*.

52 Rachel Bowlby, *Virginia Woolf: Feminist Destinations* (Oxford: Blackwell, 1988), pp. 62–79.

CHAPTER SIX

1 Alex Zwerdling, *Virginia Woolf and the Real World* (Berkeley: University of California Press, 1986), p. 12.

2 Mark Hussey (ed.), *Virginia Woolf and War: Fiction, Reality, and Myth* (Syracuse: Syracuse University Press, 1991).

3 Kate Flint, 'Virginia Woolf and the General Strike', *Essays in Criticism* 36 (1986) 319–34.

4 For further information on the construction and early draft of 'Time Passes' see James M. Haule, '"Le Temps passe" and the Original Version of the "Time Passes" section

of *To the Lighthouse'*, *Twentieth Century Literature* 29 (1983) 267–94. See also James M. Haule, *'To the Lighthouse* and the Great War: The Evidence of Virginia Woolf's Revisions of "Time Passes"', *Virginia Woolf and War*.

5 It is ironic that *The Waves*, a novel that critiques the canon-making process itself, should have been among the first four volumes in the Cambridge University Press Landmarks of World Literature series, begun in 1986 with *The Iliad*, *The Divine Comedy*, and *Faust*.

6 See the appendix in Raymond Williams' *Politics of Modernism* for the responses of Said and Williams to the question of gender. Williams' well-known attacks on Bloomsbury reveal a need to maintain a muscular macho modernism of the working class. As late as 1965 Leonard Woolf answered Queenie Leavis' claim that Virginia Woolf's novels were not popular with sales figures to show that they were (*TLS*, 2–8 March, 1990), 211.

7 The classic essay on romanticism and *The Waves* is McConnell's 'Death among the Apple Trees'. Also relevant is J.H. McGavran, 'Alone Seeking the Visible World', and J.W. Graham, 'MSS Revision and the Heroic Theme of *The Waves*'.

8 Jane Marcus, 'Britannia Rules *The Waves*' in *Decolonizing Tradition: New Views of Twentieth-Century 'British' Literary Canons*, ed. Karen Lawrence (Urbana: University of Illinois Press, 1992) [136–62] pp. 136–46.

9 Patrick McGee, 'The Politics of Modernist Form; Or, Who Rules *The Waves*?' *Modern Fiction Studies* 38 3 (Autumn 1992), p. 631.

10 Janet Winston, '"Something Out of Harmony": *To the Lighthouse* and the Subject(s) of Empire', *Woolf Studies Annual* 2 (1996), p. 65.

11 See [James Morris, *Farewell the Trumpets* (New York: Harcourt, 1978)] 368–9 and [*Pax Britannica* (New York: Harcourt, 1968)] 254–5, 506; Victoria (*The Letters of Queen Victoria*, 2nd ser., 3: 525) qtd in [Frank Hardie, *The Political Influence of Queen Victoria: 1861–1901* (London: Oxford University Press, 1935)] 174 and in [Elizabeth Longford, *Queen Victoria: Born to Succeed* (New York: Harper, 1964)] 575.

12 Jay Dickson makes a similar observation, noting '[t]he transfigurative conflation of Mrs. Ramsay with the Queen . . . .'; however, he argues that Queen Victoria 'offers a kind of legacy of domestic fertility for her modernist inheritors', and '[t]his domestic fertility serves to inspire the art of . . . Lily Briscoe . . .' (108). There are varying definitions and applications of the term ekphrasis. According to Françoise Meltzer in *Salome and the Dance of Writing: Portraits of Mimesis in Literature* (Chicago: University of Chicago Press, 1987), ekphrasis is rhetorically defined as 'the description in detail, usually of an art object' (21). '[A]ccepting the narrow meaning given ekphrasis by Leo Spitzer', Murray Krieger, in *Ekphrasis: The Illusion of the Natural Sign* (Baltimore: Johns Hopkins University Press, 1992), describes it 'as the name of a literary genre, or at least a topos, that attempts to imitate in words an object of the plastic arts' (6).

13 Woolf comments on the representation of Queen Victoria in her essay 'Royalty': 'Certainly an old body in black with a pair of horn spectacles on her nose required a good deal of gilding by the imagination before she became the British Empire personified' ([*The Moment and Other Essays* (London: The Hogarth Press, 1947)] 230).

14 See, in particular, Marcus, 'Britannia'; [Jenny Sharpe, *Allegories of Empire: The Figure of Woman in the Colonial Text* (Minneapolis: University of Minnesota Press, 1993)] 57; Masami Usui, 'A Portrait of Alexander, Princess of Wales and Queen of England in Virginia Woolf's *The Waves*', Hussey and Neverow-Turk, *Virginia Woolf: Themes and Variations* 121–7; Michelle Cliff, 'Virginia Woolf and the Imperial Gaze: A Glance Askance', Suzette Henke, 'De/Colonizing the Subject in Virginia Woolf's *The Voyage Out*: Rachel Vinrace as *La Mysterique*', and Susan Hudson Fox, 'Woolf's Austen/Boston Tea Party: The Revolt Against Literary Empire in *Night and Day*', *Virginia Woolf: Emerging Perspectives: Selected Papers From the Third Annual Conference on Virginia Woolf*, ed. Mark Hussey and Vara Neverow (New York: Pace University Press, 1994) 91–102, 103–8,

259–65; Kathy Phillips, *Virginia Woolf Against Empire* (Knoxville: University of Tennessee Press, 1994); Andrea Lewis, 'The Visual Politics of Empire and Gender in Virginia Woolf's *The Voyage Out*,' *Woolf Studies Annual* I (1995), 106–19; Karen Lawrence, 'Woolf's Voyages Out: *The Voyage Out* and *Orlando*', *Penelope Voyages* (Ithaca: Cornell University Press, 1994), 154–206.

15 Two critics who foreground colonialist discourse in *To the Lighthouse* are Mary Lou Emery in her essay '"Robbed of Meaning": The Work at the Center of *To the Lighthouse*', *Modern Fiction Studies* 38 (1992), 217–34; and Jeanette McVicker ['Reading *To the Lighthouse* as a Critique of Empire', forthcoming in *Approaches to Teaching Woolf's* To the Lighthouse, ed. Beth Rigel Daugherty and Mary Beth Pringle. Modern Language Association Publication].

16 See, for example [Frederic Jameson, 'Third-World Literature in the Era of Multinational Capitalism' *Social Text* 5 (1986), 65–88; Stephen Slemon 'Monuments of Empire: Allegory/Counter-Discourse/Post-Colonial Writing', *Kunapipi* 9.3 (1987), 1–34]; Sharpe, *Allegories*; Aijaz Ahmad, 'Jameson's Rhetoric of Otherness and the "National Allegory"', *Social Text* 17 (1987), 3–25; Sam Suleri, *The Rhetoric of English India* (Chicago: University of Chicago Press, 1992), 1–14.

17 See especially Ahmad and Suleri, 13–14.

18 Jeanette McVicker makes a similar point in the longer version of her paper 'Vast Nests of Chinese Boxes, or, Getting from Q to R: Critiquing Empire in "Kew Gardens" and *To the Lighthouse*', which she gave at the First Annual Conference on Virginia Woolf, Pace University, New York, 7 June, 1991.

19 Several scholars have written on the subject of war in *To the Lighthouse*. See Bazin and Lauter, 19–22, 31; [James M. Haule, '*To the Lighthouse* and the Great War: The Evidence of Virginia Woolf's Revisions of "Time Passes"', *Virginia Woolf and War: Fiction, Reality, and Myth*, ed. Mark Hussey (Syracuse: Syracuse University Press, 1991)], 164–78; Poole, 83–7; Schaefer, 145; and Zwerdling, 193, 275.

20 For a discussion of Woolf's use of parentheses and brackets in 'Time Passes', see Poole, 84–7.

21 James Haule, Nancy Bazin and Jane Lauter, and Makiko Minow-Pinkney relate this destruction and disintegration to the events of World War I. See Haule, 177–8; Bazin and Lauter, 20; and Minow-Pinkney, *Virginia Woolf and the Problem of the Subject: Feminine Writing in the Major Novels* (New Brunswick: Rutgers University Press, 1987), 99, qtd in Bazin and Lauter, 20.

22 Nancy Bazin and Jane Lauter read this anxiety as the loss of '[a] feeling of security that could be found in the Victorian Age [but] has been shattered by the war' (22). Roger Poole describes the existence in *To the Lighthouse* of a 'sense of "fall" from some primal moral authenticity' (90). For a discussion of how Woolf 'both reflects and rejects nostalgia for' pre-war England, see Schaefer, 145.

23 Janet Winston, '"Something Out of Harmony": *To the Lighthouse* and the Subject(s) of Empire', *Woolf Studies Annual* 2 (1996) [39–70], pp. 39–47.

ACKNOWLEDGEMENTS

The editor and publishers wish to thank the following for their permission to reprint copyright material: Princeton University Press (for material from *Mimesis: The Representation of Reality in Western Literature*); Essays in Criticism (for material from 'Hume, Stephen, and Elegy in *To the Lighthouse*'); Blackwells (for material from *Virginia Woolf: Feminist Destinations*); The Hogarth Press (for material from *Virginia Woolf and Her Works*); University of Illinois Press (for material from *Decolonizing Tradition: New Views of Twentieth-Century 'British' Literary Canons*); Cambridge University Press (for material from *Virginia Woolf: The Echoes Enslaved*); Yale University Press (for material from *The Absent Father: Virginia Woolf and Walter Pater*); Methuen (for material from *Sexual/Textual Politics: Feminist Literary Theory*); Routledge (for material from *In Other Worlds: Essays in Cultural Politics*); Pace University Press (for material from *Woolf Studies Annual*).

Every effort has been made to contact the holders of any copyrights applying to the material quoted in this book. The publishers would be grateful if any such copyright holders whom they have not been able to contact, would write to them.

Jane Goldman is lecturer in English at the University of Dundee. She has published a number of essays on Virginia Woolf and is the author of a forthcoming book, *The Feminist Aesthetics of Virginia Woolf* (Cambridge University Press, 1998), and co-editor of *Modernism: An Anthology of Sources and Documents* (Edinburgh University Press, 1998).

INDEX